TRANSITION GAME

An Inside Look at Life With the
Chicago Bulls

Melissa Isaacson

SAGAMORE PUBLISHING
Champaign, IL

Production Manager: Susan M. McKinney
Dustjacket and photo insert design: Michelle R. Dressen
Proofreader: Phyllis L. Bannon

Library of Congress Catalog Card Number: 94-68642
ISBN: 0-57167-005-x

Printed in the United States.

For Rick

CONTENTS

INTRODUCTION

The irony is that they were always best in transition.

During the Chicago Bulls' glory years, as they would eventually be known, defense to offense was but a blur, a seamless act that was somehow both cruel and graceful as the NBA's best mounted scoring runs and eventual routs with regularity.

Great days for beat writers, who could hammer out game stories by halftime, so sure of the outcome by then. Greater days for Bulls fans, who soon took for granted the wonder of a team at its very peak.

It became harder as it went on, to be sure. By the third championship, routs were becoming infrequent, boredom prevalent and Michael Jordan relied on as never before. And the transition game, as perhaps a warning of things to come, became laborious. It would not become literal however, until Oct. 6, 1993.

Jordan saw it coming. He saw the signs just as clearly as he saw the end of his career. It was late January of '93, and already Jordan was tired. His knees ached and his spirit sagged and an air of mediocrity was all around him.

The Bulls were 28-13 at the time, holding on to first place in the Eastern Conference, but something wasn't quite right. They were about to play the Rockets in Houston, and for Jordan, that meant an earful from Vernon Maxwell, a matchup he hated and relished at the same time.

But slumped against his locker that day, acutely aware of the changes that had taken place over the last couple of years, his mind was anywhere but on the game. Discussion among Jordan and his teammates had turned more and more lately toward contracts and playing time, toward the future rather than the present. And if it didn't exactly depress him, well, it had him thinking.

"It's human nature that when success comes around, everybody's fat and everybody's independent, when before everyone was supportive and connected and tight," he said. "All championship teams go that way.

"But that's going to be the ultimate destruction of this team."

Jordan knew that he wore the selfish collar more often than anyone. Two weeks earlier in a loss to Orlando, he had attempted 49 shots, a career high and seven more than the rest of the starting lineup combined. But, he said, he was getting tired of carrying the load, tireder still of defending that burden, and that his teammates were going to have to start getting used to taking the desperation shots themselves. Everyone was going to have to learn how to be a team again.

"My biggest lesson about being successful is that you don't change, the people around you change," he said. "When we became successful as a team, a lot of people around this organization started to change. A lot of people can't deal with being successful. It becomes a greed thing. They want to have it all and when they can't, they want to jump ship. They want to go somewhere else.

"That's not a fun mentality to have. It leads you into a complete circle. You have to go back to where you started, and then you're not on top anymore."

Much of that, as Jordan said, is inevitable. And so, perhaps it was to be expected and should not be resented that Scottie Pippen would eventually want a raise, and Horace Grant and Scott Williams would want out. That B.J. Armstrong would want an identity, Will Perdue his dignity and John Paxson and Bill Cartwright a graceful goodbye.

It remains to be seen whether the Bulls will return to where they started. Bulls chairman Jerry Reinsdorf's biggest fear was to become "the Milwaukee Bucks of the 90s," mired in mediocrity.

Pippen tangled with that fear. As the Bulls wound down the race for the top seed in the Eastern Conference in late April of '94 — a race they would lose with an unlikely lapse against the Boston Celtics in the second-to-last game of the regular season — Pippen seemed very much alone in the dressing room.

"Do I ever think about it?" he said incredulously. "I think about it every day. Next year, the whole championship squad could be done, the whole thing over."

Coach Phil Jackson said he warned his players about focusing on what might be in the future, rather than what could be now. He was matter-of-fact the day Jordan retired, telling his team and the public, "It's similar to the Roman Legion. You bury your dead and you move on."

And it was with that attitude that they proceeded. "You do get sentimental about the whole thing," said Scott Williams, "but things change. Players get older, players retire, some get traded and some just move on. That's all part of the business."

The post-Jordan Bulls are all about a group of men, an era, in transition. The '93-'94 season was devoid of Michael Jordan and yet it was also very much about him, and his spirit was a pervading presence throughout.

It is said that all championship eras must come to an end. But during the year 1 A.M. (After Mike), though all the signals pointed to an abrupt and painful conclusion, the Bulls spun a tale as compelling as any that preceded it. They would stumble plenty, but they would catch themselves just as often. The ugliness that Jordan predicted would rear its head often, but it would also continue to make the Bulls one of the more irresistible teams of recent times.

Jackson said early in the season that the team "was still in mourning" over the loss of Jordan. Michael spent the year mourning the loss of his father and trying to rediscover the fun and challenge of youth. Surely it was a learning process for both.

Pippen, as beleaguered as any in the '93-'94 season, still proclaimed the year enjoyable but certainly he did not always feel that way. Once, after listening to Jackson tell the team after a humbling loss to New Jersey that its effort and professionalism were severely lacking, Pippen mumbled, "I'm not unhappy, I'm just disappointed. This isn't any fun at all anymore."

Grant called it "the least enjoyable year" he had spent in his career.

If losing does that, then winning must be blamed as well. But both, you suspect, ultimately had very little to do with it. "Winning," said B.J. Armstrong, "is not necessarily a measure of personal success or happiness."

Toni Kukoc began the year as the proverbial new kid on the block and fought it from the very first day of practice, when his new teammates shared one jersey for individual pictures— then whispered and giggled that the new guy had smelled it up— to his struggles with the realities of NBA basketball.

Steve Kerr, Pete Myers and Bill Wennington were in transition as well, but for the three of them, Jordan's retirement signaled a new professional life rather than certain retirement planning, and a newfound joy in competition one gets only when he feels he has truly contributed.

This is a story about all of them, a story of triumph and turmoil; of rebirth and resignation; and of a determination borne of a thousand sources. It is about expectations and about relationships and about perspectives that color everything a shade differently.

Like all seasons, like all games, the final one of this year would end with the Lord's Prayer. But unlike the ones preceding it, many inside the tightly wound circle would know this was their last as a member of the Bulls organization. Others had to wonder.

There were tears of anger that day over the finality of it all and sighs of resignation. Three years and now this — sitting inside a cramped Madison Square Garden locker room while just outside the door, an impatient crush of media beckoned.

In one corner sat Cartwright and Paxson, knowing with each movement that they were taking off the Bulls uniform for the last time. In another corner, Williams and Grant solemnly but gladly stripped one of the last tangible reminders of their pasts. And in still other pockets around the room, players like Kerr, Myers and Wennington could only hope this was just a beginning.

It was, of course. For every one of them.

ACKNOWLEDGMENTS

Like many other first-time authors, I am sure, I never realized exactly what was involved in writing a book. "Why don't you just look at it as 11 real long newspaper stories?" my husband, Rick, suggested helpfully as I took on that sickly expression at the thought of what lay ahead.

The advantage in writing for a newspaper, I have since learned, is not only that it is but a minute fraction of an entire book — not even a "real long" article comes close, trust me on this one — but that a beat reporter learns to weave a story over an extended period of time. With the Bulls, this means over an average of nine months and 100 games per season. It also means not having to live with any one story for very long, since there is always another the next day.

Having to "live" with a book is an uneasy feeling, especially considering that not only is reporting an ongoing process, but the team's development is also on-going. I was not comfortable forever condemning the Bulls' current state as the death of a dynasty or anything close, regardless of how many people might go along with that notion. Perhaps I have learned from underestimating their accomplishments in the 1993-'94 season. Then again, maybe I am simply a coward.

Whatever the case, I think describing the players and the team as a group in transition was the most accurate way to go. It also captured a fascinating year in which every member of the team, as well as Michael Jordan, seemed at a crossroads in his career, as well as in his life in many cases.

I feel safe in generalizing that most modern-day athletes are not crazy about the media, nor the jobs we must do to communicate their successes and failures to the public who pays to watch them. But I feel fortunate to have attempted this over the past few years in a league as open-minded and public relations-conscious as the NBA.

The Bulls, for the most part, were an extension of this. Though they admittedly grew more impatient with the spotlight as time went on, they were largely gracious and generous with their time.

Scottie Pippen, in particular, fought against his natural instincts and, trying to take a page out of Jordan's book, was accessible to all of us throughout much of the season. Horace Grant fought against his natural instincts as well, but in the opposite way, shielding himself more than ever from the spotlight. Nevertheless, he managed to somehow remain his charming and candid self.

Bill Cartwright, who has found a new life in Seattle, and John Paxson, now a member of the Bulls' broadcasting team, tried their best to savor their last seasons with the Bulls, but in the process had to battle the demons of failing knees and constant pain that must have made that difficult. They too, however, were forever patient and accommodating.

It has always been difficult for B.J. Armstrong to open up to the media, but anyone who has ever covered a Bulls game will tell you that he is perpetually the last player to leave the dressing room after interviews and one of the very few who has rarely made himself inaccessible. Likewise for Will Perdue, whose humor even under difficult circumstances was much admired, and for Scott Williams, whose spirit will be missed in the Bulls' locker room.

The newcomers like Steve Kerr, Bill Wennington, Pete Myers, Luc Longley, Jo Jo English and Corie Blount were open and good-natured and fortunately, frequently good-humored as well, especially when enduring comparisons to previous Bulls teams and shouldering much of the blame for coming up short.

For Toni Kukoc, who never had to deal with pregame interviews in Europe—but did have to worry about headlines concerning such topics as his illegally parked car—the American media was clearly an adjustment. Sub-par performances were something he simply did not feel the desire to analyze. Yet he did offer occasional peeks at his off-beat humor and engaging personality, and fans and media alike can only hope that continues.

Phil Jackson, who is working on a book of his own, continued to keep us on our toes and was especially helpful in this project with his time and always-unique insight. The Bulls' coaching and support staff, as well as the public relations staff, and so many of the coaches' and players' wives, were terrific as well. Johnny Bach was indispensable as always, and his grace, wit and wisdom will be sorely missed.

Jerry Krause has never been accused of being fond nor particularly open with the media. However, he has never failed to return a phone call, is ready with a story for any occasion, and his cooperation is appreciated.

Michael Jordan left an unmistakable void when he retired. We missed not only the athletic gifts we were all privileged to witness when he was a member of the Chicago Bulls, but the daily conversation so many of us in the media enjoyed. His input in the year after his retirement was much appreciated and will likewise be treasured.

There are others who can't possibly be ignored.*Chicago Tribune* editors, past and present, were encouraging and patient and always helpful, particularly Bob Condor and Dick Leslie, so instrumental early on; Dick Ciccone, with his much-needed blessing; and Margaret Holt, for her understanding. I leaned on Sam Smith more than I care to admit, and he was always there. Likewise, writers and friends like Ed Sherman, Andy Bagnato, Mike Conklin, Al Solomon, Paul Sullivan, Terry Armour, Rose Sukowski and too many underappreciated editors and copyeditors to count. The *Tribune* library staff, particularly Alan Peters, should be granted sainthood. Tom Carkeek, invaluable for his editing of this book, was a godsend.

Thanks to "competitors" such as Kent McDill, Mike Mulligan, J.A. Adande and Lacy Banks for seeing to it that life at the Berto Center, on the road, and on press row, was rarely dull and always funny. Ditto to the radio and TV gang, too large, unfortunately, to mention individually.

And thanks, of course, to those at Sagamore for their faith.

Friends and family, who got used to talking about getting together more than actually getting together, must be mentioned: Susie, Buddy, Barry, Alysa, Richard, Sue, Jodi, David, Susie, Jimmy, Linda, Brian, Karen, Gregg, Rebecca and Shirley.

Thanks to old and faithful friends like Bari, Alan, Bob, Diane and Dan, who put up with much more than the legal requirement and ethical allotment for friendship and counsel.

To the world's best in-laws, Art and Sandie Mawrence and grandparents, Sam and Lil Deutsch, whom people think I must be making up, and to my parents, Herb and Francine Isaacson, who missed their calling in not opening up their own P.R. agency, I say thanks for the kind of unconditional support essential for anyone, but especially for an insecure, often neurotic first-time author.

To Pearl Goldwasser, in whose memory this is dedicated, and whose sense of humor and undying spirit I carry with me always; and to Judy and Philip, who are constant and loving reminders, I say thank you as well.

And finally to Rick, whose sole advantage in having a wife write a book and cover an NBA team at the same time was gaining temporary custody of the TV remote, I can only say, I'll take that back now, honey. And thanks. For everything.

9-18-93

Dear Mr. Jordan
    I think you are the greatest basket-
ball player in the world, Your bound to be
in the Hall of Fame, its a shame that
your retiring, but its your choice. I would greatly
appricate it if you would ~~sing~~ autograph my
card.

1

MICHAEL

James Jordan knew first. He sensed it about the same time he suddenly found himself surrounded by microphones and speaking for his son, who had taken to ducking behind corners and hiding in trainers' rooms and refusing for the first time in his life to talk to the media.

That wasn't Michael. James knew that. He also knew it wasn't likely to let up. Blackjack in Atlantic City was nothing more than a continuation of something he had seen coming. "I don't mind speaking for Michael," the always smiling James would say in those days back in the late spring of 1993. "He's my child. You do whatever you can for your child."

But privately, he told Michael he didn't like it. Didn't like what it represented. And that worst of all, neither of them could do anything to stop the inevitable. "He sensed my frustration," Michael recalled. "He saw the unfair shots people were starting to take a year before that and he asked me, 'What challenges do you have for yourself? You don't have anything to prove anymore on the basketball court. It's all off-court stuff now.'"

Like most parents, James Jordan was fiercely protective of his son. And like most parents, he found it difficult to be objective. One rainy Sunday afternoon in May of 1993, he stood patiently outside the Bulls' training facility and gently pleaded with the media gathered for the Bulls-Knicks playoff series to look at things from Michael's perspective.

"He knows he's in the fishbowl under the microscope," James said in about as stern a tone as he was capable. " But you should have some movement that's not guarded all the time. You just have to say, hey, this guy's human. I mean, what is enough? That's the big question right now. What is enough?

"Pretty soon, when you keep tipping the bucket up, there's not going to be anything in there after a while. You're going to pour it all out. And that's what we should start realizing as fans."

The idea of retirement certainly wasn't new to Michael. He had thought about what it would be like to take off the Bulls uniform for the last time, wondered how he would recognize the signs. But when it happened, he didn't have to wonder any longer. He knew for certain when the first signal went off.

"Practice became boring to me," he said without hesitation. "And when that happened, I knew I was getting close. I knew it was time for me to get out. Practice had always been the most fun for me. I'd get up and look forward to going because I knew the challenge comes from that competition. It was never just something to go through.

"I had some of my best games and my best times in practice, and I knew when the game came around, it wasn't like I was doing something that was new. I had done it before. Everything I ever did in games, I had already done in practice."

But during the '92-'93 season, things began to change. This was an older Bulls team — especially with newcomers Trent Tucker, Darrell Walker and Rodney McCray — and it was a more fatigued Bulls team. Averaging 100 games over each of the previous four seasons had begun to take its toll, and practice was where it became most noticeable.

"Guys were getting treatment, rest, sitting out, whatever, whatever, whatever," recalled Jordan. "And it was justified because of the length of the season and what we were trying to do. But it lost the challenge for me. No one seemed to take practice the way I did anymore. So I lost the fun and, in turn, there was nothing for me to do."

Jordan was under considerable scrutiny the last several years of his career for often missing much of preseason training camp. But when he was there, he was all business, and it annoyed him when other players weren't. During the '92 Olympics, he couldn't believe how many "Dream Teamers" went through the motions during practice. That gave him an added incentive, he said, to exploit them during the regular season, knowing that he was better prepared. "A lot of people want to deceive themselves or others, thinking 'I can fool them by taking time off from practice so I won't have to show where my skills are,' but sooner or later, that always gets exposed," Jordan said.

Fearing that might happen to him was bad enough. And when he finally decided to leave professional basketball, there were no doubts.

"I knew halfway through the ['92-'93] season, that was it," he said. "I didn't have anything left to prove. Even if we wouldn't have won a third title, that was it. But I did want to finish off on a good note. I thought maybe my decision would help me focus a little harder, especially when the playoffs came. But the regular season was a drag for me. It was tough for me to motivate myself because I knew you don't get anything until the playoffs."

Jordan said he tried to tell his teammates in a variety of ways. "I told the guys," he said. "And not just one night. We'd have a couple of beers after the game and they'd be complaining about this or that, pointing fingers as they liked to do, and I'd say, 'Man, you don't know how good you have it. You watch, I'm not going to be around here much longer. I think this is going to be my last year.' And they'd say, 'Sure, MJ, sure.' And I'd say, 'I'm not kidding, man. I don't think I'm going to play next year.'

"I told them all and they all shrugged it off. I kept saying it. Not once, not twice, but three or four times. I could sense they didn't believe me. 'Sure MJ, you're either pissed off or you've been drinking.' "

Soon, Jordan would tell his closest friends that it was to be his last season. Dean Smith, his coach at North Carolina, knew as well. Late in the regular season, Smith attended a Bulls game at Chicago Stadium. "He always told me, 'I'm going to make at least one of your games before you retire,' and that was the first and only game he ever saw," Jordan said.

The two spent about 20 minutes talking privately before the game that night. "He finally came to a game because I think he sensed that it was going to be my last year," Jordan said. "I told him then it was time for me to move on."

Interestingly, Jordan had one of his poorer offensive performances that night. Even more interestingly, he was as nervous as a school kid. "I didn't play any offense, I concentrated on defense because anytime I knew Coach Smith was watching me,

I played great defense," Jordan said. "If he told me he was going to watch me from home on TV, I'd think defense before I'd think offense, because that's the way I started. I'd think about all the defensive stances, all the fundamentals."

But it was more than that and Jordan laughed at the thought. "Coach Smith used to give you points on defense in practice, so I'm thinking about the points that I may win," he said. "We'd have point games in practice and you'd get a point for drawing a charge, offensive tips, rebounds, blocked shots, and it would add up and you'd get to use them. Like at the end of practice when we'd have to run sprints, you could use five points and get out of them.

"Here I am in the NBA, 10 years out of college, and every time he'd watch me, I'd think points."

In the back of his mind, as well, was that this was one last time to impress his old coach. Just like it was one last time for everything in those final weeks. After the Bulls had defeated the Phoenix Suns in six games to win their third consecutive NBA title, Jordan exuded a noticeable calm that could have easily been explained by the Bulls' previous successes. But of course, he knew differently. He had long since decided that the last game of the '93 playoffs would be the last game in his NBA career, and so every moment was one to savor.

"One or two plays makes the difference between being a part of history and not being a part of history," Jordan said that night. "And when you're a part of it, you cherish it. This means so much to all of us. More than I can say."

Truer words have rarely been spoken, for indeed, Jordan could not say that night what he was really feeling. He could only try to hold on to the memories. "I wore my uniform all night long," he said, shaking his head. "Then I packed it away and I saved the ball. I'm pretty sure my uniform is still soaked in champagne. I didn't wash it. I didn't do anything. I was afraid to send it out to the cleaners because I was afraid it would get stolen. I think it's right in my basement."

Over the next few weeks, Jordan would relish the third title and reflect on a decision he was almost ready to make public. But a little more than a month later, none of that mattered.

Jordan and his family were never worried when they failed to hear from James for several days or even a week. And so it was in mid-July of '93. "He would go off alone a lot," Jordan said. "Sometimes if he and my mother had a disagreement, or just to be on his own. He enjoyed retirement so much and doing whatever he wanted to do whenever he wanted to do it. So it wasn't peculiar. He went down for a funeral and to visit a friend. We knew that. But when my mother called and told me no one had heard from him for a while, we were concerned."

It wasn't until the North Carolina state police found James' stripped Lexus on the side of the road, however, that Michael really worried. "That's when I knew something was wrong," Michael said quietly. "He treasured that car."

Jordan easily and joyfully reminisced about how it was that the two had purchased it not long before. "My father always taught me to get the best price," he said. "I knew he really wanted it, so here I am negotiating for this car, an SC400 Coupe, and I got a great deal from a place in Carolina. When I was a kid, if I wanted something, I needed it right at that moment. Now all of a sudden our roles are reversed. My father sees the car in Chicago and he has to have it right then. There was a $2,000 difference, not including sales tax, from the deal I had. But he was so excited.

"He was like, 'Son, I really want that car now. I'll pay you back the difference.' And in his heart, he really was going to pay me back the difference, like I'd almost let him do that. But we laughed because he was like a kid, he was so excited."

Jordan smiled as he told the story, gazing into the distance as if he were picturing the scene. Clearly, when his father died, he lost a friend as well. As Michael grew into adulthood, the two would travel together, play cards together, and so often, laugh together. Frequently over the years, with just the slightest provocation, Michael would launch into tales of growing up and annoying his father, who did not always see eye to eye with his young son's idea of hard work.

"He was very mechanical, and so were my brothers," Michael said of James. "He made basketball come hard, and as many times as I had to cut the grass or do household chores, I would work just as hard, if not harder, to get out of it. I couldn't hold a job if I had to. My father always said that and it's true. I didn't want the money, even when I was young. If I had it, I would just buy another pair of basketball shoes.

"My father and brothers would be outside working on the car or something and I never wanted to get my hands all greasy and full of oil, so he'd say, 'Go in with the women and do the dishes.' And I was like, fine. I didn't mind.

"As many times as he tried to convert me and tried to have me follow in his footsteps, he realized he was stuck with a kid who wasn't going to be mechanical. I could only do what I could do best and he realized that. I learned from that. And with my kids growing up, I want to try to do the same thing. If they don't want to play basketball, that's fine. I just want them to do their best at what they want to do."

Michael laughed at his father's lack of pretense. "He wore the same shoes for six years, even after they got a hole in them," he said. "I would make him buy fancy suits and he kept wearing the same one. He was never comfortable with that. If he saw one pair of pants he needed, he would get 12 of the same kind so he wouldn't have to go shopping again."

During interviews, James would often invoke the names of Michael's siblings. "To his dying day," laughed Michael, "he thought my brother Larry was a better basketball player than I was, that he just wasn't big enough. And that was great. That was my father."

And if one thing comforted Jordan about his decision to retire from basketball, it was that James — murdered on that North Carolina road sometime around July 23, 1993 — had seen Michael's last basketball game. "That means a lot," he said at his October 6 press conference.

To a man, whether they were forewarned or not, Jordan's teammates were stunned at the initial trickle of news they had heard the night before. Several players were at Comiskey Park, where the White Sox were playing the Toronto Blue Jays in Game 2 of the American League Championship Series. The news swept like a brush fire around the park. Some heard it on television. Perhaps none realized at the time that their lives would change, but they would find out soon enough.

Scott Williams didn't know what to think; only that the one guy on the team who always looked out for him was leaving. He took the news as hard as anyone. Jordan had made sure

Williams got a serious look with the Bulls back when Williams was an undrafted free agent in the summer of '90. And after he made the team, Jordan made sure the rookie got the locker stall next to his in the Stadium dressing room.

Like the rest of the Bulls, Williams had heard Jordan talk about retiring, but that talk seemed to come only when Jordan was in a down mood. When James Jordan was killed, Williams only felt more sure that Michael would continue playing.

"When I lost my parents, basketball was good therapy," Williams said. "I could run up and down the court and for two hours, I could forget. I thought it would work for him like it worked for me."

When he received a phone call in the Comiskey Park luxury box from which he was watching the White Sox game, Williams could not imagine what it could be. His publicist, Kim Shepherd, told him she had just heard the then-rumor on television.

Williams remembers walking out onto the balcony and looking up toward Jerry Reinsdorf's box, where Jordan was watching the game as well, thinking maybe Jordan would send a signal, maybe lean over and laugh, anything to indicate it wasn't true. "It seemed like I stared up there for a long time," Williams said. When no sign came, Williams got on an elevator and went up.

"I had tears in my eyes," Williams said. "As soon as I saw him, I knew it was true. I don't even remember what he said to me. It was all sort of a blur. But I remember him consoling me a lot more than I was consoling him."

Like Williams, B.J. Armstrong had grown especially close to Jordan over the years, first as sort of a little brother but eventually into one of Jordan's closest friends.

"It was a gradual relationship," said Armstrong. "I happened to know Michael the longest of most guys on the team because I was a counselor at his camp when I was in college. Maybe he saw something in me then. I don't know.

"I try to treat everyone the same, with the same respect, and I just looked at him as Michael. I never bought into the whole aura of him as a superstar, and I think he respected that. Whenever we talked, it was just, 'How are you? How's the family?' That was probably a change of pace for him. I never asked for his autograph [which other players and coaches some-times did] and I know he appreciated that."

Like everyone else on the team, Armstrong saw the signals that the end of Jordan's career was near. "I sort of knew during the ['92-'93] season," he said, "but I would never come right out and ask him because I was afraid of what his true answer would be. I don't know if I could see it coming exactly, but I could definitely sense it was time for him to move on to a new stage in life. And not because he was worn down, but just for a change and a new challenge.

"I had talked to him in confidence two or three years before and he said he was prepared to do it, but the moment had to be right, the timing had to be right. You want to leave the game with a good taste in your mouth. Time and again, you see guys leave with a bad taste. How many people can actually leave on their own terms? Michael could, and I was happy he could."

Scottie Pippen said Jordan "kind of" told him the day before, but whether he refused to believe it or not, he still needed to hear for sure. "I was at the game, in one of the suites, and when I peeked out I was bombarded by reporters asking me if it was true," Pippen said. "I said I didn't know anything about it, and I really didn't feel I did know for sure. I didn't think it was a rumor, but I wanted to hear it from him. So I went back in and called up to his suite and he told me. I was very shocked. Shocked, hurt and surprised."

That morning, Jordan had already met with Phil Jackson and general manager Jerry Krause. Krause had heard the news Sunday. "Jerry [Reinsdorf] had called me on Friday and said David Falk [Jordan's agent] wanted to see him in Washington," Krause recalled. "He went in on a Sunday and called me from the plane on the way back. He said, 'Are you standing up? You'd better sit down because you're not going to believe it. Michael is about to quit.' I said, 'What?' And he said, 'We have one chance to talk him out of it. He'll be in on Tuesday, October 5, and maybe you and Phil can sit with him and see where you can go with it, but I don't think we'll be able to do it.' "

Jordan had given Jackson strong hints two weeks earlier at a charity dinner, but in a way, Jordan dreaded his meeting with the Bulls coach. "Jerry [Reinsdorf] wanted me to talk to him before I really made my decision, and knowing Phil, the psychology major, he was going to try to get in my head and see where I stood," Jordan said.

At the same time, though, Jordan felt confident he could get through it. "I didn't shy away from talking to him," he said, "because I knew in my mind that I knew what I was doing, so whatever he said, I already had an answer for it. I'd thought about it for two years. So when he went through his spiel that 'You have a great gift and you're depriving people of that opportunity to see what God has given you,' I was ready.

"It was weird that people were mad at me for leaving the game at my peak. But I told Phil, 'God has given everyone a gift and that doesn't mean you're going to always have that gift, that it's always going to be there. And sometimes, when you've been given a gift to see something, you should cherish it while you still have that opportunity, because that's not always going to be there either. This is my time to leave because I'm not always going to be there.'

"It was a test to make me realize if it was the right thing to do and I felt good that I talked to him because he made me think about it. But I was sure what I was doing was right. When he gave me a question, I could always come back with an answer and it was always from my heart. It wasn't something someone had written for me or something I had to go think about. I felt what I felt, and I told him. And I think after about an hour, he really knew I had been thinking about it for a long time and that I believed in what I was doing."

Before they parted, and before Jackson could be thoroughly convinced, however, Jordan had a final question for him. "I asked him, 'How can you get me through an 82-game season?' I told him that it was worthless for the competitor I am to go through the regular season because I couldn't find the challenge to drive me through it anymore."

In addition to the mental challenge was the physical. At least once or twice a season, a cold or flu bug raged through the team and typically affected everyone from the coaches to the players to the trainer. Most players performed through most illnesses and the Bulls, in their prime, were famous for playing through most injuries as well.

Jordan often played better under both circumstances, saying the concentration necessary to overcome illness or injury made him a better player. But after nine years, 667 regular-season games [he missed only five games in eight years, not including the '85-'86 season when he broke his foot] and 92 playoff games, the bucket, as James Jordan had said, was empty. There was no drive, no excitement, no challenge. And Jordan knew it would only get worse.

His biggest fear, he said often, was that he would be subjected to the same criticism that Julius Erving endured. "He was the greatest and yet, in his last few years, the whispers were that he wasn't as good anymore," Jordan said. "I didn't want anybody to ever say that about me.

"With Phil's coaching, he would start to go away from me, limit my minutes and my shooting. The perception would be that I wasn't as fast. And because of my competitive juices, I wasn't going to accept that. When I'm 40, I'll feel the same way. I didn't want to handcuff him. I told him, 'You can't sit me out for two weeks at a time like Bill [Cartwright]. You can decoy me only so many times. My competitive attitude is that I want the ball.' So how was he going to motivate me? He couldn't give me an answer and I said, 'That's the answer.' "

For Jackson, the deck had been played except for one last card.

Did Jordan ever consider a sabbatical? "I never would do that and Jerry Reinsdorf never suggested it," said Jordan. "Phil did. He said, 'You should take a year off and then think about it.' I said, 'No, this is it. I want to do it now because I don't want it to linger on in my mind, because I believe what I believe, and I want to move on. I don't want to move on with loose ends. And I don't want you to have hope in the back of your mind when actually there's no hope.' "

With that said, their meeting was over. "Whatever you decide," Jackson told Jordan, "I'm in your corner. I love you no matter what decision you make."

And then he cried.

"I hated it," said Jordan. "It was so tough. I had never seen Phil cry. And he was very genuine about it. I never saw the emotional sides of a lot of the guys until it was time for me to leave."

Krause's office was next. "I knew he was gone when he walked out of Phil's office," said Krause, still hoping it wasn't true. "I looked in Phil's eyes and I knew he had given it his best shot, so I didn't even try. I knew if Phil couldn't get to him, I wasn't going to."

Krause described their meeting as equally sentimental. "There was emotion I had never shared before with Michael," Krause said. Jordan, however, was not feeling the same sentiments. The two had an interesting history and Krause felt there were things to be cleared up. Jordan, however, was only half-listening.

It had all started during Jordan's second year in the league, when a broken foot caused him to miss 64 games. With the playoffs looming, Jordan thought he was ready to play. Krause did not.

"He didn't understand at the time," Krause recalled. "The doctors were saying to me, 'Don't play him,' and he's going down to North Carolina to play anyway and I didn't even know. It drove me crazy when I found out. I didn't want to be the guy who later on, they said, 'You played Michael too soon and you wrecked his career.' I'm thinking, here I am, in the job I've wanted all my life. I have the best player in the game and if I let him play too soon and he gets hurt, I'll never live it down the rest of my life. So I was a little hard on Michael and we argued about it."

To Jordan, Krause's reaction did not come across as concern. "He let me know in no uncertain terms that I was the Bulls' property and what I said did not matter," Jordan recalled.

That would stay with Jordan and affect him in later years, especially when reporters asked him why he didn't demand to renegotiate his contract when it became obvious he was underpaid.

"I didn't complain because I signed the contract, and I always wanted to be my own man after [the injury]," Jordan said. "When I retired, Jerry [Reinsdorf] said, 'I'll take care of you. I owe you.' But he paid me back when he brought me [to Birmingham to play Double A baseball for the White Sox] and I'll never ask for more. That's why I'll never come back, especially for more money. I'll never play basketball for that reason, and I'll never be someone's property."

It was that same thinking that turned Jordan off when he began his baseball career. "A lot of teams were willing to put me on their 25-man [major league] roster," he said. "But I knew it wasn't genuine. I knew it was only a business decision and not a baseball decision."

Further muddling the foot issue was the fact that the Bulls' coach at the time, Stan Albeck, was on Jordan's side. "We had problems with Stan at the time," Krause conceded. "He didn't back us. I didn't say anything at the time, but Stan was looking out for Stan and not for the organization. It was one of those days that I made my mind up that I had made a mistake on Stan."

Jordan came out publicly saying that Krause did not care about the team winning. "He got a little testy," Krause said. "Michael's a needler and I'm a needler."

But while Krause did not protest Jordan's "needling," which came in the form of jokes about his weight and demeanor, Jordan was almost always irritated by Krause's tactics. "I would say to him, 'That move you made last night was pretty good, almost as good as [Earl] Monroe and [Elgin] Baylor,' " Krause recalled.

Krause would also tell Jordan that former Bulls great Jerry Sloan could have stopped him defensively and was a superior practice player, thinking it would get even more out of Jordan. "Krause had nothing to do with me being a good practice player," Jordan bristled. "It's that kind of junk that totally pissed me off. He always wants to take credit where he doesn't deserve it. I'm pretty sure 20 years from now, he's going to swear he drafted me [rather than Ron Thorn]."

As for Krause's form of motivation, Jordan said he was insulted that Krause felt he had to compare him to others in an apparent effort to control his ego. "He treated me like a kid, like Horace [Grant]," Jordan said. "Like I'm going to get a big head if he said something nice occasionally. It was asinine."

And when Krause broke down in his office that Tuesday before Jordan's retirement announcement, Jordan could only think that it was much too little, much too late. Krause, on the other hand, saw it as a cleansing. "That day I said some things I couldn't have said if he was still playing," Krause recalled. "I told him he was the best I'd ever seen. Baylor, Oscar [Robertson], those guys weren't even close."

"You know how you don't realize how bad a situation is until after you leave?" Jordan said. "I didn't need to hear that then."

However Krause handled it, clearly he knew that day that things would never be quite the same. "I think Michael quit right in his prime," he said, disputing notions that Jordan's game had evolved to compensate for dwindling skills. "Michael had a very unusual distinction. He was always the hunted. He was also the only player I ever knew who, when he went on the road, the crowd wanted him to score 50 and us to get beat. He was the greatest road player in the history of the game."

Krause also thought Jordan made the triple-post offense go and vice versa. The triple-post, brainchild of assistant coach Tex Winter and worshipped by Krause, operated on the premise that the open man would get the shot, and that if it was run correctly, there would always be a good shot. It just wouldn't always be by the same player. But to the contention that it helped him and the team win titles, Jordan scoffed. When the game was on the line, he said and most would agree, the Bulls almost always scrapped the triangle.

It was one of several reasons former assistant coach Johnny Bach, fired by the Bulls in June of '94, never ingratiated himself to Krause. Typically, the game would be close down the stretch, Winter would be talking about back-door cuts off the reverse pick, and Bach would pull Jordan aside. "Johnny would say, 'Fuck the triangle. Just take the ball and score. Get everyone else to clear out,' " Jordan laughed.

And deep down, though you'd be hard-pressed to get Jordan to admit it, he was happy to see Krause, who had always said he couldn't wait to build a championship team without Jordan, on the spot. Clearly, Krause was taken by surprise.

"I never sensed he would retire when he did," Krause said. "I figured he'd play his contract out [three more years] and I made plans with that in mind. I already told Jerry I really thought we could win three more titles. He could have made Toni [Kukoc's] year so much easier. I felt it would have been our best year by far."

Interestingly enough, Jordan felt bad about leaving without getting a chance to play with Kukoc. Part of that was caused by Kukoc's reaction in the team meeting the morning of October 6, when Jordan met with the players before his press conference.

"We sat in that room and I told them what I was doing and why I was doing it," Jordan said. "Toni was bawling like a kid and I didn't even know him that well. He got me really emotional because I didn't know him, but here he was showing such strong feelings about what I was doing. And in that one instance, I wish I could have played, just so I could have taught him and helped him learn the game.

"I felt sorry for him because his decision to come over [from Europe] was based on me being a part of the team. And yes, I was doing something that I felt was time for me to do, but it made it look like he was [falsely] lured into a situation he had dreamed of. I talked to him that day and I think he kind of understood. But he was emotional. And it was really touching."

As for the other reactions, Jordan was equally touched. "The only guy who didn't talk to me about [the retirement] was Horace. He never called and he never showed up at the press conference," Jordan said. "Stacey [King] called me. Scott [Williams]? I couldn't even talk to him. I had to hang up on Scott. It was like a little brother and you're going away to school or something.

"Scottie [Pippen] was hurt. Or maybe not hurt, but disappointed because now he had the pressure. He knew it was coming, but now all of a sudden, he started thinking about what I had been telling him on the planes and buses.

"And then there was Pax."

Though you wouldn't normally see the two together off the court — John Paxson once said in all the years he played with Jordan, he never phoned him at home because he didn't want to bother him — Jordan grew very fond and very appreciative of Paxson, who came to the Bulls in 1985, Jordan's second year in the league.

"We were like this," said Jordan, crossing his fingers. "And the only thing I regret about retiring is that I didn't take Paxson with me. And Bill [Cartwright]. Because I felt if they knew I was retiring earlier, they would have retired, too.

"I was surprised Bill played well [during the '93-'94 season], but I was happy. I didn't like the way Pax played. I didn't like the way he wasn't healthy and I knew inside he was hurting because he couldn't do what he wanted to do. I don't know if it would have been any different if I had been there. But when he was able to play, no one knew how to play us."

Jordan's relationship with Cartwright had been strained at times and provided another wedge between him and Krause when the Bulls traded Jordan's close friend, Charles Oakley, to the Knicks for Cartwright in June of '88. But Jordan insisted there was never anything personal.

"Bill was a consummate pro in that he knew what he could do," Jordan said. "Deep down he wanted to do more, but he couldn't. He wasn't capable of scoring. A lot of times early in games, we would go to Bill and see if he could give us something while he was still fresh. But at the end of the game, it was a different scenario.

"What he wanted to do, his skills wouldn't always allow him to do, so we knew when to pass it to him and when not to pass it to him. When it came out publicly that I didn't pass it to him in the fourth quarter, we all understood, even Phil. I came out the bad guy, and I knew that Horace and them made it seem like I did that, but we all knew. Everyone who played with Bill knew his limitations and we knew his strengths.

"That's part of being on a winning team. You have to know what everyone can do."

In general, Jordan said he had a problem with the idle gossip and complaining that undermined the team. He specifically recalled when Armstrong replaced Paxson in the starting lineup, at the beginning of the '92 season.

"Pax and I knew each other so well, it was like a right hand and a left hand," he said. "And when B.J. came in [as a starter], I had to truly start over again. I had to learn where B.J. was on the floor, what he liked to do, and it was difficult at first. Certain times we were disappointed with him, but I wasn't afraid to tell B.J."

Jordan compared this approach to Pippen's and Grant's, who were clearly uncomfortable with Armstrong in the starting lineup and handled it differently. "They wouldn't tell B.J., but then they would kill him to Phil or kill him in the press," Jordan said, "and then I would usually get the blame."

One of the adjustments they had with Armstrong was that he was more aggressive offensively than Paxson. "But that was natural for B.J.," Jordan said. "B.J. was making the transition from a scoring point guard to a complementary point guard. That's what we needed. But when some of us couldn't score, he could hit four or five in a row and get us going. And that's what we were hoping for. But just the competitive attitude he had, he wanted to do more.

"Some people rebelled. Horace said he was shooting too much and didn't want to pass it to him."

As for Grant, the only Bull over the years to speak out critically of him, Jordan compared his abilities to Cartwright's as far as late-game situations. "We'd give Horace plays early in the game, but late in the game, we didn't run any plays for him because he'd screw up his own damn play," Jordan said. "We could sit in the huddle and draw up a play going to Horace on an out-of-bounds situation and he would screw it up. And he was getting the shot."

The weird thing for Jordan was knowing how many lives he affected with his decision to retire, good and bad. Pete Myers, for example, had a new life and a new career with Jordan's retirement. And that's what Jordan preferred to think about. "I knew at some point in time, my decision would affect a lot of people's lives, but it was either now or later," he said. "The good thing about it was that it gave those guys the opportunity to adapt quickly without me. If I went through half a season and then decided it was time to quit like [Detroit's Bill] Laimbeer did, then in some ways I would have cheated the team. But if I let them know before going into the season so they could start out fresh and develop their own personality, it would give them a better chance of recovering."

For Krause, the notice was not long enough. "Never before in the history of the NBA has anybody had to do what we had to do last fall," he said. "The Lakers started the season with Magic and he quit during the season, so that was tough on Jerry West, maybe even tougher in some ways. But we were left two days before training camp started with no advance notice, no nothing. We had no clue."

To that, Jordan shrugged. "I always said when it was time to quit, I would just quit," he said. "I didn't want a farewell tour like Dr. J. And [Krause] always said he liked challenges. Besides, if I would have told him earlier, what would he have done, trade me?"

The October 6 press conference showed a side of Jordan the public was not used to seeing. There was no mistaking an edge, an anger toward the media for their recent treatment of him though he insisted on several occasions that the media had not pushed him out of the game as Magic Johnson had suggested they would.

No, what fueled Jordan that day was his outrage over the coverage surrounding his father's death. Almost immediately after James Jordan was reported missing, speculation on what could have happened and why included Michael's history of gambling. The most serious incident had involved more than $100,000 in golf and poker debts Michael paid to Eddie Dow, a North Carolina bail bondsman, found in check form in March of '92 among the possessions of the man, who was subsequently killed in an apparent robbery attempt. And a $57,000 cashier's check made out to James "Slim" Bouler, a North Carolina businessman and convicted cocaine dealer, also covering gambling debts.

Jordan subsequently blamed "third-party" introductions and poor judgment for getting him into the situation, and never denied that he indeed bets large sums of money on the golf course, though he maintained that in relative terms, it wasn't outrageous.

But that incident, for which he was warned by NBA Commissioner David Stern to be more careful about whom he associated with, would resurface when the *New York Times* revealed that Jordan and his father and friends went to Atlantic City the night before Game 2 of the '93 Eastern Conference finals series.

Now, in the eyes of some, he had a full-fledged gambling problem. And when James Jordan was killed under questionable circumstances, it was brought up again in random and often irresponsible speculation about why it had occurred. Later, the crime was found to be an apparently random act of robbery and violence.

"It was unfair," Jordan said. "I feel like a lot of people feel, that the media carries a very strong influence and we're in a very vulnerable situation. When some people don't know the true facts, they speculate, which gives a false assumption. But whenever they do find out the truth, they can never give those things back to the person."

In general, Jordan respected the so-called mainstream press, but was just as affected when stories popped up in the tabloids. "I saw it all over the place — the *Star*, *Globe*, all those tabloids," he said. "They didn't show any sympathy for a situation that was very emotional. Here I just lost my father, and they were trying to connect it to something that was totally irrelevant. I felt they were trying to get at me instead of giving him the peace he deserved. They never said 'James Jordan.' It was always 'Michael's father, James,' which told me it was always related back to me somehow, and I thought that was very unfair. The story spoke for itself."

Jordan said it was one of the few times when he truly resented his celebrity. "In situations where I'm criticized, I don't have a problem with that because I know I'm in a lifestyle where that's going to happen," he said. "But you're talking about my family and they're part of the situation not by choice. My father didn't deserve that. My wife, my mother, my sisters, my brothers, none of them deserved the negative connection they were making. It hurt a lot of us, and I just felt it wasn't a fair shot at my family. They have never been in that situation and mentally, they don't know how to deal with it. It stays with them a lot longer than it stays with me."

Jordan reiterated that it wasn't the media pressure that made him retire, but that it did have an effect. "They did make me evaluate what the game was about," he said. "It wasn't a game anymore, it was my life. So in essence, I didn't have the challenge of the game anymore. The only challenge left was the one against the media and I can't win that."

To Jordan, one thing retirement meant was physical freedom. Not bound by a contract that forbade him to do things that would risk injury, he tried to rediscover fun in the months after his October announcement. "I rode around Chicago on my motorcycle for a whole day right after [his announcement]," he said. "I had a helmet on and no one knew it was me. I had ridden a motorcycle as a kid, but hadn't in a long time. One time, I rode it downtown to Soldier Field for a Monday night football game. That was great."

Another time, he went skiing with a group of family and friends. "We went to Aspen for four days," he recalled. "I started out on the bunny hill and by the time we left, I was on the blue [intermediate] run."

He laughed like a kid. "My scariest adventure was the same day I learned the hockey stop," he recalled. "I'm coming down the hill headed straight for this tree. I couldn't do the snowplow. The only way I could stop was to do the hockey stop. It was the greatest. I loved it. From that point on, I knew I could do it. I enjoyed it immensely. It was a lot of fun."

Except for every beginning skier's nightmare, the chairlift. "I fell about 10 times and that's where most of my falls came. I'd get off too late most of the time. And just as I got off, the next chair would come around and whooomph, push me down," Jordan said, gasping for breath between giggles. "I looked like a yard sale — skis here, poles there. I'd come around and yell, 'Look out below, I'm going to wipe someone out.' "

The solitude was great, he said, though it only worked to a point. "It was beautiful and quiet," he said. "But here's this big, tall black guy on skis. It was pretty tough to hide. Then again, it was just as tough for anyone to bother me as I was flying around."

Occasionally, Jordan would pop into the Berto Center, the Bulls' training facility in north suburban Deerfield, for a visit. "I wanted to put on my stuff and just go out and play," he said of the first few months. "But not in the games. I didn't and still don't want to play organized basketball, but I'll play pickup in a second. It's weird. But you have so much knowledge and experience, you feel like you could go back and show them what it took to get to where you are. Like you could go back to school and take those tests, only this time you know the answers. That's the way I felt."

When he first considered actually practicing with the team, Jordan worried how it would look if the media found out. "I felt if I played, I'd be criticized, because it meant either I was still missing the game or interfering with them and what they were trying to do in the after-Michael Jordan era or whatever," he said. "I wanted to do it, but I wanted to do it because I still loved the game and for no other reason."

Jordan, in fact, had in his contract a "love-of-the-game" clause until it was eventually modified so he could play only in non-NBA games in North Carolina and Illinois. "I challenged it a couple times," he said. "I played in Magic's game and one [former teammate] Rod Higgins had in Fresno. If I had gotten hurt, I would've loved to have seen what the Bulls would've done."

When Jordan first stopped by early in the '93-'94 season, he simply watched the team practice. "They looked terrible," he said. "They were in total disarray. I wasn't planning on practicing with them, but I talked to Phil that day and he said, 'They look terrible out there, there's no continuity, no rhythm, no nothing.'

"So I said, 'Do you mind if I come in and try to get some competition back into practice, just to get them flowing somehow?' "

"I don't know," said Jackson. "We'll see."

"Well evidently," said Jordan, "Jerry Reinsdorf got word that I just wanted to have a good time and try to get some motivation back into practices and said, 'It can't hurt.' But Phil really wanted to know what my thinking was. He wanted to make sure that I wasn't going to give the impression out there that I wanted to come back and get the team sort of hanging on to that concept that 'Maybe Michael's going to come back at the end of the year,' like everyone was saying.

"I said, 'Phil, that's not my plan. And if that's what you think, I won't do it. I'm only here as a friend, a fan and a supporter of the team. I just want to see them do well, because if they don't, a lot of people are going to get criticized, and it's not going to be a good atmosphere for you to coach, and it's not going to be a good atmosphere for players to play in. If they don't believe in themselves, then who's going to believe in them?'"

Without too much prodding, Jackson agreed that maybe it wouldn't hurt and Jordan headed home to get his shorts and shirt, since "they cleaned my locker right out as soon as I left."

Jackson informed the team that Jordan was going to practice and "Right then," said Jordan, "I could sense the competition. Pippen and Grant started talking shit: 'If you're on the red team [the non-starting team], then you're going to get treated like it.' And I'm like, OK, maybe I can help this team. These were the guys [like newcomers Kukoc, Myers, Steve Kerr and Bill Wennington, among others] who didn't know the offense, so I had to do a little more.

"I wasn't in shape, my wind was short, but I could still do certain things. Toni was on my team and I knew he was getting criticized by everybody, but I figured the best way to get him to perform was to get him to feel like he was a part of the team. So I started saying, 'Come on, man, let's play. Don't wait for me. I'm not part of this team. I'm just here to fill in the fifth spot. I'll shoot wherever I can.' "

Jordan's first impression was how Pippen was treating Kukoc. "Pippen's jumping all over him and playing tough 'D' and the guy doesn't know where he is," said Jordan, "so I said, 'OK, Pippen, come over here with someone who really knows how to play the game.' So he'd make a basket and talk some shit and I'd make a basket and say, 'I retired myself, nobody retired me.' So we're going back and forth, and it was great. That was the atmosphere that I remembered and I think they kind of forgot. That's what got that day past. How they took that to the next day, I don't know.

"I would have come back again if they would have asked me, but I didn't want to feel like I was forcing it and I didn't want to give them the wrong impression."

Jordan walked away, however, with a few impressions of his own. Several concerned Kukoc. Like Pippen, Jordan's initial feelings about Kukoc had been negative.

"When I was playing," said Jordan, "Krause would tell us all the time how good he was [Kukoc was drafted in the summer of '90 but unsigned until the summer of '93]. It was annoying, and I'd say, 'Man, you're setting this guy up. Look at [Drazen] Petrovic, look at all these European players. It takes them a couple years to adapt. You're setting him up for disappointment. The fans in Chicago, everybody is going to expect this and that and the kid isn't going to be there yet.' And Krause would say, no, no, you'll see. He's a lot better than Petrovic. He can do this and that.

" 'OK fine,' I'd tell him, 'but don't talk to us about him because he's not here and we can only deal with what we have.' "

When the United States played Croatia in the '92 Olympic Games in Barcelona, Jordan and Pippen were primed to embarrass Kukoc, who appeared no closer to signing with the Bulls. Krause's contention is that Chuck Daly, the coach of the team, chose Pippen for the team only because he felt the Croatians were capable of defeating the U.S. and Pippen was the only player capable of stopping Kukoc. Furthermore, said Krause, Daly goaded Pippen into making Kukoc look bad.

Jordan, however, said Daly had nothing to do with it. "It was Krause who actually got it started," Jordan said, "because it was he who said the kid was so great. So we wanted to see how great he was. We took turns at him. It was like this: We were sitting there before the game and I said to Scottie, 'You know how Krause always says how good this guy is? Well, here it is. Let's test him and see how fucking good he is. If you get tired, call me and we'll switch.' The conversation was just like that. Chuck never said one word."

Krause, said Jordan, also had the same effect on the way the Bulls played Phoenix Suns guard Dan Majerle. "Krause thought Majerle was the second coming of Jerry Sloan," Jordan said. "That's why Pippen and I always went at him so hard too."

Jordan warmed to Kukoc that day he announced his retirement and he took an interest in watching Kukoc's progress throughout his rookie year. "Toni was very confused," he said of his impressions of Kukoc the few times he saw him in practice and early in the season. "He just needed some guidance, a teammate just to say, 'Hey, you should do this or that.' Not, 'Do this and do that.' "

The perception was that as tough as Pippen was on Kukoc in practice, he was only doing what Jordan had done to him and other young players. Pippen and Grant said as much. But Jordan took some exception to that.

"The difference with them," he said, referring to Pippen and Grant, "was that [Charles] Oakley was still here and he did all the slapping and rookie-type things. I'd try to help them but at the same time, I'd maintain a certain competitive attitude. If you're going to learn, that means getting tested in competitive situations. And if that means getting embarrassed sometimes, so be it. But it wasn't a personal thing. But I think with Scottie, with all the hype of Kukoc coming here and the adjustments that had to be made, it was personal.

"Playing with Toni, I would have been more sympathetic, with all the things he had to adjust to, than Scottie was. Scottie was a little bit impatient. As much as he was trying to help him, the public perception of him during games was the yelling. No one wants to be yelled at on the court. That was one thing

Coach Smith always taught me and I learned from him. As mad as you may be at a player, you never embarrass him in public.

"I maybe yelled or yanked at someone sometimes. I've gotten into discussions with Bill [Cartwright] and Scott Williams, for instance. Scott gets so animated in certain situations, he gets on your nerves to where you have to say, 'Scott, forget about the fucking play, man, just play,' that type of thing. But if you read my lips, more often than not, I was saying, 'Come on, you're doing fine. Don't worry about Phil. Phil's not on the court, we're on the court. You have to just play. ' "

Jordan saw Kukoc as a special case. "You have to treat him in a calm fashion because he's getting killed by P.J. [Jackson], he's getting killed by other players," he said. "To yell at him on the floor, he's going to lose all confidence in his skills."

But as he watched Kukoc over the course of the season, Jordan said he was impressed with certain qualities. "He was a good enough player that once he stepped on the floor, he forgot about the coach, which is good," he said. "You shouldn't make a mistake and look right over to the bench. I think he was good at that.

"And one thing I did see in him was that he was the only guy out there with the confidence to take the game-winning shot. He didn't worry about the pros and cons. He felt, 'If I miss it, so what?' He had full confidence. And to take those shots, that's how you've got to think. You can't worry, if I miss it, they're going to say I'm a goat and it's going to stay with me a week or two."

Though Jordan wasn't able to see all the Bulls games, especially after he went to spring training with the White Sox, then joined the Double A Birmingham Barons, he became something of a Kukoc fan. "I counted," he said. "Toni had five game-winners during the regular season. I kept tabs. Usually when I came in from a [baseball] game, all we could see was the fourth quarter."

When the Bulls were playing the Knicks in the infamous Game 3 of their conference semifinal series, the Barons were in Orlando and Jordan was in the bathroom after the game, getting play-by-play yelled in to him. He was told the Bulls had the ball and were trailing with 1.8 seconds remaining. "I told them 'You don't have to tell me. Kukoc is going to take the shot and they're going to win.' I predicted the whole scenario."

As for Pippen's actions during that game — he was, of course, on the bench for Kukoc's shot, refusing to re-enter the game — Jordan was amazed if somewhat sympathetic, comparing what Pippen must have been feeling to how he felt when he envisioned a future of playing a limited role with the Bulls.

"All your great players have that desire to want the last shot," he said. "But if that's what he felt, that was certainly not the most opportune time to do that. You wait until after the game. If [the play called] doesn't work, you'll get your credibility back. But let the media make that decision [that it was a bad call]. But Scottie didn't understand that and I didn't have the chance to teach him. I wish I could have. I thought he would have learned it himself.

"He jumped the gun and you can't do that, especially not in a playoff game. And unfortunately, he's going to be criticized the rest of his life for that. That's the kind of situation that sticks with you."

Jordan saw the Bulls' '93-'94 home opener in person, an embarrassing 95-71 loss to Miami that had Heat players openly jeering the gun-shy Bulls with mocking cries of "Da Bulls" and "You can do it, Jo Jo," to young Jo Jo English.

Jordan sat just under the west basket, close enough to jump in if he had to, too well-dressed to get away with it as he sat bouncing his youngest son Marcus on his lap and looking re-splendent if not downright strange in street clothes. His former teammates gawked, at times even when they were on the court and often while they were on the bench, as if he might suddenly change his mind and join the fray.

Miami center Rony Seikaly evidently had the same concerns. "I was just worried he'd take his suit coat off and be Superman against us again," he quipped afterward.

But alas, it was a long night for the Bulls, who produced just 25 points in the first half, the team's lowest-ever scoring total in a half, and a record-low of just six points in the second quarter. They also shot 19.5 percent in the first half and 27 of 86, or 31 percent, for the game.

"The game took about two days in actual coaching time," Jackson tried to joke. "It just seemed like it went on forever.

"I don't know if [Jordan] was part of the effect or not, but he seemed like a looming presence to a lot of people. An eye was watching that was maybe not judgmental but very critical; one that was supportive yet one that couldn't supply the needed effort to help us solve the problem."

Jordan was equally uneasy, leaving before the game concluded. But he said later that watching it did not make him want to play again. "It was frustrating because they weren't doing what they were supposed to be doing and I guess I felt like a coach," he said. "A coach knows what you're supposed to be doing and then when the team gets into the game and doesn't do it, you get frustrated. That's what I felt like.

"I didn't feel like I should've been out there. I overcame that. That was part of my whole thought process when I retired. I told myself I wasn't going to look back, wishing I was here or there. I could be happy remembering how it was and what I did under those circumstances, but I didn't want to miss being out there. I didn't get depressed about it."

When he started frequenting Comiskey Park, almost immediately after announcing his retirement, Jordan was getting treatment on his wrist. When he began working out at the ballpark, it became a covert operation. "I was there by 8:30-9 every morning and out by midday," he said. "I'd drive in where all the TV trucks go and they'd let me drive in. My car was never parked in sight. I really didn't want anyone to know I was there. I wanted to be able to walk away without anybody knowing in case I didn't have the skills to play. But I loved it, and that's when I really developed an appetite for the game."

What he didn't miss, as he drew his own renewed media following obsessed with his new baseball career, were the random controversies that seem to pop up every Bulls season. One incident that couldn't help but draw his attention was Pippen's arrest on charges of keeping a loaded gun in his car, charges were later dropped when it was determined the car had been illegally searched.

At the time, it came out that Jordan owned a gun, and in light of his father's death, he thought about how his views had changed. And hadn't.

"It's a good thought, anti-gun," he said. "I'm as anti-gun as much as you can think of, but I have a gun. I'm in favor of the perfect world, but it isn't a perfect world. To some extent, you have to protect yourself, but you also have to be cautious. If you're going to handle a gun, you can't be a maniac and you can't be a showoff. You have to be a level-headed person to know what risks you're taking with that firearm.

"I heard that Horace said I had a gun and showed it to everyone, but I go by the law. And by the law, you can't carry it in your car. You've got to have a license for it and you have to keep it locked and out of the reach of kids, all of which I do. What Scottie did was breaking the law, and athletes, more than anyone, have to be examples."

Jordan said he owns a gun, not just as a hobby, but for protection. "There are a lot of lunatics out there," he said. "I would defend my family if I had to. If my father had a gun, he probably would have defended himself. Then again, if [the killer] didn't have a gun, he wouldn't have needed it. So there are two ways of looking at it. If the law stated you couldn't have handguns and it was against the law, OK, I'm with the law. But if the law says you can have handguns and protect your family at all times, then I'm for that too.

"I'd love it if there were no danger, no guns, a society that doesn't kill needlessly. But we don't live in that society. I always hoped we would, but we don't."

In the year that followed his retirement, Jordan would think of his father often. But he would force himself to focus on the warm memories of James' life rather than the cold, harsh reality of his death. "It makes you aware of where our world is headed," Michael said. "You always hear about it happening to other people but until it happens to you, you don't realize how bad it can be out there.

"But I don't let it get me bitter. Every now and then, it gets to me that it happened. But I can't keep going through why he was killed because I can't get anything positive out of it. And I can't treat the rest of the world with a bitter tone. It would just make me crazy and miserable all the time. But it does make me mad that the world has to be this way.

"I guess you can't have the good without the bad. You can't learn from good."

For Jordan, baseball was all that was good, but it was also a learning experience. "It was my father's love and I loved it too," he said.

James Jordan loved Roberto Clemente, the legendary right fielder from the Pittsburgh Pirates. And so Michael did as well, playing right field for the Barons in the spring and summer of '94, and constantly batting off rumors that he would return to basketball.

"I still love the game," he said. "I always will. I just don't want to play in a uniform with referees and all that other stuff."

So he played pickup basketball whenever he could. On beaches and in parks. More often than not, before a crowd that came running once word was out. But he embraced baseball and he had fun with his new young teammates, who were the beneficiaries of his reflected fame and experience, not to mention, in the case of designated hitter Scott Tedder, several dozen of Jordan's once-worn size 13 cleats. Several other players shared a new Mustang, which Jordan had been given by a local dealer and didn't need.

Another player, backup catcher Rogelio Nunez, had a running wager with Jordan, though it was entirely one-sided. Nunez, from the Dominican Republic, had been trying to learn English when his new teammate came up with an idea.

Every day, Nunez would give Jordan a letter. The next day, Jordan would give Nunez a word related to baseball beginning with that letter and Nunez would have to spell it. If he did it correctly, Jordan gave him $100.

Every day was an education for the Barons, who never before had to fight their way through hotel lobbies and parking lots. And soon, they stopped asking if Jordan wanted to join them at McDonald's.

Jordan eventually got over the resentment he felt at the initial bashing he took by deciding to try baseball. But one typically humid day in mid-July, after another pregame workout that soaked him to the skin, he talked about the *Sports Illustrated* cover urging him to "Bag it, Michael — Jordan and the White Sox are embarrassing baseball."

"If it could be called un-American, that's what it was," he said of the cover, his voice rising. "The American dream is to do whatever you please and do it to the best of your ability and enjoy doing it. If you have the opportunity, go out and do it, go make the best out of the opportunity you have.

"I was doing that, and yet I was being criticized for it. It just kind of took me by surprise, because I really didn't think I was making the game look bad. I would never do that. And I certainly wasn't breaking any laws. I just always loved baseball and wanted to play."

Just as he had loved basketball. And just as he had left it.

When he started thinking about retirement, Jordan wondered if he had done all he could on the basketball court, if indeed he had distinguished himself as one of the all-time greats, and decided maybe it was more important than he thought.

"I wanted to separate myself from your average Joe basketball player," he said. "I knew winning championships showed your skills at an even greater level so they didn't have any doubts about what you're capable of doing as an athlete. But it was more than that.

"I'm pretty sure all your other great players wanted to be distinctive from the next superstar, and that's what I was thinking. I knew I didn't have Magic Johnson's smile or his point-guard abilities. I didn't have Larry Bird's shooting abilities. But I did have my own all-around play, at a height that was unheard of in terms of scoring, in terms of playing defense, blocking shots, making steals, whatever.

"Those are the things that drove me as a basketball player. When I achieved all that and there was no comparison between the three of us, we were all on the same level for the talents we had, then my job was done, in a sense. What else is there? Because if you continue, all the things away from the game are going to detract from that and leave some sort of tainted career."

Baseball would be but a postscript, he knew. A significant one if he was lucky, but nothing more. For even if he left his basketball career as an unfinished masterpiece, it was still one of a kind. It was still his masterpiece. And he drew deep satisfaction from that.

"People said, 'You'll taint your image as a basketball player by playing baseball,' " Jordan said. "But you can't do that. You can't touch what I did in basketball. You can't touch it. You can never take that away from me."

Public Relations Dept.
Chicago Bulls
One Magnificent Mile
980 North Michigan Ave., Suite 1600
Chicago, Ill. 60611

Dear Bulls,
I am a condemned inmate here on death row at San Quentin and am writing
this to you on behalf of my mother, Ruth

My mother, who is an avid Bulls fan, is presently confined to a nursing
home in Illinois. She is able to follow your progress in the play-offs
on a television at the nursing home. I was wondering if it would be
possible for you to send her a team photograph of this years Bulls team.
This would really be a pleasant surprise for her and I would appreciate
it very much.

2

PHIL

It came as a surprise to some when Phil Jackson suddenly gathered his Bulls team the day after they lost to the Knicks in Game 1 of the '94 Eastern Conference semifinals and told the bus driver to bypass the Downtown Athletic Club, where they were scheduled to practice in midtown Manhattan, and instead go to Staten Island for a ferry ride past the Statue of Liberty.

A surprise to some. But in retrospect, not to his veteran players. And certainly not to veteran Jackson watchers, who had seen him bypass the Bulls' charter jet to take his team on bus rides from Portland to Seattle for the sightseeing opportunities, or to Capitol Hill for the cultural opportunities. This day was for diversionary opportunities.

"I know a lot of coaches who would have just taken us to the gym and worked the hell out of us," said first-year Bull Bill Wennington, "but that's not what we needed."

"We had much more to learn," Jackson explained later, "about being together in the fresh air and the ocean than being on the basketball court. Living life is living it in the moment, and if that's what you've got to do, do it. Just enjoy the life. I try to do things interesting that will hopefully expand their lives and make them more comfortable being citizens of the world."

OK, so maybe that was a little dramatic. Jackson has a gift for outrageous overstatement. The key is the delivery. Slip it in when they're least expecting it. When they're busy trying to figure out what the hell that last sentence meant, quietly mention that Pat Riley is an arrogant jerk. It sounds oddly less offensive and more cerebral. And nine times out of ten Jackson gets away with it.

But back to the cultural stuff. That is Phil Jackson too. One day, for example, before a normal midseason practice, he brought up Casimir Pulaski's name. It happened to be Pulaski Day in Chicago, though—surprise surprise—none of the players had been talking about it much.

"Who knows who he is?" asked Jackson, requesting a show of hands, then proceeding to reveal the identity of the general in the Polish army as his players feigned interest.

But they did not always fake it. Jackson launched into similar impassioned speeches about Martin Luther King, the riots in Los Angeles, and current events that hit a lot closer to home, like Scottie Pippen's arrest on gun possession charges (which were eventually dropped).

In the case of the former, Jackson dealt in abstract concepts as examples for other lessons in life. In the case of the latter, he did much the same. But after the Pippen incident, Jackson was truly worried about what he feared was a growing trend. "I got an inkling guns were part of the team, " he said. Indeed, Horace Grant owned guns, which he used at a range, as did Michael Jordan.

"I saw Michael once take out his gun [in the locker room] and I talked to him about that," Jackson said. "And I got the feeling there were more and more guns. I could hear chatter and I worried about it. Recent years have brought such an irrational kind of violence that players got worried, and from that worried standpoint, they went to more and more protection and they felt individually they could provide it for themselves."

Strictly pro-gun control, Jackson took advantage of the opportunity to preach where he was coming from and, as always, in a way unique to himself. "I talked about little things," he said, "that your own consciousness is brought back to you. What you think, happens. As you think, so you are, which is tough to buy for these kids because they don't see thoughts becoming reality.

"When Scottie's situation happened, it wasn't the first time that I talked about guns, but it was time to emphasize again where I stand on handguns. Even though I feel it's an individual's right to have them, I think you have to measure an awful lot as to who you are and what you think about when you get a handgun. Handguns are for one thing: killing humans.

"It becomes a toy. And what I told them is that it's great if you want to go to a rifle range and shoot them, but leave them there. Don't own them, because they end up in the wrong places and in the wrong hands. It could end up in your child's hands.

"When I played, our trainer with the New York Knicks, when you got into a conflict with a referee and got a technical, always used to say, 'If you had a gun, you'd shoot him.' You go from the standpoint of the biggest and strongest. If you have a fist, you'd hit him. If you had a knife, you'd stab him. And if you had a gun, you'd shoot him. And that's the wrong resource for your anger."

While Jackson had a concrete reason to bring up the issue of guns, he usually did not need an excuse to talk about a variety of topics and issues.

"I have no problem talking about my spiritual beliefs, things totally out of the realm of their minds," he explained. "Like Martin Luther King on Martin Luther King Day and his anti-violence stand, and how basically we revere his memory and everything else, but that we've gotten to be a very violent society and we have not held up to all the things he preached."

A shooting outside the players' gate at the Stadium in mid-January that injured a bodyguard of rap star Hammer prompted another team discussion.

"I like to bring up those things, or like the riots in Los Angeles when it happened," Jackson said. "The worst thing we can do is not talk about racial facts.

"Whites are dealing, by and large, with more blacks than we've ever dealt with in our lives, and blacks are dealing with more whites than they ever would, and there has to be this give and take. And if not in our world, if not in the NBA, then where else is it going to happen in society? Not in the business place, where people work for eight hours with 2.6 percent minorities."

Given the choice, Jackson said he likes to form his teams by players' individual "psyches" as much as anything; their ability to play and relate to the others in the group, as well as their ability, obviously, to execute in the Bulls system. But the racial factor is unlikely to go away.

"I'm aware there are Chicagoans who say the Bulls are more and more conscious of building up whites on the team, that Jackson is trying to make this a white team," he said. "But Toni Kukoc was the best player available a couple years ago. The style of basketball we play and the system we use happens to be conducive to a lot of skills white players have — spot shooting, ball movement and cutting — as opposed to power basketball usually indigenous to the skills black players have — one-on-one moves, quickness, jumping ability. Michael used to call it the white man's game of basketball. And I said, 'So did Dean Smith at the University of North Carolina.' "

Jackson was relatively lucky on the issue of race. Aside from Pippen's comments in late February of '94, any racial tension there may have been on the Bulls was often defused with humor. Like John Paxson one day glancing to either side of him in the locker room and laughingly proclaiming it "White Man's Row." And Pippen, joking that the "crackers" were out-numbering the brothers as the Bulls' white population grew to six after the acquisition of Luc Longley for Stacey King.

There was tension, to be sure, when the trading deadline drew closer and no one, white or black, was brought in to help the team. Pippen was especially impatient and angry at Krause for the apparent inactivity. In early January, shortly before the deadline for guaranteeing contracts for the remainder of the season and one day after the New York Knicks picked up Derek Harper, Pippen and Grant sat in Pippen's Washington, D.C., hotel room and fumed.

"If people expect the Bulls to contend," said Pippen, care-fully planning his words for publication, "we have to have something to go to war with. ... I'm not going to be comfortable going to the playoffs with the roster we have now."

Jackson, meanwhile, also expressed very thinly veiled criti-cism of Krause. "We've known since day one that there's an ingredient missing that we're not going to be able to cover up," he said in reference to Jordan's void. "We still need a spot filled or we come up short. Players are looking over their shoulders and we're telling them to leave it to the organization. But they read the papers. They know what's going on."

Later, Jackson spoke privately about how he reconciles that frustration and has continued to maintain a peaceful working relationship with Krause for five years, something previous Bulls coach Doug Collins was often unable to do. "I can only deal with the cards I get dealt to me," Jackson said. "You don't always have the best hand dealt to you compared with others in the league. But I've been in situations when Doug was the coach, when I saw coaches fret, fume and waste so much energy lusting for a trade or whatever, the look-at-what-we-put-on-the-floor and look-at-what-they-put-on-the-floor type thing, and I think it's a waste of energy.

"You can't spend all your time fighting management. I've suggested some people need to be moved on for the betterment of their careers and the betterment of the organization. But I'm probably a general manager's dream for a coach. Outside of stimulating Jerry once in a while to get active, basically we have our own lives and an exclusive area in which we operate."

At the same time, Jackson did not seem to mind taking responsibility for the firing of assistant coach Johnny Bach, easily one of the most unpopular moves in his tenure as head coach. While Jackson did not necessarily open up personally to his assistants any more than to his players, his relationship with Bach was always solid.

Ideologically, Jackson had little in common with Bach, a formal naval officer and conservative who often drew military analogies to basketball, frequently in graphic forms such as using the ace of spades, the so-called death card, to symbolize outstanding defensive performances.

Nevertheless, Jackson respected Bach's basketball knowledge and thought it nonsense and tiresome when Krause would hound on the theory that Bach was disloyal and leaking valuable information to the media. So when Bach returned from a brief layoff after the '93-94 season, "I was thoroughly surprised when Phil said he wanted to speak to me," Bach said. "He was short and to the point."

Bach was not going to be offered another contract and Jackson immediately took responsibility, telling Bach as well as the media that it was his decision. He never did elaborate on the reason and Bach said he did not care at that point. "It was inarguable," said Bach, who added that Jackson was "cold as ice." Besides, it was obvious to everyone close to the Bulls that while the final decision may indeed have been Jackson's, the idea had originated with Krause.

But why then did Jackson take responsibility? Jackson said he wished it was a case of disloyalty or disrespect on Bach's part, but that wasn't it. He just felt "it was the right time to do it."

Clearly, insiders say, Jackson had grown tired of refereeing the strained relationship between Bach and Krause, which rarely took the form of a one-on-one confrontation, but rather had both parties complaining to Jackson about the other. Still, the move was out of character for Jackson, who looked publicly to be turning his back on a trusted colleague rather than taking a stand.

In the end, though he never did talk about the situation on the record, it came down to Jackson choosing his battles and deciding that among the matters in which he wished to sway Krause and had a pretty good chance in doing so, this was not one of them. He had grown tired of Bach being labeled the "defensive guru" of the Bulls anyway, and so Jackson would take the hit for Krause on this one, knowing that his record with the media and fans was solid, and that Krause would undoubtedly be skewered. No doubt, however, Jackson would use this as a chip in the future.

What some of this did, perhaps, was convince Jackson that decision making of this magnitude was not all it was supposed to be. The business side of basketball made the profession stressful, and after the grind of another season, Jackson, as he always did, pondered his future.

"I don't see myself in the game very long at all as far as coaching," Jackson said after the '93-'94 season, "and I don't see myself as a general manager. I don't see myself, surprisingly enough, getting drawn into it in this organization. Jerry pretty much wants to stay in tight control, and rightly so."

Personnel decisions, with the increasingly complicated salary cap, were not just basketball anymore, Jackson said, and it certainly wasn't very much fun. Being a coach and general manager, he viewed as a conflict of interests. Beyond that though, he just didn't see himself able to sustain the interest and energy for a prolonged period.

"I'd like to fulfill my contract [which expires after the '95-'96 season] and then I'd like to re-evaluate," he said. "I always thought I'd coach for 10 years [which would take him to the year 2000]. Jerry Reinsdorf once said to me that it should be part of a coach's job description to take a sabbatical like a university professor, so I'm looking for that opportunity — to take a year's paid vacation and then come back and take the team over after a sabbatical."

Jackson laughed. "I just want to know the interim coach and what he's going to do and who's going to apply for that job."

As far as a possible future in broadcasting, Jackson has thought about it. He had done some work for ESPN in the early days of the all-sports network, and did some radio for the Knicks network. And, of course, there were his local radio and television shows during his coaching tenure with the Bulls. But he turned down an offer to do postseason work for NBC in the spring of '94 after the Bulls were eliminated, and couldn't quite picture himself, he said, as a full-time commentator.

"It's something I could do, but I'm a little too long-winded and run-on to be real concise and good at it," he said. "There were a lot of things I didn't like about television, the monkey-behind-the-microphone thing a lot of times, interviewing someone I don't know or doing something spontaneous I don't feel spontaneous about. I've learned I like coaching a lot better than television work, because I didn't know who I was in television."

Jackson got his first taste of coaching as a player/coach in New Jersey. The joke was that he never officially retired as a player. "I laugh about that," he said. "But I don't have a good feeling about the way my career ended. The management in New Jersey was still in training. It was tough. They wanted me as a player, they wanted me as a coach, but they didn't want to make me an assistant coach, so there was a lot of back-and-forth stuff.

"The first year they hired me on as a coach, I said, 'OK, but I want to be paid as a coach.' They gave me $10,000 and I had a guaranteed contract [as a player]. I just wanted a special designation."

Eight games into the season, the rookie who had beaten him out at back up center went down with a knee injury and

Jackson was activated. The next off-season, he learned he suddenly wasn't being considered a coach any longer but was back to being a player.

"So I went through the same process again," he said, "but this time with no guaranteed contract. Then at the end of training camp, they let one of their assistants go and they asked if I wanted to be an assistant. I never really knew what role I fit into."

The Nets then activated Jackson for the last 22 games of the season, but they missed the playoffs. "I really feel like they liked the way I played the game my last year," Jackson said, "but I realized it was bogus. At 34 years old, that was no life to be living. But I never retired officially."

And there is no official record of Jackson as an assistant coach in New Jersey.

"I had no [coaching] contract," he said. "I was walking on eggs as a player. But I knew I was through."

Something funny, however, happened along the way. In his final year as a so-called assistant coach under Kevin Loughery, Jackson realized something. "Loughery got kicked out a lot, so I got to coach games," Jackson laughed. "And I found out I really liked coaching."

And for the meantime, anyway, he still does. "There are rhythms to that where all of a sudden, you're exhausted and you've had it and you realize everything has boiled to the surface and you need a break," he said of holding off the almost inevitable burnout. "But usually a day or two away is enough to revitalize me right now. That and the end of the season [when he spends most of the summer with his family in Montana] have been enough."

The '93-'94 season was trying for Jackson, no question. After Jordan retired, much was said and written about Jackson relishing the idea of doing a real coaching job and finally getting acknowledged for it. And in truth, he did readily accept the challenge. But that did not mean there wasn't plenty of anxiety along the way.

The first inkling Jackson received that Jordan might actually be serious about retiring came at a September 18 ('93) dinner benefiting the Michael Jordan Foundation. Jordan told Jackson then that he was considering it, though Jackson, like the players, had already seen and heard the signals.

Jackson said he had seen it coming two years before Jordan made his official announcement. "In Michael's life and lifestyle, basketball was one place that gave him the perfect distraction," Jackson said. "He had the obligation, the excuse, to climb down off his whirlwind lifestyle, get to work and have a reason for telling everyone, 'No, we have a game. No, I'm busy with practice. No, it's not possible.'

"But I saw more and more over the last two years his inability to bring his level of competition up to where it had been in years past. And having to shoulder that responsibility time and time again, the wearing effect it had on him when he did do it was immense. So there was considerable discussion, at least in my home, about the possibility of retirement when his father was killed."

Jackson said among his many thoughts upon hearing of James Jordan's death was that it would only make it tougher for Michael to continue playing. "I thought, now the press has another place to go back at him," he said. "He's going to have to answer all those same questions, and it would add up to a summation that was just too much to handle."

In the past, off-the-court controversies had not worried Jackson, who seemed to always remain outwardly cool, no matter the problem. And there was a reason for that. It never seemed to ruffle Jordan, especially on the court, so why should it bother him?

"I always felt that whatever the focus was on Michael that could be negative, that could be looked at as upsetting, simply wasn't," Jackson said. "He'd always come out and disprove that. It could be gambling in New Jersey and people would say this is a distraction to your basketball game, and he'd immediately come back and prove them wrong."

That fierce will in Jordan, Jackson said, gave him the only reason to initially hold out hope that his retirement was not permanent. "I thought maybe the only outside reason he might perhaps return to basketball was because he's retired, and no one has ever returned from retirement," Jackson said. "His success is at such a level that he could do something that would be totally off the wall — be part of a championship team and maybe win a scoring title again."

Deep down though, Jackson said he knew Jordan would not return. "What bothered me was the constant wearing at the veneer that he has developed," he said. "It eventually makes a person put a shell around himself so he doesn't have that ability to be real and upfront and honest and reflective. There's always the worry, 'How am I going to look?'

"But I never worried about shielding him. Once we got the MGM [private charter] plane, it was just some people who wanted to press in on him that I felt most worried about. Not the media. Media, I think, are understanding, though I think there's always the occasional guy sliding a poster in to be autographed with his work pass on. Everybody has a son or nephew who wants a Michael Jordan autograph. But we were able to at least provide the privacy of the plane and the locker room.

"He really liked to be one of the guys. That's what most guys like about basketball. But in the end, it was too much of the other stuff."

And in the end, ultimately, it was Jordan's absence that prevented the Bulls from going further than the second round of the playoffs, though certainly referee Hue Hollins wears that collar in Chicago as well.

"The reason we didn't win this year," Jackson summed up the '93-'94 season, "is because we didn't have a Scottie Pippen behind a Michael Jordan. Scottie had no one like himself to step up behind his effort. Horace wanted to be that guy, but couldn't. And B.J. is B.J. He does pretty good with the talent he has, which is not athletic talent, not superior speed or explosiveness, but great shooting skills. He does the most with what he has.

"We needed someone else and unfortunately, none of that became a reality. [Derek] Harper or [Jeff] Hornacek would have given us an opportunity, but it didn't happen. We were in the ballpark with Philadelphia [for Hornacek], but they didn't include us in the dance. For some reason, we didn't get the call. But we thought we could have made [the trade] happen as much as Utah made it happen."

Jackson wanted these trades, desperately wanted offensive help at shooting guard, but watched as any potential moves fizzled.

Krause said he "immediately" looked at then-free agent and eventual Indiana Pacer Byron Scott as a possibility. But after talking to former Lakers teammate Michael Cooper, Krause said the Bulls, after consulting Jackson, decided against going after him.

"We decided that defensively, Byron Scott would be a liability," Krause said. "And the biggest thing we had to replace with Michael [leaving] was defense. People didn't realize we had to replace that defensive ability more than his offense. We could rely on the system to get us points, but we knew we had to emphasize defense. So the older scorers like Scott, who had lost a step defensively, we just couldn't take.

"That's one of the reasons we passed on Harper. We scouted him very thoroughly because of his defense, but all the stuff about us making offers is b.s. We backed away."

The reason? "Derek's ability as a jump shooter went way down," said Krause. "His first three to four months with the Knicks, he shot 34 percent, and a lot of those shots were layups. In our offense, you have to be able to shoot jump shots, so we made a decision — a total staff decision. We took a vote of the coaches and the coaches didn't want him. And I didn't want him either. He hit some big shots in the Finals against Houston, but against us he didn't hit too many big ones."

Krause said he never felt pressure to make a move. "We never felt desperate," he said. "Scottie said some things [complaining about Krause's inaction] before the trading deadline without even talking to me. When I finally talked to him, I said 'Scottie, to get a great shooting guard in this league, do you know what we have to give up? To get a great shooting guard, we have to give up a great player. That's you. Or someone of your caliber."

Concerning a move for Hornacek, Krause said the Sixers weren't interested in Scott Williams, though they eventually signed him in late July to a seven-year, $20 million deal. Not interested in taking the risk involved at the time was more like it. "Nobody's going to take a free agent if they don't think they can sign the guy," Krause explained. "I wasn't in a position where I could give Philadelphia permission to talk to Scott Williams. So we discussed him at one point and they said they weren't interested and never offered me a deal."

Krause said up until the day of the trading deadline, he was trying to arrange a three-way deal that would have given the Sixers what they were looking for, which was a shooting guard in return for Hornacek. "If I could have found one to give Philadelphia, I would have," he said. "I didn't think they would take Jeff Malone. Did I try to get Hornacek? Yeah. Did I want him to go to New York? No. I would have rather Harper gone."

Ultimately, Krause said, he felt comfortable with looking Jackson in the eye and saying he had given it his best shot. "We looked at everyone and everything at midseason," he said. "We looked here, overseas and at every possible player in every way to help our team."

At the same time, however, Krause suggests that he wasn't sure they needed to make a move at all. "At the trading deadline, we felt we were going pretty good [at 21-10] and some chemistry was developing on this team, which we didn't want to disturb a whole lot," he said. "As far as I'm concerned, we were one call away from the Finals and we could've beaten Houston." This was assuming, of course, the Bulls beat Indiana first, which no one seemed to doubt.

Jackson obviously had to play the cards he was dealt. And by then, he had already weathered several storms. His first worry of the season was Pippen's recovery from ankle surgery, which should have taken place immediately after the '92-'93 season but which Pippen inexplicably delayed until August 31 of '93.

"The only time that I felt troubled about this team," Jackson said, "was when I felt that maybe Scottie might not have the physical capabilities to play the season or when he was showing the temperament that perhaps he wasn't going to survive the operation very well. It was tough to think about Pax and Bill being able to play a consistent amount of games. And Horace was going into a free-agent year, which I knew was going to be upsetting for him. Even though we reached an agreement that if he went free agent, he said it wouldn't affect his season at all, that's impossible with Horace.

"I knew that if Pippen wasn't there as the driving force, the energizing person in terms of confidence, attacking with the basketball and as a disconcerting defender who could cause offensive opponents to change tactics, to lose confidence or to destroy their system, then we were going to be in for a long season.

"So at some point around November 5, we saw the reality of our season. Toni was too young, too inexperienced and we were too unconfident to win on the road. We felt, well, at least we can probably win at home with this group."

On their first major trip of the year, mired at 4-7 following a 25-point loss at San Antonio on November 24, the Bulls had already lost more games than the previous year's team had lost by mid-December, and the team before that by late January. "That's when it really blew up in our faces," said Jackson.

In the locker room, veterans like Grant and Armstrong were discouraged and a little impatient with the newcomers. And the reports from home were not encouraging. Word was that Pippen was not keeping his therapy appointments.

"Scottie was intimating the possibility that his ankle might not come back," recalled Jackson. "He was saying things like, 'I'm not getting any movement out of this.' And there were no assurances that when we got back, he was going to feel any better. I'd talk to him a little bit on the phone and ask, 'How's the training going?' and he was having trouble with his therapy, it wasn't going very easily. But then we came home and he stepped onto the court."

Pippen's return sparked one of the most encouraging victories of the season, a 132-113 rout of a talent-laden Phoenix team on November 30, and put into motion a 10-game winning streak. But it did not erase the question of why he waited so long to have the surgery in the first place. Jackson understood the first delay, citing the burnout of three consecutive nine-month seasons.

"It was so soon after the season," Jackson reasoned, "that it was probably hard to think that, man, I just got free from basketball, now I have to go get pain administered to me and spend a month recuperating from this. But then when that window went by and the next one was missed because he had camps and all these other excuses, that's when Krause called me up in Montana and was upset about it because he and I both knew that many things could go wrong when you do this. Not only is rehabilitation usually put on the high side, but actually facing the recuperation and rehabilitation is not easy. You always have to go through the doubting and breaking through mental doubts involved in an invasive operation.

"I think those doubts were in Scottie's mind and without any training camp, I think it affected us all. So that was immediately problematic because without Scottie in camp, we had doubts that Horace would want to be there because he has trouble functioning when he feels he's working and somebody else isn't on that groove. Michael was out. Paxson and Bill were hurt. So we anticipated a rather lethargic, slow camp, which it turned out to be."

Nevertheless, Jackson immediately promoted Pippen to co-captain, joining Cartwright at the helm, and promoted the idea that he was the Bulls' leader, that the saddle was on his back.

Jackson said it was an easy decision because Pippen had become a team leader over the previous two seasons. "Once we came through the first championship and even during the first championship year, he became a practice leader," Jackson explained. "Michael was often silent in practice, working on something he wanted to work on or distracted by outside influences a lot of times. Physically, he had been more beat up over his last two seasons and it kind of fell on Scottie's shoulders to provide that kind of leadership on the court and in practice."

Jackson said he also noticed Grant yearning for more leadership. "I wasn't worried so much about Scottie and Horace wanting that, or maybe not being responsible about being leaders, but maybe trying to do too much," he said. "I felt that they would try to take a larger bite than was necessary. They wanted to make every big play, wanted to try to do everything that would exclude other people in the group. I just kept reminding them that confidence would have to go one through 12 among the players and coaching staff and not just well, we know everything because we've been through it before, and try to place the responsibility exclusively on their own shoulders to make big shots and big plays."

That would resolve itself soon enough. But off the court, as usual, things were not going as well. Primarily, Jackson grew increasingly impatient with Grant.

With many of the team's internal problems, Jackson often preferred not to communicate. "I'm obtuse in a lot of ways on purpose," he tried to explain one day late in the regular season. "But that's also a way of communicating. My wife always tell me I don't give enough praise. I know I don't. I guess I just believe good behavior is expected. And I think playing time is a reward. I think that says a lot.

"There's just so much stuff that you don't need to talk about because the next day it dissipates. That's the best thing about the NBA. There's always another game tomorrow. So there's a lot to be said about just leaving something alone."

Grant, however, made Jackson look at everything a little differently, and it was impossible to leave their relationship alone. Early in Grant's career, Jackson recognized his passion and sensitivity, and viewed it as an opportunity to use him as a sort of lightning rod for the team.

"I brought Horace off the practice floor one time that first year ['89-'90, Jackson's first as head coach, Grant's third in the league] and asked him, 'Do you mind if you get yelled at? Does it bother you?' He said, 'No, it kind of helps get me going.' So I said, 'Good because I want to yell at you a little bit. It can be a motivating thing for the rest of the guys, so don't be surprised if I get on you.'

"I had a Jordan, Pippen, Paxson and Cartwright, and I knew I could use Horace as a motivating force. He was the kind of guy around whom others would rally to his defense. It wasn't manipulating as much as getting energy into the group. Sometimes you have to stir up the hive a little bit and get the bees angry. But this bonded our relationship."

As Grant matured as a player, however, his patience with these tactics wore increasingly thin and he began speaking his mind, voicing his displeasure over what he considered double standards for Jordan and Pippen and mistreatment by team management in regard to his contract.

"After we won the first championship [in 1991], " said Jackson, "he really wanted to change the rules and so my criticism had to become oblique. He had younger guys around him now like Scott Williams, and he didn't want to be embarrassed in front of the group anymore. I could understand that, but I brought him in and said, 'OK, you want a relationship like this now, an adult relationship, then you can come in and we can talk like men. Don't call in and tell the trainer you're sick and you can't play. Be a man and call me.' "

Jackson laughed when asked if the relationship indeed matured in that direction, but says he understood Grant's heart-on-his-sleeve personality and appreciated it. "Over the past couple of years, I realized Horace was just a person who would say whatever he felt right at the moment and that he wouldn't affect the team with his statements and he certainly wouldn't change any of the team dynamics," Jackson said.

"His own issues of free agency and talking about not being part of the Bulls had its own epicenter over to the side that were causing quakes in the organization. But I don't think it affected the team, and I don't think it affected their level of play and intensity."

That confidence was shaken, however, before the year was through, and it had Jackson finding himself often recollecting a conversation the two had late in the '92-'93 season, a talk Jackson remembers this way: "Horace asked, 'What do you think about me being a free agent?' And I said, 'Pax handled it in such a great manner, you have to look at the examples before you. You saw him go through it. He didn't talk about it. His agent had a meeting with the Bulls during the season and decided it wasn't fair and equitable. He decided to play it out and he played it out in the best possible way he could for himself.'

"And I said, 'If you really think you can handle it in a responsible, adult way, that could be a great boon for you. I don't want you to mess up with the organization. I don't want to lose you as a player. And I don't think we will. But if all you need is security and you know the money is plenty to live on anyway, you should sign for whatever will make you feel secure so it doesn't affect your basketball. If you don't feel comfortable and it's going to be a problem every other week as to how you're doing and what's going on, then you have to reconsider whether you want to be a free agent or not.' "

Jackson said the two met again in the summer. "He assured me he was going to be a free agent, he felt good about it, and he felt he could hold up his end of the deal that he would continue to work hard," Jackson said. "The problem is every injury, without a salary to protect you, becomes career-threatening. From John's standpoint, he didn't miss a game. He played right through it. And whatever it took to get back out on the court, he wasn't going to miss a step."

When Grant missed a step — sitting out seven games before the All-Star break due to illness and tendinitis in his knee after

missing an average of just three games per 82-game season before
that — Jackson's antennae went up immediately.

"Unfortunately," Jackson said after the season, "Horace
fulfilled all the expectations we worried about. I gave him
personal advice, hoping he could pull through like John Paxson
did. But the season seemed like it never ended for him. So much
time was spent with intrigue and posturing, with contract possibilities, and all of this with a chance, in his mind, to hurt himself
and miss out on this great jackpot at the end of the season. So it
was a constant warfare of trying to get him to be responsible to
the contract he was under.

"I tried to tell him he had signed to do a job this year and
if he wasn't fulfilling that job, he wasn't being an honest person
about his skills. And if he really committed to it and did it with
the right heart, then it would have all worked out and the right
thing would happen. At times he could buy it and at times he
couldn't. I don't know if he went home and deliberated over it
and maybe his knees hurt and maybe he made himself sick. But
whatever he did, he was fragile. He made himself a fragile
person."

Jackson said he tried to understand, but he also had to get
Grant to perform, which led to some unpleasant shouting
matches followed by week-long silences.

"I had to understand who he was and still love him while
doing things tough for him," Jackson said. "He couldn't understand that I had to do a job to make him come to work and keep
that perception of what he had to do to toe the line. Under the
circumstances, we really felt we couldn't bend our team and the
concepts of the team structure to accommodate an individual in
a way that would hurt our overall performance.

"It seemed like Horace always wanted me to give him
extra consideration and special treatment to incorporate what
he was going through, and I couldn't do it."

Part of Grant's frustration, in Jackson's estimation, stemmed
from his comparisons to others on the team. This was particularly the case, Jackson said, with Bill Cartwright, who had an
abbreviated practice schedule due to the chronic pain in his
knees, hips and back. He had a much-reduced game schedule as
well, as Jackson pointed him toward the playoffs — a strategy
that paid dividends against New York as Cartwright turned in
his best overall performances in years.

"Horace couldn't understand if I could do it for Bill Cartwright, why couldn't I do it for him," Jackson said. "He didn't understand that Bill Cartwright had been in this league for 14 years and was a different type of player. Horace was our meat-and-potatoes player. Bill Cartwright became a specialty player for us. Horace's game was what we based our whole team around. So that was difficult."

Jackson relied largely on his experience to guide his actions with Grant. In general, Jackson did not believe in either flattering or pampering players. He watched, from his position as player-coach for New Jersey and then from afar as head coach in the Continental Basketball Association in the late '70s and '80s, as player salaries rose and attitudes changed. "I've been on clubs where trainers would wake players up for practice, where they would wash players' clothes and become babysitters," he said.

Under revered Knicks coach Red Holzman, players had two sets of practice gear and six pairs of socks and were responsible for washing it themselves, and it was this system under which Jackson formed most of his coaching philosophies. "I figure in so many areas of their lives," he says of his players, "everything is a 'yes.' There are very few areas of discipline and I think players want discipline."

With that said, however, Jackson knew things were bound to be different with Jordan on his team, so he adjusted. And again, he recalled how Holzman used to handle things. "He used to have a policy," Jackson said. "He would ask [Dave] DeBusschere if we should practice and if he said yes, it meant we wouldn't practice. And if he said no, we would. And that happened until Dave caught on."

Jackson similarly kept his team on its toes often getting on the bus after a game and changing his earlier decision not to practice with an announcement that indeed they would. But he also had a keen sense in most cases when his team needed the day off and would not hesitate to do so. He believes in ground rules and guidelines, but also how to attain freedom within that structure. "They're grown men and should be treated that way," Jackson said.

That's the reason he has never enforced curfew and does not call players in their hotel rooms or at home if they're not on the bus or plane on time.

At midseason Jackson hands out what he calls a "Bulls-eye test," in which he asks players to put themselves in the center of the group and ask how they see themselves in relation to the others. It's private between Jackson and each player, and they discuss the test as part of their midseason conference.

"We have to constantly remind them that they live in a real world and that it's not made for them; that our structure is going to be the same as another work structure," he said. "Even though the boss may not be paid more than the employees, they still have to have that clout or everything gets out of whack. Once they give over the authority, then they can go to work. If one guy says we should run more screen-rolls and another says more isolations, there are too many voices clouding the issue. We don't ask for control of the mind, we ask for the voice so we can all hear one voice. That's the first premise people have to work on."

Within that premise, however, is also the knowledge that the majority of players earn more than coaches and that the players are the product.

"Our whole game is perceived as a players' game," Jackson readily acknowledged. "When you come in, you know players are making 10 times more than the coaches, for the most part, but somehow they have to understand it has to be this way or there's going to be chaos. That's where Michael Jordan's influence was very important, and Bill Cartwright's influence was terrific. They basically said, this is the coach and this is his job, and we'll work the other stuff out later on.

"There were times when the game was going on and Michael would say, 'I don't think we're getting that push in our transition, let's change it up this half,' and we'd say 'OK, let Scottie push the ball.' But that's what I ask of them. 'You guys are out on the floor. If you have a feel of how we can do better, talk to me because that's the way it has to be and we should make adjustments.' "

He approached the star system in another way as well. And dealing with a '93-'94 squad in which the salaries were wide-ranging, with veterans such as Steve Kerr, Bill Wennington and Pete Myers making the league minimum of $150,000, while rookie Corie Blount was due to earn more than $7 million over six years, he couldn't ignore the issue.

"What I say at the beginning of the season," said Jackson, "is that whatever you make and whatever the terms of your contract are, I don't care. I understand that we've invested more money in some of you than others and that's natural and that's part of this business, and we all have to accept that. Some people are going to have more favors on this team because they've gone through more battles and had more success than others. But for the most part, we're trying to treat each guy equally."

The team concept got an invaluable boost with three NBA titles achieved within a system where Jordan was clearly the star. "All these other guys went from anonymous players to known commodities, not just in Chicago but all over the country," reasoned Jackson. "So they knew that was due to team success."

Nevertheless, he concedes that if Jordan did not like him and did not want him as head coach, all the group dynamics in the world would not have changed things. "Every coach has that problem and every coach has to deal with it," he said of the vulnerability within the star system.

"Some coaches concede by just going to the players and trying to win them over. And then some coaches set them up in an antagonistic area that ultimately doesn't work either — 'This is my way and if you don't do it my way, we'll send you somewhere else.' That might work for some people."

One example, in Jackson's opinion, is Pat Riley. "He realized he could probably convince Patrick Ewing of the efficiency of the system if he made him the focal point," Jackson said. "Patrick had a strong college coach in John Thompson, so he felt comfortable with a coach who was very strong, well-disciplined and directed, so he could back up the authority that Riley needed and get accomplished what he had to get accomplished to make his team better.

"Every coach has to use his personality and his ability to coach to win the team over. Some do it through a strong authoritarian way and some through concession."

When it comes to Riley, Jackson is rarely short of opinions and never short on emotion. And the more, it seemed, he tried to avoid being critical of his rival, the more critical he became. After the '93-'94 season, two national NBA writers called Jackson for his observations on various subjects. Both touched on the subject of Riley and the New York Knicks, and Jackson was honest, reiterating his opinions that they played "ugly" basketball and calling Riley the "original whiner" and "media coach."

To his credit, Jackson did not claim to have been misquoted and did not blame the writers, saying only that he naively assumed his comments were off the record. And given another chance to speak of a relationship he said started positively when the two were players, Jackson backed off a bit. Anyone, however, who has been following the Bulls-Knicks rivalry over the last few years knows all about the animosity — the snubbed handshake by Riley after the Bulls took the Eastern Conference title in '93; the subtle and not-so-subtle comments from both about their relative styles of play — and Jackson recalled when the trouble started.

"The warning shot was fired across our bough in the first playoff game after our first championship," Jackson said, "when Charles Oakley laid a flagrant foul on Bill Cartwright, almost tearing his neck off his shoulders. We had beaten them four straight times in the regular season. Charles was fined for speaking to me on the bench, and the next thing I knew, it was a bitter war. I felt backed into a corner. I felt we were the champions, they were the team chasing us, and they had to make a statement. And they've come after us ever since."

Jackson tried to stop himself, sort of, but was on a roll. "Going into a game with them is a lot like going to the dentist; you know you're going to have severe pain," he said with apologies to those in the dental profession but speaking from experience as a man who went through the season with a series of root canal procedures. "Your whole body is going to have severe agony.

"The first time I saw them play [against the Bulls in the playoffs under Riley], I wondered if the refs forgot how to call the game. Then I realized that they were going to challenge the referee to make every single call. I realized Pat's whole strategy was to make the referee make all the foul calls, knowing they won't do that. It was a direct threat to authority. It was, 'We're going to take the spirit of the game and play the way we want to play it.' In that regard, 'Winning at all Costs' should be the name of his book rather than 'The Winner Within,' and that's what I saw as Pat's drive."

Riley was a year ahead of Jackson in college and considerably more high-profile than Jackson as a three-time team MVP of the Kentucky Wildcats, who finished second in the NCAA his senior year.

"I liked him as a player," said Jackson. "He had back surgery and missed his rookie year. He was very much like me. We both had to play our careers with bodies decimated by this game."

They played against each other in the pros, but not much, with Jackson in the Eastern Conference and Riley with the Lakers in the West. "We knew each other off the court socially a bit," he said. "We're definitely different people. But in his post-playing career, he has had nothing but success. From radio to the bench to assistant coach to head coach, he has gotten better at it. He has worked at it. And I have a great deal of admiration for his ability to get a team to play as hard as he does. He has tremendous motivating skills."

That, however, is where the two apparently differ. Jackson said he has tried to put himself in Riley's place. "Let's face it," he said. "He was the first coach to get a million-dollar-a-year contract; there was tremendous pressure on him and I empathized with him after he went to New York. There's no tougher place to fail or succeed. But the end result does not justify the means."

Jackson used a variety of means and they never ceased to keep his team alert. Toward the end of the '93-'94 season, Jackson had grown increasingly moody, and by the time the Bulls lost a dismal game in New Jersey in late March, a game in which the Nets' Rick Mahorn suckered Scottie Pippen into an altercation and eventual ejection of both players, it seemed nearly every player on the team was either fed up with Jackson or Jackson with them.

When he burst into the locker room that night, he told them 'You gave up,' pretty much the worst insult you can dole out to any self-respecting athlete, especially a professional athlete. And the Bulls did not take that accusation well. Grant and Pippen, in particular, were fed up and refused official comment to the media but grumbled to whomever walked by that Jackson had gone too far.

For Jackson, his actions often orchestrated, sometimes not, coaching was an all-or-nothing proposition. "As a former player, you know what your players are going through and how frustrating it is on the floor at times if what they're doing is not successful," he said. "But I've never felt, since they're expending all this energy then, oh hell, they can avoid responsibility for the game and when it's over, just let it go.

"Players are measured a lot on individual effort, but they don't see themselves accountable for the loss individually. And they can't. I know as a player, I used to go home after a game and think of every mistake I'd made. But ultimately, I'd forgive myself for the loss.

"But as coach, you have to be responsible for the team, so you have to be accountable for the actions of the whole. And that's where the frustration comes in."

More often than not, Jackson goes by instinct, strange or otherwise. There was no question, for example, that no textbook he ever read or coach he ever studied inspired one presumably spontaneous postgame talk.

The Bulls had just lost by 19 to Portland, were in the midst of a five-game losing streak and things were not looking especially cheery in early March when Jackson walked into the dressing room for his postgame remarks. Pulling up a chair, he seemed truly worried about the current slide.

"We've got to talk," he told the team. "What is going on here? Will someone please tell me what is so different now than two weeks ago?"

Then, as heads started to droop and eyes to glaze over, he began to explore the possible reasons for one of the Bulls problems of late — beginning the third quarter sluggishly — in a manner that instantly drew their attention. "I've noticed guys coming in at the half and taking a piss," he said straight-faced. "Now how many of you take a piss before I talk at halftime? Let's see a show of hands."

Guys who had been daydreaming suddenly awoke, and hesitatingly, a few hands around the room went up. "OK," Jackson continued. "Now how many of you take a piss after I talk?"

An entire discussion ensued as players stole quick, furtive glances at one another. Is he for real? "Pretty soon," said one player, "losing four games in a row didn't seem quite as serious anymore."

Humor was often invoked during some of the tensest moments. One night in which Pippen was having a particularly poor game, committing several turnovers and missing seemingly every shot, Jackson had called a timeout with five minutes left in the tightly contested game. As the players huddled, waiting for some words of wisdom, Jackson leaned in.

"Whatever you guys do," he intoned, "just don't throw the ball to Scottie."

The group laughed, Pippen loosened up, and he proceeded to hit three key baskets down the stretch to carry the Bulls to victory.

As a team, the Bulls have meditated. They have burned incense. And they have done breathing exercises. They have read books, watched obscure movies and listened to sports psychologists lecture on the importance of positive imagery. They have watched hour upon hour of videotape in preparation for regular-season games, listened to endless strategy sessions, and have walked into a locker room in Cleveland before a playoff game and have seen the words, "Just play the game. Have fun," on the team blackboard.

Sometimes, Jackson seemed to be hoisting the weight of the world on his angular shoulders, stewing silently or, during the playoffs, for example, choosing to take long solitary walks from Madison Square Garden back to the team hotel knowing full well there would be a kook or Knick fan or both on every corner just waiting for him to get within earshot. Then another time, you'd walk into the Bulls' dressing room at the Stadium and think he must not have a care in the world.

One night, for example, players and media found that the peephole on the coaches' office had been covered with adhesive tape, ostensibly to discourage peepers. Coincidentally, the tape formed a cross on the door. Far be it for Jackson, however, to endorse one religion over another. So for the next game, he placed tape in the form of a Jewish star under the cross. The game after that, there was a crescent moon and star under the Star of David to represent the Muslims. Presumably, there was more to come until he taped up the one universal symbol of the Bulls, the triangle, representing their offensive religion.

But Jackson finds perhaps his greatest entertainment in the spoken word. "This is insidious," he once yelled at his team, following that up with, "How many of you know what insidious means? I want you to go home and look it up and tell me tomorrow."

On another occasion, deep into a halftime lecture concerning his team's poor demeanor on the court, Jackson started to explain the effect of drooped heads and sulking expressions. "What that connotes..." he began, but suddenly stopped. "God, I love that fucking word..."

Jackson also had great fun with the language in his dealings with the media. Or at the very least, the media had fun with him as Jackson tossed out words like "jocularity" and "elan" more often than any sports cliches. And he never missed a *New York Times* crossword puzzle in the pregame locker room each Sunday, no matter how big the game, knocking off obscure literary references and stopping only to ask the nearest reporter for, say, the central character's first name in the television show "Happy Days."

And though that side of his personality often came off as pseudo-intellectual, or at worst, arrogant, the central character in "Happy Days" was indeed completely foreign to him and he almost always had a sense of humor about it.

"I don't know why I choose the words I do," he chuckled. "A lot of language is in the feeling and sound of words. I definitely have a fractured sense of language. One time I used the word 'sieve.' I definitely like that word. But what's a sieve?"

Jackson doesn't deny the occasional use of expletives, but doesn't particularly like to swear, he claims. "There are better ways to use the language than to curse," he said. "But in the NBA, it registers displeasure better than any other way sometimes."

"He curses for emphasis," explained Steve Kerr. "He appreciates the use of profanity to get his point across."

Unfortunately for Jackson, no particularly clever words were readily available the night of Game 3 of the '94 Eastern Conference semifinals with New York, when he looked down his bench with 1.8 seconds remaining and saw Pippen firmly planted on the bench.

In the days that followed, Jackson would be praised for his low-key approach to Pippen's infamous mutiny. But at the moment, there was no time for planning, only instinct. "The basic thing I knew we had to do was just go on," said Jackson of the moments immediately afterward when he left Pippen to stew on the sideline and inserted Pete Myers to inbound the ball to Toni Kukoc for the now-famous game-winning shot. "I knew I couldn't change my mind because I made a decision that I believed in and I was going to stand by it.

"When I knew for sure [Pippen] wasn't going into the game, I called a second timeout. The team was out on the floor, so I gave him another opportunity to still go out there. When he didn't, I pulled out another guy who I thought could do the job and I told Pete to make the right pass.

"We deserved to win that game, to go out there and make the shot. There was no reason why we shouldn't and I told them that: 'It's ours to win. We've led for most of the game. And there's no reason we should be in the position we're in, but we'll discuss that tomorrow. Toni, go in and make the damn shot and let's finish this thing off.' So they went out and did it."

Jackson said he doesn't particularly remember feeling intense anger toward Pippen or embarrassment at the moment. Again, there wasn't a lot of time for any emotion to settle in. "I was disappointed with him and I let him know it," he said of Pippen. "People said we exchanged hostilities. And there might have been an expletive spoken, but it wasn't in a derogatory sense. It was more, 'OK, the hell with it. If you're not going to go out there, I'm going to get someone else to go out there and do the job.' That was basically the way I felt. 'We don't need you. We'll go on. We're not going to look over our shoulders.' "

When Jackson left the floor, he didn't have much time to plan his next move. But as it turned out, he didn't have to. Bill Cartwright, who had already had a few words with Pippen on the bench, was primed to talk and Jackson merely got out of his way.

"After he expressed himself," Jackson said of Cartwright's emotionally fired speech, "there was absolutely nothing left to say. We simply said the Lord's Prayer and that was it."

Cartwright, said Jackson, was the only one who could have delivered the message. "Bill was wonderful," he said. "It was right from the heart. And the amazing part about it is that Bill is the most unemotional guy that anyone has ever seen in his life.

"We had all seen how hard Bill had worked to be part of all this, and how much he sacrificed from a physical nature to be there and that this was perhaps his swan song. All of that registered that Bill was disappointed that someone he trusted could do that. The fact that everyone was emotionally drained and physically exhausted, coming from personal motives and team motives, all those things registered as a common denominator for all of us."

Jackson said he never considered trying to cover up for Pippen at the postgame press conference. His comments were brief but to the point. "Scottie asked out of the play so I left him off the floor," Jackson said at the time.

Wouldn't it have been easier to lie? To say that Pippen was shaken up (he had indeed sustained a cut on the bridge of his nose) and would have been available for the overtime period if necessary?

"I don't like to lie, first of all," Jackson said. "I've never been very good at lying. It just buys you some time and when the other side comes out, everything's exposed anyway."

Pippen's actions set off a frantic wave of reaction. From newspapers to television to radio to fans on the street, Chicago's and arguably the nation's sports fans were talking, debating, raging. But as Jackson got into his car that night with his wife, June, a strange calm washed over him.

"Scottie has been as stubborn and resistant as anybody I've ever dealt with," he said. "They all have their rigidity, I guess, all great athletes. And it was important that he realized there was plenty of room for him to save face and still he had to know his action was going to bring a reaction. We survived it and yet, somewhere in my dream sequence it was echoed back to me that we couldn't win if this kind of action happened all the time, that it would eventually destroy the nerve fiber of the team.

"But when I left the Stadium that night, I wasn't worried. I knew walking out of the locker room that we were OK and that we would come back out as a group again. I knew we'd be emotionally high for the next game and it was probably the best game we'd played against New York in three years."

Dear Chicago Bulls,
   Hi, How has basketball been going? It is my favorite sport,
and I am going terrific. I really like you Bulls. You are the
coolest basketball team. My friends even say that. Trust me.
I haven't lied for 1 or 2 years now. I'm not just saying that
to make you happy. I really mean it.

3

HORACE

When Horace Grant was a "little" boy, sticking forks in delicate parts of twin brother Harvey's anatomy and generally making his mother crazy, he had one serious flaw, if you will. That is, he always got caught.

He could not tell a lie (not very well, anyway) and he couldn't get away with a thing, a trait that seems to have followed him into adulthood. Whenever any hint of controversy surrounding the Bulls has arisen over the last several years, one thing was certain: If Horace wasn't directly involved, he was close. Or merely waiting his turn.

When did it start? Most serious Bulls fans and trivia hounds remember Grant speaking out in October of '91, the preseason after the Bulls' first title and shortly after Michael Jordan's infamous snub of the White House.

"If me or any of the other guys had missed, we'd have caught flak from the organization," Grant said at the time. "There's been a double standard since I got on this team and you can only take so much of it."

Then there was the fall of '92-'93. Jordan and Scottie Pippen had spent the summer in Barcelona at the Summer Olympics, and the Bulls issued a press release saying Jordan would miss the first week of camp and return the day before their first exhibition game. Pippen, it was revealed, would take part only in the morning session of the team's two-a-day drills. Six days later, Grant, the only starter practicing, stormed out of an early practice after a particularly grueling running drill.

On the eve of the preseason opener, Grant told the media he was tired of being treated like a "second-class citizen." He admitted it was probably wrong to walk off the court, but as the only starter required to take part in two-a-day sessions, he felt he deserved a measure of respect from Phil Jackson that he was not receiving.

"I know I can never get the respect Scottie and Michael get, but don't treat me like a second-class citizen," Grant said. "I think I'm just as important to this team as a lot of other guys are.

"I don't want everybody to think I'm a troublemaker because I'm not. But when I feel something is not right, I'm going to speak out."

And that was Grant. Emotions on his sleeve. Always ready with a quick quip or an honest response to a direct question, whether it would get him into trouble or not.

But until the '93-'94 season, Grant could always shake off trouble almost as easily as he could attract it. Never were problems so serious that they had him as distracted as they did the season before he became an unrestricted free agent. A dream situation for Grant, his status the summer of '94 meant that as he continued to improve and enjoy the prime of his career, he could also look forward to perfect financial timing.

With his contract expiring July 1, any team could extend offers, and Grant could go to the highest bidder with no future obligations to the Bulls if he did not wish. And by very early in the '93-'94 season, he realized that was something he definitely did not wish.

Grant says he knew there were going to be problems when he renegotiated his last contract in the summer of '91 — $6 million over the next three years. "I had asked for a five- to seven-year contract," Grant said. "The fact that they were only willing to give me three years told me right there that they didn't have me in their future plans. But in the end, I liked that because I wanted to become an unrestricted free agent when I did.

"And they always encouraged me to test the market."

The timing ultimately paid off when Grant signed a six-year, $22.3 million deal with the Orlando Magic in July of '94. A performance clause, to which the league objected, would allow him to opt out of his contract as soon as one year and re-sign with the Magic for a contract that was expected to top $40 million.

So Grant had his windfall. And in the early flushed days of excitement, he was sure he had his respect back as well. But where did things go wrong with the Bulls? Grant, selected 10th overall in the '87 draft, said he never felt comfortable from the start. "I never built a home in Chicago and one reason was because Krause didn't want to draft me in the first place," Grant said. "[Doug] Collins and [Johnny] Bach were walking on egg-shells from the beginning."

Krause naturally disputes this, saying he was pleasantly surprised by Grant when the Bulls brought him in for a workout 10 days before the draft. "We were shocked," said Krause. "We saw him do things he didn't do at Clemson. I liked [North Carolina's] Joe Wolf. But when it came down to it, Horace slipped to 10th and when I walked out of the draft room, the coaches said we'd like you to pick Horace.

"Jerry [Reinsdorf] said 'Go with your guts,' and I walked around the office and finally said, 'Let's pick Horace. He's a better athlete than Joe Wolf.' "

The version told by others in the room that day was a little different; that after seeing Grant on tape eating up the other ACC centers, including Carolina's J.R. Reid, Collins and Bach had fought with Krause to bring Grant in. Krause didn't want to initially, saying he was "just another Brad Sellers, built just like Sellers [a first-round draft bust they would trade in June of '89]."

When Grant finally came in, Bach and Collins fell in love with him and convinced Krause to select him with the 10th pick. But as the pick got closer on draft day, Krause began wavering, saying maybe he ought to go with Wolf, calling him "a 6-10 version of Jerry Sloan."

The coaches argued, saying that wasn't what they had agreed to, and that with Pippen and Grant, they would be set at forward the next eight to 10 years. Finally, Collins brought Jerry Reinsdorf in to settle the impasse and Reinsdorf said, "If that's what you all agreed to, then we're picking Horace Grant."

Krause said he caught the wrath of North Carolina coach Dean Smith for passing on Wolf but didn't regret picking Grant. But Grant said he never felt wanted as he and Pippen trumpeted a new era in Bulls basketball, and the stage was set.

It wasn't until the '91 negotiations, however, that those sensitivities were brought to the surface again. This time, it was again something Krause said. "I wasn't married at the time,"

Grant said. "I liked to go out and have fun and things like that, but I never let it affect my play on the court, not once. But Krause brought that up in negotiations, comparing me to A.C. Green, saying he would definitely rather have him because he's a better person."

The Bulls would trade Sedale Threatt, sure that he was a bad influence on Grant and Pippen because of his penchant for night life, and it also got back to Grant that Krause had called him stupid.

It was no secret that Grant was sensitive. His first year in the league, he would sometimes get so flustered or frustrated on court that there would be tears in his eyes. But the coaches always loved his eagerness to please and never questioned his heart.

As Grant matured, that translated into a fierce desire to speak his mind when he thought things were unjust. Some players might have described this as young foolishness. "One of my flaws is that I am so honest," he said. But at the same time, his teammates didn't seem to mind that Grant was willing to put himself on the line.

It always grated on Grant that Jordan received what he considered to be preferential treatment from Jackson and the organization, but Jackson made no apologies. "It's not unusual," he said at the time of the White House flap. "The pretty girl always gets kissed. That's life."

Grant said some of the problems with Jordan began his rookie year when Jordan often became impatient with Grant's mental lapses. "My first year, Oakley was still power forward and I was coming off the bench and I was trying to prove myself," Grant said. "Whenever I had the chance to play I tried to do my best, but I would mess up. Michael would say something to me and I'd lash back.

"He's a great athlete, but people are people. I've never been in awe. Scottie and I never bowed down to him."

Nonetheless, Grant said they both learned to live with that. "We'd never want to go out and have dinner together," he said of Jordan. "We never saw eye to eye. But I always respected him from the standpoint that he's a great athlete and a great basketball player."

As for Pippen, their relationship may be one of the toughest to figure out. Talk to either one on any given day and you'll get a different answer. "As rookies, it's true," said Grant. "We were very close."

"We were pretty much inseparable," said Pippen. "When we came in as rookies, there was no one else there for us."

The two often wore the same clothes, bought similar cars and were very rarely seen anywhere in public without the other. "But as we got older," said Grant, "we naturally grew apart in some ways."

Both got divorced, Grant embraced the Bible and they set their sights on different goals. "We were still friends," said Pippen, "but we went on with our lives."

And it was bound to get sticky. With Pippen's burgeoning stardom came newfound fame and a growing ego that Grant at times resented. And with Grant's impending free agency and guaranteed financial bonanza, not to mention freedom, jealousy struck Pippen as well.

When Grant spoke out in the fall of '93, saying it wasn't fair that Jordan and Pippen were allowed time off during the pre-season, Pippen responded by saying that Grant "had his priorities in the wrong order."

"I think he needs to be more concerned with his business and not any other player's," Scottie continued. "He should let Phil be the coach and let the other guys make their own decisions. He's paid to play and do his job."

The two never resolved that conflict, though both were annoyed with the other for their own reasons. And to their credit, most of the animosity was kept private. Publicly, Pippen insisted that he would be happy for Grant no matter how much money he made. And Grant spoke of the pride he had in watching Pippen grow into one of the true superstars of the league.

Complicating matters somewhat was the fact that they were both represented by the same agents, Jimmy Sexton and Kyle Rote Jr. Ethically, Sexton and Rote had to keep both players' professional business private from the other, and did. But it gnawed at Pippen not knowing exactly what was happening with Grant's situation, and it irritated Grant whenever rumors surfaced of some sort of package deal that might send both to the same team for the '94-'95 season. This was his moment and Grant wanted it to stay that way.

More than anything, though, as the two played their final

season together, there were not harsh words, or estrangement so much as a natural split as they went their separate ways.

And it was indeed with a profound sadness that Pippen watched Grant leave Chicago. Said one close friend, "I don't think Scottie ever really thought it would happen. He was devastated."

As much as the signals seemed to point toward Grant leaving, however, he said he was still open to continuing his career with the Bulls before the '93 preseason training camp opened. But as the season progressed, Grant became a very unhappy, often disillusioned and occasionally confused man.

Those around him often wondered as his free agency approached if that was what he really wanted. "I think deep down, Horace wants to stay," Pippen would say during the '93-'94 season. Then it was, "I don't know if Horace even knows what he wants to do." And that was true. For Grant went from scared kid to self-assured businessman with uncertainty and anxiety dogging him all the way.

There were times when week to week would bring about a different response on whether he thought he would leave the Bulls. Often, it was designed to simply keep Krause off balance, but other times it was because he truly wasn't sure.

"When you spend half your career somewhere, sure you're going to have your doubts about leaving," Grant said at midseason. "There have been times when I've been swaying back and forth."

As the '93-'94 season wound down, however, it seemed clear Grant had reconciled in his own mind that he was leaving and in some ways, it seemed, the situation paralleled a kid going away to college for the first time. Deep down, the kid is scared and nervous about leaving home but he also knows that it's something he has to do. And so as the time draws nearer to actually leaving, there's a subconscious pulling away, maybe arguments with parents or siblings, or perhaps just a general surliness that suggests he's not going to miss home at all.

Grant started exhibiting such behavior about midseason, and by the time the Bulls were humiliated by New York 86-68 in late February, he had decided that Jackson was no longer on his side. Not only was he not going to miss Jackson and the Bulls organization when he left, but that day couldn't come soon enough.

Now Jackson had long yelled at Grant on the court. But Horace had slowly tired of it, and in New York that Sunday afternoon, Grant had had enough. Every time he touched the ball anymore, it seemed he could hear Phil's voice barking at him. It finally got to him so much that when he was shooting free throws— an area of tremendous difficulty for the Bulls and Grant in particular— he asked the assistant coaches to tell Jackson to shut up because the constant sound of Jackson's voice was distracting him. And in New York, it seemed like he couldn't do anything right.

"Did you see when I got the ball inside?" Grant relayed afterward. "Patrick [Ewing] is on my back, so I throw it back out to Steve [Kerr] and Phil yells, 'Cut out that chicken-shit stuff and shoot the ball.' I can't take much more of this."

It was about that time that Grant began his countdown — "Thirty-two more games," he would say. "I can't wait."

That feeling only intensified as the Bulls sank into their post-All-Star break slump, a streak that would extend to five straight defeats, including a nationally televised loss to Cleveland on March 6. Grant's back was killing him that game, throbbing with spasms caused under embarrassing, but very real circumstances.

He knew exactly when and how he had hurt it, stooping to put on his clothes several days earlier. He would dress out for the Lakers game, though he regretted it all through the first half as he was forced to lie on his back in front of the bench to seek any kind of comfort.

In the second half, feeling guilty as he watched the team struggle, Horace told Bach in the locker room that he wanted to play.

"Better tell Phil," Bach said. "He's not going to ask you."

That wasn't Jackson's style, to demand that an injured player go out and play. But he did have other, somewhat more subtle methods, making it clear that he respected players who did that because that's the way it was when he played the game.

Jackson enjoyed recounting stories of the glory days when reporters would ask him to talk about incidents of guys playing sick and with injuries. There were tales of guys vomiting on the court and playing in agony and invariably, the story would be told of Willis Reed, the Knicks legend who played in the title-clinching game against Los Angeles despite a torn tendon in his hip, inspiring his team to victory.

Grant took the court that second half against the Lakers and gave the team an instant lift with eight points and nine rebounds in the third quarter alone. Afterward, however, a game the Bulls would end up losing 97-89 for their third straight defeat and sixth since the All-Star break, Grant was in worse pain than ever. Krause came into the trainer's room afterward to thank him for the effort, but Grant wasn't in the mood and wasn't buying it.

"I'm pissed off at myself for going out there," he grumbled. "It's insanity. I don't care what they think. I'm not going to do that Willis Reed routine. I'll definitely be in street clothes Friday [for Portland]."

And so he was two days later, despite the fact that Jackson told him that morning at shootaround that if he wasn't going to play, he didn't have to bother coming. Grant paid no attention and made his way to the bench before the game dressed in slacks and a sports jacket, only to be met by Jackson and told to "go home."

"If your back hurts, how can you sit on the bench?" Jackson demanded.

"I'll be fine," Grant shot back. "I want to be here."

"We don't need you here," Jackson said.

The two ended the exchange by cussing each other out, Grant responding, "I'm not doing that Willis Reed shit." But he didn't leave, and afterward he sat slumped in his locker stall, counting down the days once again. "I can't wait to get out of here," he said.

That Sunday, the Bulls would play in Cleveland, their second game against the Cavs in less than a week after losing 89-81 in the infamous booing game. It embarrassed the Bulls and especially Jackson that fans had booed as they went down by 18 points in the third quarter. This was the Stadium, and against a team they were used to pounding. So the rematch in Cleveland, a nationally televised contest, was more than just another game.

Grant spent the pregame hours reading a religious text as he lay on top of a heating pad. Not more than 20 feet away, Jackson worked on the *New York Times* crossword puzzle, a Sunday ritual. If the Bulls' current four-game losing streak was bothering him, he wasn't letting it show, talking affably with reporters and asking for help on his puzzle.

But Grant was tense. His back was still radiating painful spasms and he was second-guessing his decision to play. During the game — one the Bulls would lose 99-95 with Grant playing 46 minutes mostly because if he stopped, his back would stiffen up — he was miserable. And during one timeout early in the second quarter, Grant was especially agitated.

"Count how many times Phil yells at me when I have the ball," he said, leaning over the scorer's table. And indeed, the name "Horace," as usual, was heard more than any other as Jackson continued to bark at him.

"I'm going on the injured list," Grant said afterward. "I'm in so much pain, I can barely stand up."

Bill Cartwright was on the injured list at the time, having missed six games with recurring knee pain, and was, as always, itching to get off. But it had become painfully evident that the Bulls needed Grant desperately and so the news, as expected, was not met kindly the following Monday morning when he met with Jackson and trainer Chip Schaefer.

The three met in Jackson's office and, according to Grant, the exchange went like this: "My back has been bothering me pretty bad," Grant told Jackson. "I need some time off."

"What do you mean, 'time off?' " Jackson replied.

"I mean, like go on IR," said Grant.

"Oh no, absolutely not," said Jackson.

Back and forth it went, with Jackson suggesting that Grant take one or two days off and no more. The injured list minimum was five games, which in this case would have translated to at least nine days of no games or practice. Finally, Grant, under the impression that he did not need the team's permission to go on the injured list, said, "Look, Phil, I made my decision. I'm going on the injured list."

Jackson was incredulous and angrier than Grant had ever seen him. "Chip," Jackson exploded, "am I going fucking crazy or is this guy not listening to me?"

Grant stood up and started to leave. "I guess you're going fucking crazy, Phil," he said slamming the door behind him.

The next conversation was with Krause as Grant went from teacher to principal's office, a route he was familiar with by this time. Krause warned him that his attitude could adversely affect the team, especially during a rather fragile period. And not in Grant's favor was the fact that Jackson and Krause had recently finished talking with Toni Kukoc, who was all but begging to play the next day despite a swollen ankle and Achilles tendon.

Kukoc, however, had his own problems, still trying to win the favor of coaches, teammates and fans, and was merely anxious to do anything to prove himself.

These were two different situations, but once again, Grant looked forever like the kid with his hand caught in the cookie jar as he trudged down the steps to the training room, where he confided in Scottie Pippen.

Jackson followed. "Horace, I'm not mad at you," Jackson said, obviously realizing that it would do no good to upset him further. "I just want to let you know we can take it day by day. But just remember, you're not a free agent until July 1."

"Phil," said Grant, "if that was such a major part of my thinking, I wouldn't have played in the Lakers game, and I wouldn't have played in Cleveland."

For the time being anyway, there was another truce, but it definitely wasn't over.

"They want the fans to think I'm not playing because I'm an unrestricted free agent," Grant would say later that afternoon, convinced also that in making him look like a malingerer, they were trying to drive his market value down.

For Grant, who had taken out a $9 million insurance policy with Lloyds of London, the season had become an annoying and exhausting routine of having to defend himself for every illness or injury. And with a history of never missing five games in any season in his career, plus the fact that, excluding his rookie year, the Bulls had averaged 100 games a year since he had been there, he didn't think he should have to do that.

The first time the problem surfaced, it was Christmas Day. The Bulls were playing Orlando that night and Grant did not think he could play. "I had a sore throat, 102-degree fever, chills, I felt horrible," said Grant. "I told them that every time I coughed, my lungs felt like they were burning, and they told me there was nothing seriously wrong. We were playing the Magic, so I wanted to play, but I also wanted to know what was wrong with me. They knew then, but they waited until after the game to tell me I had bronchitis. Just another example of their mind games and their win-at-all costs [attitude]."

Grant stopped trusting the team trainer and physician, thinking they weren't being straight with him, and insisted on seeing his own doctor for whatever problems he had after that. "It got to the point," he said later, "where I didn't trust anyone in the organization."

It galled him when he had to explain himself. He had had trouble shaking sickness all winter, and two weeks before the Christmas game, he had returned from a two-game absence with the flu, only to vomit on the bench in New Jersey. Despite that, he managed to play 36 minutes and finish with 18 points, 16 rebounds and four blocked shots.

"We've all been through the same thing," Jackson said after that game. "Keep going, the body's resilient. The guys learn this more and more as they play."

In late January, Grant was bothered by chronic tendinitis in his knee, a condition that plagues many basketball players and one that occurs in varying degrees. In other words, some players may indeed be able to play with it, and Grant had on many occasions in the past. But other players often get to the point where the only remedy is rest. Grant was at this point. His was a soft-tissue injury that varies in severity and does not always show up on X-rays and MRI exams.

He had missed three of five games when Jackson was asked by the media about Grant's prognosis. "I've been concerned with Horace's mental attitude toward his knee," Jackson said.

"He's worried about me mentally?" Grant responded in disbelief. "That's one of Phil's little psychological [ploys]. My knee's really hurting me. I guess coaching in the All-Star Game means a lot to some people, and they'll try to put a little pressure on you to go out there and not play to your capabilities."

Grant was referring, albeit sarcastically, to the fact that the Bulls were in the running for best record at the All-Star break, which would have meant that Jackson would have coached the Eastern Conference team.

"Mentally?" Grant continued. "If that was the case, I've been going through mental things here with this team ever since I got here. There's nothing mental."

Jackson referred to the injury as "jumper's knee," a common expression for tendinitis, but Grant didn't appreciate the implication that it wasn't anything to be taken seriously. "It's a mystery to us," said Jackson. "We just hope that mentally and physically, he can play for us."

Four nights earlier, Grant had played at Indiana, going scoreless with eight rebounds in 26 minutes. "I'm not going to play at 70-75 percent like at Indiana," he said, "when I got frustrated because I couldn't jump or do the things I do best out there."

The next night in Cleveland, Jackson played Grant a game-high 41 minutes. "I go out and bust my butt every day when I'm on the court," he said. "I hustle, I dive for balls. I do all those garbage things, if you will. Then to have someone say it's mental or doubt me, it's ludicrous.

"I don't want to end my career and walk around in life with the body of a Phil Jackson. I don't want to do that. There's something wrong with my knee and deep down, Phil knows it."

Grant admitted the last thing he wanted to do was injure himself to the point that he would harm his market value as a free agent. His point, however, was that he was only being careful, whereas earlier in his career, he was willing to take chances and let himself be talked into playing through anything.

But again, his timing hurt him. Complicating matters was a recent absence from practice Grant said was caused when his truck broke down. Already late, he said he was then given a ride to his townhouse 10 minutes from the Bulls' practice facility, where he discovered he had left his house keys in the truck. Although Grant phoned Jackson to explain his absence, Jackson told the media that day that Grant was "AWOL."

"They can buy lies in a heartbeat," Grant said much later, "but here I told the truth and it didn't matter. I could very easily have lied and said I was sick, but why should I have to do that? Talk about treating someone like a kid. But that's how he messes with me. He was hoping it would blow up in the press."

Grant was having a long season off the court already. "It's definitely the most miserable in my career," he would say more than once. Earlier in December, the sleazy *Cheri* magazine pictured a clothed Grant posing with nude female models. Grant had allowed the photos to be taken the previous summer when he and former teammate Corey Williams unknowingly walked into the photo session at a downtown Chicago gym.

Grant was paid a small amount for the short session and after checking to see that it did not violate any NBA rules — it did not — he playfully went along, thinking it would be good for some locker room laughs. "I figure, when I'm 90 years old and I want to still feel young," he laughed, "I can just look at the pictures."

But a story published the next day quoted anonymous sources — Stacey King later admitted to it being him — criticizing Grant and saying the Bulls would be better off trading him. King was then quoted in another story saying he never thought Grant would intentionally do anything to harm the team. And Grant closed the subject by apologizing.

"Considering the timing with my contract and the year we're having [the Bulls were 9-8 at the time], yes, I regret it," he said. "If I knew the consequences and the way people would think about it, I wouldn't have done it. That's what I'm sorry about."

All the Bulls agreed that it certainly didn't serve as a distraction. "We joked about it," Grant said. "With all the other serious issues in the world, my taking some pictures with a bunch of girls should be so trivial. I hope the majority of fans know that I'm a genuine, hard-working person."

It was important to Grant what the Chicago fans thought of him. He rarely listened to sports radio himself and read the papers only occasionally, but it didn't matter even when he tried to avoid the media because friends would always tell him what people were saying.

Grant had won the fans' affection in much the same way he had won the media's — with hard work on the court and unfailing honesty off of it. So when the fans started rumbling that Grant had forgotten the team and had become selfish, he yearned to tell what he considered the whole story. "I would love to tell the fans everything," he would say more than once.

"How they're treating me, how they're playing mind games with me. Then maybe they would understand."

As for Jackson, Grant was always a little puzzled. The two got along great when Grant was in his first two years in the league and Jackson still an assistant to Doug Collins. "I thought he was one of the best," Grant said. "A lot of the players really looked up to him because he knew them so well. A lot of head coaches don't like that."

Things were bound to change when Jackson became boss before the '89-'90 season, and Grant expected it. What he didn't expect was to be the guy seemingly always picked on — even though Jackson had warned him, and in fact, pretty much received his permission to do so.

"We sat down one year," Grant recalled, "and he asked me, could I handle him getting on me? There was a point in time that I could, but in the midst of everything, I was losing respect from my teammates and I said to him, 'Enough is enough.' During practice, if I made one mistake, he would yell at me and in games, if he didn't think I was working hard, he was all over me. I became the joke of the team. If Phil could abuse me, why couldn't everyone?

"Eventually he stopped a little bit. But in his own way, he still thinks this is my third year in the league. He failed to realize that I paid my dues as a player."

As one of the least egomaniacal of the Bulls and the most popular among his teammates, he was an easy target for Jackson, whose psychological ploys should never go underestimated. Jackson knew that Grant's play would never be adversely affected and he knew that players would rally around Grant, perhaps all the more so if he was the perpetual whipping boy.

But by early March of '94, Grant didn't much care what Jackson was trying to do. One day after their fight over the injured list, the two had still another blow-up, something that was becoming an almost daily occurrence now.

Grant was getting treatment for his back and had plans to see a doctor for an MRI to make sure there was no more serious damage than simple muscle spasms. He was in the weight room, adjacent to the training room in the plush Berto Center — the Bulls' private training facility also referred to by the media as "The Fortress" for its prisonlike characteristics — when Jackson shouted something from the training room.

"Are you a part of this? Are you coming out?" he yelled. Grant and trainer Chip Schaefer thought at first that Jackson was calling for Chip, so Grant didn't move. A few minutes later, Grant was sitting in the training room when Jackson burst in. "He just starts yelling," Grant said. "So I said, 'Phil, don't raise your fucking voice to me. Stop yelling.' "

"I asked you whether you were a fucking part of this," Jackson shouted.

"And I said don't talk to me that way," Grant said. "He talks to me like I'm Scott Williams or some little kid."

"Why aren't you listening to me, you fucking baby?" said Jackson.

"Fuck you, you big pussy," Grant replied.

Now it should be pointed out that an exchange such as this should probably not be taken any more seriously due to the language content. The equivalent, in a normal business situation, might be something along the lines of, say, "Jones, where is that report that was due today?"

Jones: "I thought it was due Friday. I'll have it on your desk as soon as possible."

Boss: "Well, see to it that you do."

Of course, Jones, while he might be in line for a promotion and suspect the boss of playing games with him, would probably not see fit to warn the president of the company that if his boss didn't lay off, he would be a goner. But Grant did.

"I'm telling Jerry that there's no way of signing me if Phil keeps messing with me," Grant promised. Of course, all of this was ironic since it was Jackson who told Krause that he better lay off talking contract with Grant during the season because he was obviously distracting him.

For the record, nobody listened to anybody.

One time, after being asked by Grant's agents not to talk to him about contract business, Krause tried to do just that in the weight room. "Jerry," barked Phil, "take that shit upstairs."

One of the things that got to Grant was how Jackson talked about him to the media, and during the '93-'94 season, the coach had some fun indeed at the player's expense. Some of it was subtle, like when Jackson dropped in the fact that it was Grant's decision to have an MRI done. Or that he was missing games in February with "a sore throat," instead of the more glamorous-sounding, as well as more accurate description of viral infection.

Other times, there was little subtlety at all. In discussing the sore throat, for example, Jackson jokingly theorized "He sees four or five movies a week. Perhaps he catches alien germs floating around the theaters or maybe his hand in all those popcorn boxes may be doing it too."

And on the same day and same general subject: "I suggested to Horace that when he signs his new contract, he signs it on a 60-game basis rather than 82 . . . . "

Whether he was kidding or not, he nearly always drove Grant nuts, as surely Jackson must have suspected it would. "He's messing with my mind," Grant would say more than once. And more and more, Grant really did feel as if he wasn't Bulls property any longer. "It's all because I'm going to be an unrestricted free agent," Grant reasoned. "If I wasn't and I was complaining of back pain, there would be no suspicion and they would insist that I have tests."

Close observers who wondered why Grant and Jackson were seemingly always bickering reasoned that both were just stubborn. But as the season progressed, Grant was sure he no longer cared. "I don't ask to be pampered, I ask to be respected," he said.

And what if Jackson suddenly made a strong pitch to get him to consider a Bulls offer and stay in Chicago? "He's too proud for that," Grant said in early March. "And at this point, it doesn't matter anymore. Absolutely not. At this point, he's only making it easier for me to leave the Bulls."

To consider all of this, and then to accept the possibility that Grant may still have signed with the Bulls, is perhaps the biggest jolt of all. This, however, is the contention of Jerry Reinsdorf in what is sure to go down as one of the strangest "negotiations" ever.

The way Reinsdorf explained it, he had just returned to Chicago from Arizona, where he and his wife spend most of the winter, when he decided to visit the Berto Center on Thursday, April 28 of '94.

The Bulls' executive offices at the time were located downtown, a good 45-minute drive away, but Reinsdorf said he had a specific reason for the trip. "There were a number of players on the club I had actually never met," Reinsdorf explained.

Grant scoffs at this. He believes Reinsdorf came to the Berto Center with the specific intention of cornering him and trying to negotiate a contract.

Nevertheless, Reinsdorf said it was happenstance that he and Grant began discussing his future. "I went to the trainer's room to say hello and Horace Grant came over to me, shook hands, then went to work out with [strength coach] Al Vermeil," Reinsdorf said. "He was doing something I wasn't familiar with, so I went over to observe.

"Al Vermeil said, 'Horace has progressed so much from seven years ago, it's amazing.' Then Al said, 'It's hard to believe Horace has been here for seven years.' I said, 'I agree with that. I only wish he would be here for five more years.' At that point, Horace said, 'If you mean that, I want to be here. But you and I have to make this deal.'

"I was a little shocked, but I suggested to Horace that when he finished working out, I would be upstairs in my office."

Horace said he never had any intention of talking contract with Reinsdorf without his agents. "He wanted to talk and my thought was that we were going to sit down and talk in general about the team," Grant said.

The two met that afternoon. "Horace said, 'I really want to stay here, but Jerry Krause and Jimmy Sexton are never going to get this done. Each guy is jockeying for position and neither one wants to show his cards. You and I can make this deal,' " Reinsdorf related.

"I said, 'Horace, what do you want?' And Horace gave me that little smile of his and he said, 'I'm not going to tell you. What do you think is fair?' I said I had no idea but that I would pull out all the comparables, and why don't we get together on Saturday after the Cleveland [playoff] game? We're going to beat them and you'll be in a real good mood."

Grant then called Sexton. "Jimmy, should I talk to him?" he asked.

"Let me call him first," said Sexton.

The next night Reinsdorf talked to Sexton from the Stadium and Sexton asked for his version of the meeting, agreeing that was what Grant had told him. Reinsdorf said Sexton told him he had no problem with the two meeting Saturday. Reinsdorf said Sexton told him, "I don't think you're going to make a deal. I don't think anything is going to come out of it. But if you want to meet, go ahead."

Sexton agreed that he told Reinsdorf he didn't think anything was going to come out of it, but said they agreed no numbers would be discussed or deals struck. Said Sexton: "Jerry said, 'I just want to talk to Horace and see if there is any chance he'll stay here and why he's unhappy here.' I said it's fine with me, but I don't think you're going to get anything out of him."

Reinsdorf said he prepared for the meeting by pulling out a list of player salaries. "And after practice," he said, "we went through name by name and what each guy was making. We talked about whether each player was better than Horace or not better than Horace, and I remember he thought he was better than [his brother] Harvey [earning nearly $3 million per year]. We agreed on that.

"Then I said to Horace, 'Look, I know you don't want to tell me what you want, but I don't want to make you a proposal and not have any idea of what you're going to say afterward, so here's what I'd like you to do. I'd like you to take a piece of paper, I'm going to go out of the room, and I'd like you to write down on the paper how much money you want, fold it up and put it in your pocket. I'll come back in the room and tell you what I think is fair. Then you show me what you wrote down.

"Horace said, 'What if I write down a lower number than you?' And I said, 'I can assure you that's not going to happen.' So he thought that was an acceptable idea. I walked out of the room, he wrote his number down, and I came back."

Reinsdorf said his offer was: "a five-year contract, and remember this was an opening offer, $6 million the first year; $4 million the second year; $3 million the third year; $3 million the fourth year and $4 million the fifth year . . . 20 million dollars over five years. But it's actually worth more than $4 million a year because of the front-loading. I figured it was probably the equivalent of about $20.5 million over the period of time.

"I then said to Horace, 'Let's see your number.' So he took the paper out of his pocket and the number Horace was looking for was $4.5 million a year or $ 22.5 million. I thought that was pretty close and I said to Horace, 'Why don't we bridge the gap with incentives? You want to make $4.5 million a year, I've basically told you I want to pay you about $4 million. Let's sit here and make up some incentives, some things you can do that we can pay you for. So we came up with things like, leading the NBA in rebounds, being second in rebounds, third in rebounds, making the all-defensive team, a whole series of things."

Reinsdorf said he then wrote them down and read them to Grant. "Horace's eyes lit up like I had never seen before," he said. "He got up, he walked over, he shook hands with me. He said, 'This is great, this is wonderful. I don't want to go through a whole summer of not knowing what's going on. I probably can't even get this anyplace else. This is a deal. We have a deal.'

"I said, 'Horace, that's great, I'm really happy, I'm thrilled, why don't we write it down and then you and I will initial it and we'll get the lawyers involved later?' I wrote the whole thing down, I actually signed it for some reason instead of initialing it, and I handed it to Horace.

"Horace said to me, 'Can I give Jimmy Sexton the courtesy of telling him what I've done before I sign it?' I said, 'Wait a minute Horace, you told me you wanted this meeting. No Krause, no Sexton, we're not getting them involved. You and I were going to make this deal.'

"He stood up, walked toward my desk again and said, 'We've made the deal. I give you my word.' He shook my hand and said, 'We've made a deal. I just want to tell Sexton I'm going to sign it.' I said, 'That's fine, and why don't you call me over the weekend and if I'm not in, just leave a message and tell me you've talked to Sexton and I'll have everything taken care of.' "

When Grant left Reinsdorf's office, he said he called Sexton from his car phone. Sexton described him as "very emotional."

"Jimmy," said Grant, "the guy just tried to negotiate with me without getting you involved."

Sexton had Grant fax over the piece of paper they had scribbled on, the proposed contract in Reinsdorf's view. "I swear on my grandfather's grave, I didn't agree to anything," said Grant, who related that same story, off the record, to at least one reporter. "If I did agree, then why didn't I just sign the paper? He knows within his heart and God knows that the only time we shook hands was for me to say goodbye and walk out of his office."

Reinsdorf was annoyed when he didn't hear from Grant over the weekend. On Monday, four days after their original meeting, Sexton called Reinsdorf. "[Sexton] said, 'Give me your version of the meeting,' " Reinsdorf said. "I told him, whereupon Jimmy said, 'You're not going to believe this, but when Horace left the meeting with you, he called me from his car and said that you had tried to take advantage of him and offered him much, much less money than he was worth.' I told Jimmy, 'You're correct. I'm not going to believe it and I don't believe it.' "

Reinsdorf said Phil Jackson asked Horace later what happened, a fairly unusual move for Jackson, who usually stayed out of such business dealings. "Horace told Phil everything that happened," said Reinsdorf, "except that he said when he left here and called Sexton, he told Sexton he made a great deal, told him what the deal was, and that Sexton bawled him out and said, 'How in the world could you ever make a deal with that guy? Why would you end up negotiating with someone who's a better negotiator than you? I've got to get you out of this deal.'

"Either Jimmy didn't tell me the truth or Horace didn't tell Phil the truth. But when Horace left my office he was so excited, I can't believe he would tell anyone I tried to take advantage of him."

Grant maintained that all he said to Reinsdorf was that the deal "looks good," and was referring to the first few years. And as far as the conversation with Jackson, Grant said he never told Sexton he made a great deal. "I was sure he was trying to take advantage of me," Grant said of Reinsdorf.

"I've known Horace a long, long time," said Sexton, "and if he had screwed up or even thought he had, he would have told me."

Sexton's biggest problem with Reinsdorf's story is that this was somehow a "spur of the moment" offer. "If you're going to do a handshake deal with a player," he said, "you talk about, for example, five years for $20 million. Maybe you say it's front-loaded. I don't think you take time to write it on a legal pad and ask a player to sign it."

According to Sexton, you also don't include fine-print details that suggested the offer was planned in advance. But more than that, Grant said, it was principle.

"He talks about the morality of sports," Grant said, referring to Reinsdorf. "Why would anyone want to negotiate with me without my representative there?"

Reinsdorf said in his mind, it marked the end of Grant's career with the Bulls when he refused to go through with the agreement they had made. "I've made literally hundreds of millions of dollars of deals in my life on handshakes," he said. "My word means everything to me and I have never, ever given a guy a second chance to get even with me. Once somebody has hurt me, has lied to me, I don't give him a second chance."

Nevertheless, Reinsdorf said, "Krause worked on me and convinced me" that for the good of the Bulls, they should continue to go forward. Reinsdorf said he imposed one condition, however. "Before any negotiations could take place, Horace and Jimmy had to come sit down with me in a room and tell me what happened," Reinsdorf said. "I wasn't going to call him a liar but the air had to be cleared, I had to know what happened and Horace had to realize that he had done something wrong."

There was no way Grant was going to do that, feeling demeaned, intimidated and more than a little annoyed, and Sexton said that neither he nor Rote ever promised Reinsdorf it would happen. Additionally, Sexton said Reinsdorf never said why he wanted this meeting. "He did say he wanted us in a room together, but he never made a statement to us that it was to clear the air," he said. "But Horace felt there was such a misunderstanding the first time, then what in the world would happen the second time? The bottom line was that Horace never felt comfortable being in a room with him again."

Reinsdorf said he was told Grant would meet with him but that he never heard from him. He said he made himself available "even going to the Berto Center and purposely parking my car next to his," but never tried to talk to Grant again either.

Sexton said it was a "giant misunderstanding in a lot of ways." It was also apparently a colossal clash of egos.

Reinsdorf said that on Monday, July 25, Rote called to say Grant had completed his "Steve Garvey tour, knew what clubs wanted him and that he would like an offer from us."

"Is Horace going to come talk to me himself?" Reinsdorf asked Rote. "If Horace won't talk, there's no deal."

"Let me get this straight," said Rote. "You're saying that if

Horace doesn't come to see you, you do not want him on the Chicago Bulls team?"

"That is correct," said Reinsdorf.

Reinsdorf said Rote told him he would call him back in the next day or two, but that he did not hear from him. Reinsdorf then tried on Wednesday, but could not reach Rote or Sexton.

That morning, Rote left Reinsdorf a message saying that Grant was not going to meet with him; in essence, that he was taking his services elsewhere. It was obviously a decision that had been made a long time before that.

Reinsdorf called a press conference for Friday afternoon to tell the Bulls' side of the story. "I don't think I'm either angry or frustrated," Reinsdorf said that day. "But I do want our fans to know what happened because I'm tired of people complaining that we didn't try to sign Horace Grant."

But Reinsdorf was not finished. "We've always tried to treat Horace with a great deal of respect," he said. "I know how many times I've told Horace we love him personally and we think he's a great basketball player, tried to keep him happy and never criticized him for the blue flu, even though the number of games he didn't play this year because of the blue flu probably cost us the Eastern Conference regular-season championship.

"I've always known that sports morality is different than that in most businesses. I've accepted it. I don't like it. But there comes a time when you have to draw the line and you can't turn the other cheek anymore. And so I've decided to say goodbye to Horace Grant."

Grant and Sexton did not see Reinsdorf's press conference, which was broadcast live on a local channel. They were, instead, at the Grand Rapids, Michigan, home of Richard DeVos finalizing their six-year, $22.3 million deal with the Magic.

"I was with people with character, people who told me they would stand behind me no matter what," said Grant. "Those people made me feel so much more at home than I was made to feel by the Bulls."

Sexton obtained a condensed, wire-story version of Reinsdorf's press conference, and Grant was furious at the blue-flu comment in particular. "Here it was one of the biggest days of my career, and then to have someone try to shoot you down and damage your character like that, that really upset me," Grant said. "I put my heart and soul into my work. I always have and

I always will. If that wasn't the case, then why did so many teams tell us that the biggest thing they liked about me as a player was my durability?"

Grant's contention is that Reinsdorf's original "bump" in late April was carefully orchestrated to go around his agents in a last-ditch effort to sign him. Others saw the Bulls' so-called game plan as a display of arrogance that when all was said and done, Grant would not dare leave Chicago.

It was especially curious considering that while indeed the Bulls could offer Grant as much as they wanted since he was their own free agent, they ignored the fact that with the one-year out clause that players and teams were exercising as a way around the salary cap, every other team could essentially offer Grant anything as well.

Sexton said he wished Grant could have left the Bulls on better terms. "It just seems that everything with them is war," said Grant.

Ultimately, the whole thing could perhaps be written off as a so-called "seven-year itch," for clearly Grant and the Bulls merely grew apart. And just as clearly, Grant grew restless with his perceived roles — that of a so-called "blue collar worker" for the Bulls; of an obedient student to Jackson; of a loyal friend to Pippen. He wanted more — more glamor, more freedom, more respect.

Jackson and others often wondered aloud if he knew what he was in for, pursuing new goals and new dreams in unknown territory. And Grant, as well, was somewhat nervous about making such an enormous decision despite the excitement of being the hunted.

In the end, maybe there was no right or wrong. Maybe as Jordan always said, it was simply inevitable.

Chicago Bulls Professional Basketball Team,
Public Relations
980 N. Michigan Ave.
Chicago IL 60611

Dearest Madam or Sir,

Congratulations on your fine third National Basketball Associatic
Championship victory. I can imagine that you are as proud of the young me
on the team as the rest of Chicago is. I can also imagine that you are
crestfallen as I am about the tragic violence, that befell our fair city while
was celebrating your recent success on the basketball court. These mc
unfortunate incidences got me to pondering. What more could the team ar
its staff have done to avert such revelrious crimes? I am sure the publ
service announcements with the players and coach helped, but I think th
underlying problem is in the image of the team. That large angry beast, th
you use as a symbol of the team, would seem to suggest that you encourag
ruthless, raging anarchy, just like that which we witnessed in the streets
Chicago not so long ago.

The "raging bull" has for centuries been used to symbolize a powerfu
unreasonable, violent, and misdirected anger. We would all certainly agr
that your team is "powerful" on the basketball court, but none of those oth
adjectives seem to quite fit the dynamic elegance of containing brute fore
which is the sport of basketball. The team is also looked to as a model in t
community, and each individual on the team is expected to act in a demu
and respectful way both on and off the basketball court. From all of these fac
I came to the conclusion that the team's name and mascot should be chang
to better reflect the sincere nature of your organization.

I feel that the historic importance of Chicago's beef industry is right
included in the design, and the country is familiar with the cattle imagery.
I thought that you should choose a more representative member of t
bovine family, the demure adolescent cow is my suggestion. Enclosed ye
will find a rough sketch of my idea. Thank you for considering my proposa

Sincerely,

DA LIL DOGGIES

4

SCOTTIE

It's ironic that Scottie Pippen has never particularly enjoyed being the center of attention. In recent years, his playful "No comments. Peace." have become familiar to beat reporters who needed a reaction from him on, say, another Bulls controversy. But he never waded in. Maybe he was just biding his time.

Whatever the case, he more than made up for it during the '93-'94 season. A glorious year that should have been remembered solely for his maturation as a team leader and bona fide NBA superstar, was clouded by a series of ugly glitches, one seemingly feeding on the other.

There was the January 20 arrest on gun possession charges (later dropped) that might have been forgotten if not for his racially fired comments of February 28. And then there was Game 3 of the Eastern Conference semifinals, the infamous 1.8-second incident. And that, unfortunately for Pippen, may never go away entirely.

It's unfortunate because mistakes, like most misfortune, generally fade with time. But public figures, like it or not, live by the running obituary. That is, no matter what they do, if it's noteworthy enough, it will somehow end up in their epitaph.

"That's one of the worst things about fame," Michael Jordan once said. "But it's also what you learn to live with. It's the reality of the situation."

Pippen not only understands that now, but claims to have understood it then.

In retrospect, Pippen said he feels no remorse about what happened in Game 3 against New York, under the circumstances. And that is an important distinction to make to even attempt to understand what was going through his mind as he rooted himself to the bench, refusing to come in for the final play with the Bulls and Knicks tied at 102.

"Going into the game, there was a lot of pressure on us, for one thing," explained Pippen about a month later. "We were in a situation where we could have lost, and then we're down 0-3 and we probably lose the series. What was going through my mind is that I wanted to be there. Not to take the last shot, necessarily, but just to be an option.

"All game long I'm being utilized offensively (to that point, he was 1 of 4 in the fourth quarter, but ended up 10 of 20 for 25 points, including 2 of 4 from three-point range for the game). And now we're taking a last-second shot and you're going to tell me to take the ball out?"

Pippen's voice rises, then suddenly falls. "I was being used as a passer but really, I was being used as nothing the way I saw it."

Some were sympathetic to Pippen, and they could only guess that he couldn't possibly have considered the ramifications of his actions during those frantic seconds between Phil Jackson calling the play and Pippen planting himself on the bench. But Pippen says he isn't looking for alibis and says he did, in fact, realize that it was going to be "a big deal."

"I knew it as soon as I did it," he said. "I just didn't care. I was going to stand up for what I believed. And if I'm put in that position again and I'm still considered the team leader and we're down 2-0, I'm going to voice my opinion again. To say I'd do exactly the same thing again, that's hard to say.

"The thing is, I wouldn't have cared so much if it was the regular season. But it's like, when we lose, everything is on me. So just give me a chance to answer to that."

B.J. Armstrong said he understood perfectly. "I've seen guys walk off the practice court," he said. "I've seen guys quit during games. Here's a guy who's so competitive, he just wanted the ball. I understood it completely. If he couldn't do it, he just didn't want to be out there at all."

At the same time, however, Armstrong said he could also understand the reaction of Bill Cartwright. A 15-year veteran,

Cartwright had precious few games left in his body and in his career, and very likely no one in the building reacted as intensely to Pippen's boycott as he did.

At first, Cartwright said he thought perhaps it was just a momentary pique and figured that all Pippen needed was a verbal nudge to bring him to his senses.

When Pippen didn't react, Cartwright was overtaken with a type of rage he had never experienced before. John Diamond, the Bulls' public relations assistant who was in charge of quickly lining up players after games for courtside television interviews, raced up to Cartwright in his usual manner and urged him toward the cameras. Diamond, in the late-game frenzy of his job, was not even aware of what had transpired and could not have known the depth of Cartwright's growing anger. But he got a pretty good idea that something was bothering him when the normally gentle Cartwright all but shoved him aside to get to the locker room.

Once inside, Cartwright knew he had to say something, but he had trouble getting his thoughts together. So upset was he at the very idea that Pippen had so thoughtlessly risked the outcome of a playoff game that he actually began to hyperventilate in the shower. When he emerged, Jackson let him address the team. And with tears of hurt and anger, he turned toward Scottie.

"When Michael was here, we put up with a lot of his bullshit," Cartwright sputtered. "Scottie, I can't believe you would let us come so far, to bust our asses, and then be so selfish. I've never seen anything like it. It's totally unacceptable."

The sight of Bill Cartwright crying was something no one had seen before. When he got home that night, said his wife Shari, she could not tell anything out of the ordinary had happened. "He was his usual quiet self," she said. "Then he woke me up at 4 in the morning and said he had something to tell me."

After he told his wife what had happened, she was shocked. "I've known him since high school and I have never seen him cry," she said. "Ever."

"He was so hurt," said one Bull. "If I was Scottie, I would have felt like dirt."

And indeed, Pippen said he felt pretty low. "I felt bad when Bill was talking, really bad," he said. "I knew I had to say something. Basically, I just apologized for not going into the game. And I tried to explain that if you don't get the plays, ask. The wrong execution just kills us. I felt the guys were on my side when we walked out of there."

The pointed comments were aimed at Toni Kukoc. For contributing to Pippen's anger on the last play was the play before — a possession designed as a clear-out for Pippen on the right side of the basket. Only problem was that as Pippen drew the isolation, he wasn't entirely isolated. Kukoc was in the right corner and despite Pippen's frantic waving, stayed there long enough for the Bulls to draw a 24-second violation with 5.5 seconds remaining. When Patrick Ewing hit a hook shot to tie the game at 102 and the Bulls called a timeout, Pippen was fuming.

"That had happened with Toni all year and I don't know if it was an English thing or what," said Pippen, who was annoyed even more when Kukoc's number was then called for the final play. "But you just can't make mistakes like that in the playoffs, especially when you're down 0-2."

Kukoc said at the time he thought he was cleared out and wasn't exactly in the mood for criticism, especially after hitting the game-winning shot to bail out his team and, in effect, Pippen. "Where do you want me to clear out?" he asked afterward. "Out of the gym? Where do you want me to be?"

Pippen, in even his weakest moments, will not admit to having anything personal against the rookie. Yes, he admits, he was angry when the Bulls, specifically Jerry Krause, did their most ardent recruiting of Kukoc at a crucial period before Pippen's last contract negotiations. And yes, he resented terribly the thought that the Bulls could end up paying Kukoc more than the $2.8 million Pippen was to be paid for the '94-'95 season.

As soon as he heard about the one-year "out" clause in Kukoc's contract, a provision that was upheld after going through federal district court in the case of Portland's Chris Dudley, Pippen could see the proverbial writing on the wall. "Horace can make more than me, that's fine," he muttered on several occasions. "But not Toni. I'll sit out a year before I'll let that happen."

And, in fact, Pippen asked around about the financial consequences of just such an action. "I voiced my opinion," Pippen said after the '93-'94 season. "And they voiced theirs. They want Toni to be here and to make him the player they always thought he could be."

That player is something of a prototype of Pippen, a small forward, and a player who can run the offense as a so-called "point forward," in Bulls vernacular. At close to 6-11, Kukoc has neither the necessary quickness to play guard defensively nor the strength to play power forward. That left Pippen, when the two were on the court together, to scurry around after the smaller guards defensively and away from the boards where he is so effective.

"I wouldn't be happy if I had to play off-guard," Pippen said in anticipation of Kukoc eventually moving into the starting lineup. "But I'd have no choice."

Off the court, clearly the two were not buddies. But neither were they enemies. Pippen was more impatient than any Bull with Kukoc's defensive shortcomings and offensive lapses. And he rode Kukoc endlessly on the practice court, much as he thought Jordan had done to him, but Kukoc never balked.

After the first playoff game in New York, during the '94 conference semifinals, Pippen got on the team bus and leaned over to Kukoc. The rookie was a bit dazed from the beating the Knicks administered in a game the Bulls very nearly won. It was a typical Knicks playoff performance, but clearly, no one could have prepared Kukoc for its physical nature.

"See? This is what I've been telling you about," Pippen said to him. "They didn't call anything. This is why I've been so tough on you in practice."

And like the good soldier, Kukoc nodded in agreement. "I would play him the same way in practice that I knew New York would," Pippen explained. "I'd push him all the way upcourt. I did what Michael used to do. I was really trying to get Toni to use his right hand and he did get better at it. At first I think he probably took it personally, thinking I was against him. But I think he understood eventually."

In retrospect, however, Pippen's relationship with Kukoc, good or bad, was hardly a blip on the screen. For Pippen, the '93-'94 season was a crash course in celebrity, a learning experience and a failure and a coming-out party all at the same time. To his credit, Pippen did several things. He was much more accessible to the media than he had been. And he exhibited superstar ability in his consistency on the court, hitting his peak with an MVP performance he all but predicted at the NBA All-Star Game.

"But the best thing he did," said John Paxson, "was that he didn't try to be Michael, and that would have been an easy thing to do."

Specifically, Paxson was referring to the fact that Pippen averaged 18 shots in 38 minutes per game, a far cry from the 26 shots in 39 minutes by Jordan the year before, and only two more shots than the season before.

The night Pippen heard about Jordan's retirement, he was in a blur, confused and a bit shaken. So much so that he immediately left the baseball game where he had been given the official news. On the drive home, his mind was bombarded by what this would mean. "I didn't feel we'd have no chance [to repeat as champions]," he said. "I never did think that."

In fact, it was much the opposite as the shock soon gave way to excitement about the new opportunities this would bring. "I looked at it as a challenge," he said. "I knew it would be fun for me."

Pippen resisted the urge to be the next Michael. But if ever there was a metaphor for the season, it occurred the night of October 28, as Pippen prepared for his first exhibition outing of the preseason. Earlier, he had joked that he knew only one thing for sure about the Bulls' first year in the post-Jordan era. "All I know is I'm getting his locker," he said with a laugh. And with great aplomb, that's what he did.

"This is the greatest promotion I've ever had," crowed Pippen, as he began to clear out the famous double stall, twice the size of every other in the locker room to help accommodate the inevitable media crush after every game. "Michael, I love you, but I'm glad to see you go," he laughed.

And Pippen did seem to relish the opportunities this was sure to bring. Shortly after Jordan's retirement announcement, Jackson named Pippen co-captain. Then he patted him on the back. "I just told him that's where the saddle's going to lie," Jackson said, only partially kidding.

"I kind of think it's good timing for me as a player," Pippen said at the time. "I've learned a lot from Michael, that you've got to go out every day and try to reach certain goals. I think this season is going to be really great for me because it's going to give me a chance to open up."

And it was certainly a more open Pippen than the one the media were used to dealing with. Fishing out an old T-shirt from Jordan's locker that night, Pippen offered it to anyone within shouting distance. "Here, anyone want to wipe their tears?"

Finding several prehistoric candy bars, he added, "Hey, we could get a lot of money for these.... If that's what he was eating at halftime, I might just have to have one."

If this was the new Pippen, every reporter in the room had to be thinking, bring him on. Maybe this was indeed the opportunity he had been waiting for, that all those comments he made about not minding the fact that he was perpetually in Jordan's shadow, weren't quite the truth.

"If Michael comes back," Pippen joked, "I might just sublet him a little spot."

The obvious question was just how much of Jordan's old role Pippen would try to claim. "A lot of guys are going to be challenged through the season, not just me," Pippen said. "We feel we're going to be better as a team because we're going to look to help one another out and pull each other along."

In that respect, Pippen responded, showing his indispensable value — after returning from an early 10-day stint on the injured list spent rehabilitating his ankle — by leading the Bulls to 30 victories in 35 games leading to the All-Star break. The streak was highlighted by Pippen's 29-point effort in a 132-113 rout of Phoenix.

"If you're looking for one defining game in the season," said Steve Kerr, "you could pick that one. It became obvious then that Scottie was the center of our team, that it revolved around him."

Yet Pippen seemed burdened by the inability to avoid controversy, something on which Jordan perhaps could have advised him, but probably couldn't have told him how to avoid. Part of the problem seemed to arise from a cockiness exuded by Pippen, a trait that surely helped him to become the player he had, but often exacerbated his sometimes questionable judgment.

Often, it would take on a mocking form, such as the time he was talking about his ability to make those around him better. "I bring a level of unselfishness seldom seen in this game," he said bursting into laughter.

But there were times when he was stubborn, particularly when Bulls assistant Tex Winter would issue instructions to Pippen only to be sneered at or ignored. Once, Winter was so incensed after a game in which the Bulls won and Pippen was named Player of the Game in a locally sponsored regular feature of each postgame, that he charged over to the scorer's table, demanding to know why Pippen was given the rather modest honor.

Often, Pippen had a way of coming off as well meaning. But when he put off his ankle surgery until August of the summer before, he annoyed and unnerved many in the Bulls organization. The operation was invasive, not merely done with an arthroscope, and Pippen said he did not fully understand the extent of it.

"I pretty much just wanted to enjoy the summer off," he said. "I didn't think of it as actual surgery, and I was sorry I put it off after I realized I needed so much time to recover."

That led directly to the Bulls' 4-7 start, pushed Kukoc into the starting lineup sooner than he should have been and lent a definite air of panic to the team early in the season. "I just felt pressured to come back too soon," Pippen said. "I know my body and how my body is feeling when it's right, and something was wrong. After the first game of the season I was fine, but after the back-to-back [the Bulls played Charlotte and Miami to open up], it really bothered me. It felt worse than it had ever been. I lost a lot of strength after the surgery and so I gave myself some cushion time."

But once Pippen returned and the Bulls started to show their potential as a certain title contender again, he felt he had to do something and this took on the form of public criticism of Krause.

Pippen, like many of the Bulls, got a kick out of seeing Krause squirm, and certainly the public and most of his teammates could see where he was coming from. The Bulls were 19-10 at the time, after being thoroughly dominated in a 15-point loss to Orlando, and Pippen was fuming at the Bulls' inactivity one day after the Knicks had just obtained Derek Harper from Dallas in a trade for Tony Campbell and a draft choice.

"If people expect the Bulls to contend," said Pippen, "we have to have something to go to war with."

Clearly the Bulls, though satisfied with the job Pete Myers had done under the circumstances, especially on defense, still needed to shore up the two-guard spot in the absence of Jordan. Harper had appeared to be a perfect candidate.

"We have a slot that needs to be filled," Pippen said. "We were very lucky to get guys in training camp who have been major contributors, but they have not filled what we need. They've been the greatest, but there's a slot there and we need our general manager to bring someone in. Whatever it takes.

"We have guys with trade value, and if we're going to be better, if we're going to contend, we have to do something. In the playoffs especially, you've got to have confidence, to know you're going to win. And right now, I don't feel good going on the court."

Asked later if he regretted the comments, Pippen stood by them. "I don't regret saying it at all," he said. "I think the players on this team kind of look up to me and if I don't say anything, then everybody thinks we're having fun and feeling good about our chances. . . . We have to think we can defend our title."

Like Jordan before him, Pippen seemed to know just which buttons to push with Krause, who was with the team in Orlando.

"New York loses their point guard [Doc Rivers] and within two, three weeks, they get a solid replacement," he said. "We lose the best player of all time and three months later, we've done nothing. . . . We need [Krause] on the phone, not in the locker room."

While Pippen's intentions may well have been in the best interest of the team, however, it occasionally rubbed some of the veterans the wrong way. Some quietly referred to him as "the president," in part because of remarks he had made a few weeks earlier.

John Paxson, Scott Williams and Will Perdue were getting ready to come off the injured list and the once unthinkable question was: What in the world were the Bulls going to do with them?

The Bulls were riding a nine-game winning streak at the time and had won 13 of 14 games when Pippen was asked about the current state of the team. "From a coaching standpoint, you don't fix anything that isn't broken," he said. "Right now, playing with the guys we have on the floor, the decision shouldn't be that tough."

Winter backed up Pippen, saying, "We have good continuity going right now and the people coming back will change the roles of a lot of players. You'd have to be concerned with the effect on the overall team effort."

But it was Pippen who absorbed the brunt of blame for being insensitive. Williams was particularly annoyed, though fairly diplomatic publicly. "I'd like to think that my teammates would welcome us back," he said. "I didn't like reading in the paper where a teammate said he wouldn't like to see any changes in the lineup. Players we've had on the injured list have been around the program and wouldn't do anything to disrupt the chemistry."

Pippen shrugged when told that Williams was mad. "Maybe you ought to go say something to him, smooth it over," someone whispered to him. "Fuck it," said Pippen. "Whatever I say is going to be taken the wrong way."

And whatever he did, as it turned out.

On the night of January 19, Pippen had stopped at a bar in the Rush Sreet section near downtown Chicago after the Bulls had defeated the Bullets, and had parked his Range Rover in a tow zone.

When he emerged from the bar, he saw his car being towed, but that was the least of his problems. When officers had gone into his car to prepare it for towing, they said they had found a blue steel Colt revolver loaded with seven .380-caliber bullets "in plain view" next to the console. Pippen was arrested and charged with a misdemeanor weapons possession charge that carries a maximum penalty of one year in jail and a $1,000 fine.

The next day, his teammates were asked for their reaction. Williams, who lost his parents to a murder-suicide when he was in college, said Pippen was putting himself in a dangerous position.

"Society has gone crazy," Williams said. "Things happen all the time over handguns. I lost my parents because of a handgun, so I know all too well what guns on the street and what a handgun can do. And I think legislation has to get tougher and we have to get tougher on getting guns off the street."

Pippen claimed the gun was not in plain view. The charges were later dropped when his attorneys argued the search had been illegal.

"There's nothing really to tell," Pippen said. "I'm not one to carry a gun. I don't feel the need to. Buying a gun to me was just something I wanted to do because I like guns. I grew up around them and my dad and I used to hunt.

"On that night, I hadn't been to the range in a while and I accidentally left it in the trunk. I was going to the Stadium when I realized it, but I couldn't just turn around and go back home. I was already running late as it was. So I tried to hide it."

He was surprised, though, and more than a little put off at the level of disapproval he perceived, and though he later publicly apologized for the incident, he was particularly annoyed with criticism from Chicago Mayor Richard Daley.

"I heard the mayor criticizing me," he said, "yet why does he walk around with bodyguards? It wasn't like I was going around carrying a gun in my pocket. But I still used bad judgment and I feel very badly about it."

If the public tide had turned on Pippen by then, it wasn't yet evident. His name was still being bandied about as an MVP candidate, but the Bulls had started to slide after the All-Star break and there was still some question as to whether he was truly a leader.

Many consider February 28 of '94 a turning point, and surely that did not help Pippen's public image.

Interestingly, he had answered a similar question that night early in his postgame session, a ritual that consists of several clumps of reporters and TV cameramen wading in and out of the tiny area in front of each cubicle. Often one group may have asked the question already, but it has to be re-asked any number of times until each group has heard it.

And so it was that when the last clump finally caught sight of Pippen, the subject of booing came up again. Phil Jackson had gotten the ball rolling when, at his postgame press conference minutes earlier, he said he was appalled and offended at the fans' behavior during the Bulls loss to Cleveland, an embarrassing scenario especially considering that the Bulls were playing division rivals and a team they were used to humiliating in years past.

"To lose before your home fans and have them boo you?" Jackson said incredulously. "It's very demoralizing. As many thrills and great games as we've given these fans . . . the fact that they have absolutely no loyalty to this team, which is trying hard . . . there's no excuse."

Pippen avoided comment on the booing at first, but it was that one last question as he prepared to leave that he couldn't quite resist. "Is it a little depressing to hear the boos?" he was asked.

"Personally," he responded, "the only thing that's depressing is that in my seven years here, I've never seen a white guy get booed in the Stadium. But it seems that when things go bad, when the ball's in your hands, if you don't score, then the fans take over."

Of course, he should have stopped right there, considering he had already undoubtedly gotten himself into trouble. And as much as reporters love a juicy quote, it was almost as if that last small clump standing before him was silently willing him to stop; as if Pippen's words were coming out in super slo-mo with enough time for everyone to realize that this did not simply mean a good quote in the next day's newspaper or a great sound byte. No, this meant follow-up. This meant asking Pippen the next morning if he really meant it. If he was sorry. It meant asking Bulls management for an official reaction and Pippen's teammates for their comments.

"Scottie, stop now," everyone was thinking.

But Pippen was not quite finished. "Toni [Kukoc] was 0-for-whatever tonight," he concluded, "and I never heard one fan get on him."

Another controversy.

The question now was whether Pippen would apologize. After all, he obviously had pretty strong feelings on the subject and though he was also frustrated after a disappointing loss, this was not the sort of thing you just took back.

The Bulls, however, knew a public relations problem when they saw one, and Jerry Krause wasted no time drafting a statement of apology for Scottie to sign. Make no mistake: They were not Pippen's words. And it was most certainly not his apology.

"It was something I just said at that time," Pippen said much later of his original comments. "But I resented having to apologize."

Pippen said he didn't put up much of an argument. Krause called him into his office and showed him the statement. From Pippen's perspective, it was more an attitude of fine, whatever, I'll sign and let's get this over with. And he did realize he did have to say something about another incident that night when, during a third-quarter timeout and the Cavs leading by 18 and the booing at its loudest, he flipped off one particularly obnoxious fan behind the bench.

The statement came in handy for that part: "There was a small minority at last night's game who booed me and my teammates," the statement read in part, "and I reacted in an improper way by making an obscene gesture."

But here's where the sticky part came in: "In my comments after the game, I in no way meant to imply that there was racism involved," the statement continued. "That small minority booed all the Bulls players. In past years, they have booed players of both races. We have the greatest fans in the world here, and I reacted to a small minority in poor taste."

If that didn't exactly sound like Scottie talking, then the kicker was even worse: "I also made some comments about Jerry Krause and my teammates which I now realize I said in the frustration of a losing game, and I realize that the statements were not true."

The assembled media got a real howl out of that part. "Geez," mused one reporter, "while they were at it, why didn't they just say, 'And furthermore, Jerry Krause isn't overweight either.' "

The comments about Krause were, in fact, not made in the heat of a losing battle but rather before the game. Out of necessity,

Pippen had been playing more off-guard and was still annoyed at management's apparent lack of activity. By now, the trading deadline had passed and players such as Harper, Jeff Hornacek and Danny Manning had been traded, while Ron Harper had stayed with the Clippers despite making it clear he wanted to leave and wouldn't mind going to Chicago.

Pippen was merely repeating his earlier feelings of frustration when he said, "I'm very disappointed because I don't feel like management has given us an opportunity to win a fourth title. . . . We've hardly done anything in the draft since me and Horace came in. B.J. was a good pick, but what have we gotten after him?"

And Pippen showed great foresight with his next comments: "It's discouraging because come the end of the season, I know more is going to be asked of me. . . . Playing off-guard takes me away from rebounding. It takes me away from the team defense we need and has me chasing all these little guys around the perimeter. I don't like it."

No doubt, Krause was especially enraged with Pippen's comments about the draft, for this was his greatest pleasure and source of pride. But Pippen had little to say the next day as he glumly faced the media. "I pretty much apologize to some extent," he said. "I feel bad for saying it [the racial comments], but you can never take back things you've said."

Later, reflecting back on his season, Pippen said the gun incident and racial comments did not scar him. "It was a distraction to some degree," he said, "but I didn't let it faze me on the court. I still did what I had to do."

He would, indeed, finish the season strongly, averaging 22 points on 49 percent shooting, nine rebounds, six assists and three steals per game. "I definitely feel this was the best season of my career," he said before the playoffs began. "I think I was put into a position where I was going to either shine or fail. I think, to some extent, it has been a great shining for me because of the success I've been able to have, as well as the team's. It's really been a wonderful season."

It wasn't over, though, of course. Pippen had proven, like Jordan before him, that he was capable of performing under duress. The Bulls' 95-83 victory over the Knicks in Game 4 of their playoff series was a testimony to that as Pippen, with the eyes of the sporting world and then some burrowing into him, led the team in its finest defensive performance of the postseason with 25 points, eight rebounds, six assists, two steals and just one turnover.

During the game, with everyone focusing on Pippen and Kukoc's every interaction in the wake of the 1.8 second incident, it was noted that the two encouraged each other on the court and hugged off of it. "He supported me a lot during the season," Kukoc said afterward. "It was no different tonight than a lot of times. There is nothing personal between Pippen and me."

Pippen's other teammates also rallied around him. "Scottie wants to win more than anyone on this team and that's why that happened the other night," said Steve Kerr. "He's so frustrated and he's under so much pressure, it probably just spilled over. But he came out [in Game 4] and played a great game, throwing high-fives and getting the fans into it. I thought he battled back and showed what he's really all about."

In Indianapolis, someone asked the Pacers' Reggie Miller what he made of the 1.8-second incident. "If I did that to this team, they would not only be upset with me, they'd lose a lot of respect for me," he said. "Chicago's the three-time world champions. You can't have that with the world champions. Not where the world can see it."

"It was an act of stupidity," Pippen admitted to a national television audience.

But would he be forgiven? In Chicago, it seemed he would, as nary a boo was heard in the introductions before Game 4. Time would have to tell beyond that. But nationally was quite another story.

"There's a phrase that follows Scottie Pippen around and it's anything but flattering," wrote Michael Wilbon of the *Washington Post* that weekend. "Pippen was a heavy-duty contributor to three NBA championship teams here. He was regarded enough to be named to the Dream Team. He was the MVP of the 1994 All-Star Game. Few players of his generation have as many skills or are capable of changing a game in so many different ways. Still, there's this phrase you hear when Pippen's name is mentioned. It's uttered most often by players. You can hear it in any gym in the NBA: 'Scottie Pippen is a punk.'

"In locker room parlance, a 'punk' is somebody who can't deliver in the clutch, somebody who either can't hit the big shot or doesn't want to take it. A 'punk' in the NBA glossary is a quitter, somebody looking for an excuse or an easy way out.

"You know what they're calling Pippen after Game 3 here in the Stadium, don't you?"

It is national perceptions such as these that will dog Pippen and he says he realizes that. "Either people understand or not," he said. "It's out of my control now."

Out of his control, too, after the '93-'94 season was Pippen's future. And that bothered him. "I know when I signed my last contract [in the summer of '91 for five years worth about $18 million], it was a bad deal," said Pippen, "but it was security for me. I knew it wasn't going to pay me any more than Michael. But I wish I would have played out my option."

If he had, the timing could not possibly have been any better for Pippen, for he would have become a free agent in the summer of '93, after the Bulls' third championship. But now, of course, it was out of his hands and he had only to look forward to his contract expiring at the end of 1998 [he will be 33 in September of '98]. "After this year, I see myself playing a couple more years maybe," Pippen said. "I want to be like Michael. I want to quit when *I* want to quit."

Before that, however, he looked forward to renegotiating his contract and hoped that a good relationship with Jerry Reinsdorf was going to help. "To me, it's all about getting paid what you're worth," he said. "If they're going to pay Toni $4 million [Kukoc ended up averaging $4.3 million], then I want to get $5 [million]. He does good things on the floor, but I don't think Toni is anywhere worth the player I am.

"Whether he ends up paying Toni $2 million, $4 million or $2 billion, I still want my contract redone."

After a deal was killed suddenly by Seattle in late June that would have sent Pippen to the Sonics for Shawn Kemp, Ricky Pierce and an exchange of draft picks, Pippen was furious. "I feel like I've put down roots here," Pippen had said only weeks before. "I like Chicago. I've invested in a nice house here. This is my home now."

Not only that, but even after Grant's experience in dealing with Reinsdorf alone, Pippen was hoping for a nice, quiet private conversation with the Bulls' owner in the hopes that they could work something out. "Reinsdorf's signature is what counts on a contract, not Krause's," said Pippen. "If Reinsdorf signs, you know the deal is done."

Pippen was not only hurt by the Bulls shopping him in trade talks, but furious that they did not have the courtesy to tell him. He told off Krause in one particularly heated phone call the night of the deal, and spent the rest of the summer stewing and hoping for another trade.

Earlier in the season, shortly after the Atlanta Hawks dealt veteran Dominique Wilkins to the L.A. Clippers, Pippen remarked, "The Bulls would do that to me in a heartbeat." It was the same sense of insecurity he felt as he watched Grant depart a wealthy and happy man, and how he felt as he watched the team change around him. Nevertheless, through it all, he said '93-'94 wasn't all bad.

Maybe it's the resiliency of Scottie Pippen. Surely it is that trait that makes him so difficult to read sometimes. But it is also the same trait that allows him to say these words with no hesitation:

"When Michael left, I looked at it as a challenge right away," he said. "I definitely knew it would be fun for me."

Fun? Probably not the word most people would think Pippen would use in describing the season. And he realizes that.

"It was fun, though," he insisted. "No matter what happened. The statements I made, me being caught with a gun, me not going back into the game, I was still able to enjoy it."

He laughed at the sound of it. "I know how that sounds, but it's true."

Dear B. G. Armstrong:

How are you? I just wanted to write this letter just to see how you were doing and to let you know what a wonderful person I think you are. I watched your commercial – the one where you are reading an abused child's letter – and I felt so saddened and touched that I cried. It's unbelievable that a young child has to endure such pain and hardship at such a tender age. On the other hand, it's remarkable that a talented, popular, busy man like yourself would take out time to care. Thank you for being the person you are. I admire you on and off the court. I think you are great.

Thank you for taking the time to read this letter. I really appreciate all you've done and will will continue to do. God Bless you.

Sincerely,

5

GROWING PAINS

It didn't take Scott Williams long to figure out that the NBA was a business. Or at least that this wasn't college anymore. Never a star at the University of North Carolina, he was nevertheless a valued component. And after beating out the final six players in Bulls camp for the last non-guaranteed spot on the roster for the '90-'91 season, he was sure there was some kind of a conspiracy going on when he didn't play much, even during blowout victories.

"The only thing I could think of was that I wasn't playing because I walked on," he said.

In Williams' estimation, he was outplaying Stacey King and Will Perdue in practice and working hard. But come game night, he would get inconsistent minutes or no time at all. Michael Jordan would take his fellow Tar Heel aside and encourage him, tell him he would get his chance one day, but Williams eventually became convinced it was a personal conflict between Phil Jackson and himself.

"There was so much communication at North Carolina," Williams said. "Here, there was nothing."

Williams, who once considered himself a person who kept many of his emotions inside, suddenly found himself losing his temper. One day in practice, Jackson jokingly referred to Williams as "Psycho," and his teammates soon started teasingly using the nickname. But Williams didn't think it was particularly funny, and the tag bothered him more and more over the years, especially as it became a symbol of the knock on him from management.

"Scott Williams? Oh yeah, decent player. Solid rebounder, good defender. But the kid's psycho."

Williams bristled at the connotation. "Sure, I'm excitable and I play with emotion," he said. "But off the court, I consider myself an intelligent, reasonable person. And I couldn't imagine what I did to make him say something like that."

Like a self-fulfilling prophecy, however, Williams found himself behaving in ways he never had before. One day in the middle of his rookie season, assistant coach Tex Winter was all over Williams at practice. In Williams' mind, he was only doing what he had been told, so he snapped back and soon the two were screaming and cursing at one another.

"You're a horse's ass," Winter yelled at him. That attracted the attention of Jackson, who rushed over just as it looked as if Winter wanted a piece of Williams.

"Here's this little, 70-year-old guy looking like he was coming up on me," said Williams. "And I'm thinking, 'OK, if you think you can take on a 23-year-old, let's go.' I was trying to stand up for myself."

Jackson tried to throw Williams out of practice, but Williams wouldn't budge. "I just said, 'I'm not leaving. I want to practice,'" Williams recalled. "It was the only time I got to play."

In the middle of the argument with Winter, the coach had said to him, "You wouldn't do this at North Carolina," and again, Williams thought about how different it was in college. "The program was so different, so structured at Carolina, I guess I wasn't prepared for the NBA," Williams said. "Everyone there was treated equally, was treated fairly. There was no need to talk back to the coach."

No arguments with Jackson, however, were really at the crux of the issue. As with most player disputes, it was mostly about money. "I never really cared that much about salary, per se," Williams said. "It's that I wasn't compensated fairly in relation to my teammates. I was never in line. I'm making $350,000 [his second year] and there are guys behind me making a million." Stacey King was, in fact, earning $8 million over six years, a fact that annoyed pretty much everyone on the team over the course of King's career with the Bulls.

But what really irritated Williams was that he could never get more than a one-year guaranteed contract. "At least throw a guy a bone instead of making me sweat out every season until January [and the NBA guarantee deadline]," Williams said.

When he signed a two-year deal in November of '91, Williams' second season, it called for a potential $200,000 in incentives, in addition to his base salary of $350,000. Most players want to avoid having a lot of incentives built into their contracts. Besides being overly stressful and distracting, most incentives are intentionally very difficult to reach.

"Every game, I was frantically adding up my totals from the box score and checking my contract," said Williams. "Jerry [Krause] told me after that season, 'We gave you more money in bonuses than anybody in the history of the franchise.' I told him, 'You didn't give me anything. I earned it.' Maybe when you're making $3 million, it's not a big deal. But 20 percent of your salary is a big chunk of change." And Williams missed a big chunk by his erratic playing time.

At the same time Williams signed the contract, he was recovering from off-season surgery on his shoulder. Actually, he felt he was fully recovered. But the Bulls, who had drafted Mark Randall with the 27th pick that year, wanted to take a longer look at him. Thus, Williams was placed on the suspended list, the same as the injured list for inactive players.

"I was going nuts wanting to play," Williams said, "and I couldn't even practice with the team. So I was sneaking into the Multiplex [the Bulls' old training facility] between [Bulls] work-outs and playing pickup games with lawyers and kids."

When Williams did come back, he slowly improved. By the '92 playoffs, he was a key role player off the bench, providing the energetic defense and rebounding the Bulls thrived on.

In the second game of the third round of the playoffs, however, the Bulls hit a snag, losing by 26 to Cleveland in a game in which Williams came in for a minute early on, and then did not play again. After a season in which he felt he never knew if he was coming or going, he now decided he wanted to go.

"I called my agent and told him to call Krause and tell him that at the end of the season, they could trade me or release me" [the Bulls had the option on Williams' contract the next year], Williams related. "I didn't care. I just wanted out."

The Bulls were none too pleased receiving that phone call in the midst of a playoff run, but Williams did not catch the brunt of their fury until after the season.

Less than 24 hours after the Bulls won their second consecutive championship, Jackson and Krause began their annual postseason meetings with players. The meeting with Williams would be short but action-packed.

"I walked in on cloud nine," Williams recalls. "I had a solid playoffs. I figured I'd get a nice little pat on the back and they'd tell me, 'Good job. Have a great summer.' But as soon as I walked in the door, they started blasting me."

The focus of their anger was his agents' call. But by the time they were through, Jackson and Krause had drummed it into Williams that he was not nearly as talented as he thought he was. "You're running around like a clown out there," Jackson said in reference to Williams' cheerleading gestures on the court.

"You're not nearly as good as you think you are," said Krause.

"I finally said, 'I don't need this. I'm leaving.' And I didn't talk to them all summer," Williams recalled. "I had a great summer."

And that's just what he did, in his words, "hanging out," taking full advantage of his relatively newfound celebrity and thinking very little about basketball. "The last thing I wanted to do was go in and work out and have to see those guys," Williams said of Jackson and Krause. "So I played some pickup basketball and I had fun."

After the third title, Williams decided he wasn't going to mess around. He had scored more points (5.9 per game) and played more minutes during the '92-'93 season than his first two seasons combined and thought he deserved a long-term contract. The Bulls, however, would offer no more than a two-year guaranteed deal, and so Williams accepted a qualifying offer that paid him about $900,000 and made him an unrestricted free agent at the end of the '93-'94 season.

"I thought that considering where I started and the way I helped this ballclub, I should have been rewarded with a long-term contract," Williams said. "They said they needed more time to reevaluate my abilities, but with all the things I had done over the last three years and in the playoffs, that should have been enough."

By the end of the season, Williams knew he wanted to leave Chicago, and the Bulls had decided that he would be better off elsewhere as well, especially if he had notions of being anything more than a part-time player.

"We have to ask ourselves, 'Is he really worth the investment with this body?' " Jackson said after the season. "It's a cyclical thing with him. He gets in shape, then his tendinitis [in his knees] hurts and he has to rest. Then he gets out of shape again.

"It's very scary, but I had to tell him. I said, 'Scott, look, I'm in your corner, but I don't think you're going to be a 30-minute-per-game player in the NBA. There's nothing in your history that says you can do it. Maybe an 18-to-24-minute player, or maybe as a role player in a backup situation.' That was hard for him to hear at 26 years old, but he has to be realistic. I know what it's like. I had to go through it myself. I had to go back to being a bench player."

The trouble was, Williams didn't have anything to go back from. He never was a regular starter, though former Bulls assistant Johnny Bach was a big Williams supporter, often trying to talk Jackson into starting him at center. And in fact, Williams would have started the '93-'94 season if not for the knee injury.

Williams still cringes when he thinks about that day, October 29, 1993. The Bulls had just completed their morning shootaround before a trip to Pittsburgh, where they were to play Philadelphia in an exhibition game, when Williams pulled his knee up to his chest to stretch.

Suddenly, he realized he could no longer flex it. "It was unbelievable," said Will Perdue. "He was just standing there rubbing his knee with a funny look on his face. We were teasing him about it in the training room, and he said it really hurt. He started limping, then all of a sudden he could barely walk."

For Williams, it was the worst of all scenarios. "I'm thinking, oh no, I can't believe it. I took a gamble [with the contract] and then this happens to me. This is terrible."

Initially, Jerry Krause termed the torn patellar tendon an injury that would likely keep Williams out for the year, and surgery was indicated.

His injury also had other immediate ramifications, killing talks between the Bulls and Dallas Mavericks, who were discussing a trade for Derek Harper and Sean Rooks. Williams was the player Dallas wanted.

It had already been a tough preseason for Williams, who had struggled with tendinitis in his knees, aggravated his shoulder while bowling at the Bulls' annual party and strained his back moving a television set. This seemed too cruel a joke.

But four days after the knee injury, he was back at the Berto Center doing strengthening exercises and predicting a two-week absence at most. That too would turn out to be an exaggeration, though, as Williams would end up missing the first half of the season (41 games) before returning February 1.

Two weeks later, he scored a career-high 22 points against Miami, and by April was rounding back to form, averaging 10 points and seven rebounds that month.

By then, Williams knew there were teams that wanted him. Earlier talks with Philadelphia had fallen through, but Boston was paying close attention and the feeling was that he would be among the next tier of free-agent forwards pursued after Grant and Danny Manning.

But Williams was also a bit confused. Well, maybe more than a bit.

Early in the Bulls' playoff series with the Knicks, he suddenly proclaimed he did not necessarily want to leave the Bulls, contrary to what he had been saying most of the season. "I originally said this was my last year with the team," he said, "but as things have been coming together, I realize I'm a big part of this program."

Williams said he had been frustrated when the Bulls traded Stacey King for Luc Longley because management was giving the impression that Longley was the Bulls' center of the future. "I didn't feel the door was closed," he said. "I just felt I had to see if I had opportunities with other ballclubs. But my priority is definitely with this team. I don't want people to think I'm only thinking of myself."

That last sentence was probably the key, for Grant made a similar statement that same day, saying his thoughts were only on the Bulls. This was Bulls-Knicks time and to their credit, even the most disgruntled of the Bulls were hunkering down and closing ranks.

The truth would come out a week later, when Williams overslept and missed a team shootaround the morning of Game 5 in New York. When Jackson made it clear that he didn't buy his excuse, Williams was furious.

"I'm out of here," he fumed. "This has nothing to do with me missing practice, but this has been a very disappointing season as far as me receiving the minutes I felt as though I deserved .... The Chicago Bulls have treated me like shit and I'm ready to move on."

Jackson set the stage for Williams' ultimate departure [he would sign a seven-year, $20 million deal with Philadelphia in July] with his comments the next day. "What Scott said last night won't be forgotten," Jackson said. "These kids have a penchant for saying things sometimes. Their standards are me first, and everybody else later."

Williams said he regretted only his timing. "It was said in frustration," he explained.

He didn't have to.

No one had to tell Will Perdue about being frustrated. Perhaps no other Bull has had a more miserable time playing the game he loves.

As good-natured, bright and genuine as anyone on the team, Perdue has seen the NBA's business side firsthand. By the end of the '93-'94 season, he was thoroughly disenchanted and knowing only that if he didn't get out of Chicago soon, it might very well be the death of his career.

Ironically, for most of his career, Perdue was thought of as a potential lifer with the Bulls because of Krause's affection for him. The 11th pick overall in the '88 draft, Perdue was projected as the center of the future, the heir apparent to Bill Cartwright. But no one figured Cartwright would hang in so well, so long, and no one but Krause seemed to see that potential in Perdue.

When people ask Perdue now how long he has been in the league, he is tempted to say four years instead of six. "I only *played* four," he says with a resigned grin.

The first season, under Doug Collins, Perdue played a total of 190 minutes in 30 games. While fully understanding that he had to bide his time behind Cartwright and Dave Corzine, he had the feeling that not playing was a direct result of Collins rebelling under the pressure of Krause. When Collins was fired, one of the several publicized reasons was that Collins was dismissed because of his failure to play the team's No. 1 pick.

"I felt people started to look at me a little differently because I had gotten him fired," said Perdue. "I felt very uncomfortable about that."

When the Bulls made plans to trade King, Perdue could only wait and hope that would mean more playing time. It had already been a dismal '93-94 season for Perdue, who had missed 16 games with a broken finger on his shooting hand. Unbeknownst to him, it would get even worse two weeks later, when he would fracture the same finger and miss 16 more. But it was bad enough when the trade was made and the Bulls brought in Luc Longley.

"That's when I knew my fate was sealed in Chicago," Perdue said.

When Perdue talked to Krause and Jackson about the deal and asked why they would trade for another center when they already had too many, they told him that it was in King's best interest to leave the Bulls and that Longley was simply the best player available. "That doesn't mean Luc is going to take over," Krause told Perdue.

"They told me it was up to me," Perdue recalled, "but immediately, Luc started."

Krause, who clearly wanted insurance at the center spot in the likely event that Cartwright and Williams would not return the next season, also told Longley to "beat up" on Perdue in practice, and told Perdue to do the same to Longley.

While Longley showed promise, he also struggled with the complex, unfamiliar offense and Perdue grew even more restless, inquiring again about his future. We need to see what this kid can do, they told him. We already know what you can do.

Jackson, who had seemingly always been impatient with Perdue, grew even more annoyed with what he perceived as second-guessing. Like Collins, Jackson seemed to bristle against the perception that Perdue had been "Krause's boy," and he told out-of-town writers that Perdue should be happy with his role as a million-dollar backup center, a position he could fill for 10 years in the league, easy.

Before the season, Perdue had signed a guaranteed five-year deal worth about $8.5 million. A sixth year was at the Bulls" option, and with various perks and incentives, the deal could be worth $12 million. Jackson could have only dreamed of that money as a player, and while he said he did not begrudge the modern-day players the big contracts, he did think role players like Perdue should basically shut up and not complain.

"Yes, we are fortunate to be here," says Perdue in defense of that logic. "And yes, we are making a lot of money. But how can you tell a player to be satisfied doing anything? I don't want to just collect my check, I want to go out and earn it. They're sending out the wrong message if they expect people to just be happy."

For Perdue, basketball success always seemed to come the hard way. Growing up on Merritt Island, Florida, where football was king, and baseball the clear-cut second choice among young participants as well as sports fans, he did not pick up basketball until the age of 13. Perdue grew up on the beach, boating and shrimping and deep-sea fishing with his dad.

There were no organized leagues for basketball outside of school and so, as the tallest, skinniest kid on his teams, Perdue played tight end and defensive end in football and just about every position in baseball. In seventh grade, the junior high basketball coach urged him to try out for the team, but it was far from an instant success story.

"In seventh grade everyone had to play, but by eighth, they only played seven or eight guys, and I never played," Perdue recalls. "I scored one point the whole season."

By the time he entered high school two years later, it was clear he didn't have the build for either football or baseball and so he concentrated on basketball year-round. At Merritt Island High School, where the football booster club provided brand new uniforms and equipment each season and fans stood in line for the 6,500 or so "season tickets" for its Friday night games, basketball was not exactly the cool thing to do. This was the school that proudly produced the likes of Leon Bright, formerly of the New York Giants, and Jeff Wickersham, who went on to star for LSU and was drafted by the Miami Dolphins. It was in the same conference as the famed Astronaut High, which turned out Cris Collinsworth and Wilber Marshall.

When the basketball team practiced, it had to split gym time with the girls team. That often meant coming in at 6:30 a.m. "Basketball was what football players did to stay in shape," Perdue said. And as a rapidly growing young center — he went from 6-1 in ninth grade to 6-10 when he graduated — there weren't a whole lot of qualified tutors readily available, so he turned to the person who knew more about basketball than anyone he knew, his best friend Tony Longa.

Tony had recently moved from Virginia, where basketball was obviously a bit more popular. The two would send away for videos and basketball manuals, and in large part, that was how Perdue got his earliest basketball instruction, though he also attended basketball camp at Stetson College in Deland, Florida.

By Perdue's senior year in high school, he was being recruited nationally and made official visits to Georgia Tech, Vanderbilt, Virginia and Purdue before settling on Vanderbilt.

As it turned out, it wasn't any easier in Nashville at the start than it had been in Merritt Island, as it took Perdue three years to work into the starting lineup. By his senior year, he was named SEC Player of the Year and when he was taken 11th overall by the Bulls in the '88 draft, he figured out quickly that the NBA was a business.

In Chicago that summer, Perdue was befriended by a former CBA player, a forward named John Fox. Together they worked out, played in the summer league in L.A. and became close friends.

"They had given him every assurance that if he did certain things, he would be with the team the next season," Perdue recalled. "He worked very hard and they told me he was some-one I could learn from. He had done everything asked of him and when training camp came around, they cut him. He was a great kid and he was shocked. So was I. I guess I realized then that just because you do what they say doesn't mean you're going to always stick around."

By the end of the '93-'94 season, already a bust anyway, it began looking more and more like Perdue would not even make the playoff roster. Nevertheless, he held out hope that his veteran status and proven ability against Patrick Ewing would secure him a role in the postseason ahead of rookie Jo Jo English. Over the years, Perdue had learned more and more from watching and working with Cartwright, and had some of his better defensive games against Ewing.

One day, shortly before the decision was made, Perdue tried to draw some analogies between the frustration he had experienced in his career and someone else his age who may have hit a career crisis.

"It's like getting your college degree and then starting out at McDonald's," he said. "Nothing against McDonald's, but that's not what I was trained for. It's like putting a suit on and bringing your briefcase to work, then sitting on a sofa all day. That's not what I was trained for either.

"The real frustrating part is that I have friends with nice jobs and nice pay, but if they found themselves in an organization with no room for advancement, they would quit and go to another company. I've been stagnant for four years with the Bulls."

Over the years, like many of the Bulls, Perdue had grown accustomed to halted and contradictory communication with Jerry Krause. "I'd pick up the paper and there's one quote from me, then another quote from him," said Perdue. "That's how we communicate."

Several times during the '93-'94 season, Perdue said he requested a meeting with Krause to discuss his practically non-existent career, dialogue he no longer hoped to have with Jackson, and said Krause told him, "The last thing I want to hear is another player complaining about a coach who won three championships."

Perdue's relationship with Krause had hit an especially low point early in the season. Perdue, always with an eye toward a career after basketball and getting his feet wet with a regular broadcasting gig for Chicago's Fox affiliate, had also dabbled in writing. Unlike many celebrities with their own newspaper column, Perdue actually contributed to this one himself.

In a column November 19 of '93, Perdue "wrote" from Portland and covered a variety of topics concerning the Bulls' first major road trip of the season.

"For the most part," the column read, "our entourage consists of 12 players, four coaches, one trainer, one scout, a couple public relations people — and general manager Jerry Krause, of course. Believe me, I'm not alone in my inability to understand why Jerry accompanies the team on road trips so often.

"It seems that most general managers stay away from the spotlight and work behind the scenes, but not Jerry. When the players know that 'Big Brother' is watching, it just puts more pressure on them. For example, take the one-point loss against the SuperSonics on Tuesday night. After the game, we heard Jerry say that there are no moral victories in this league. I mean, didn't the players know that already? Even when we win, the guy is never in a good mood. He's the only real distraction on the trip."

The headline on the column read: "With 'Big Brother' along, trips aren't as enjoyable." Krause obtained a copy of the piece and, needless to say, he wasn't thrilled. That day, he called Perdue in and told him he thought it was improper for a player to do that and that he would have to quit.

"I thought I was pretty straightforward about it, just pointing out that nobody does well when the boss is looking over his shoulder," shrugged Perdue, "but I guess he took it personally."

"I got a little annoyed about it," said Krause. "It's not appropriate for a backup center to write a newspaper column. When [then-scout] Billy McKinney was here, he wanted to do a radio show, and I didn't think that was appropriate, either."

In February, Will and his wife, Jennifer sold their Suburban Chicago townhouse with the idea of finding a house in the summer. In the summer, they were renting and hoping for a trade. Over the last year, there had been interest from Sacramento, Dallas and Washington, but Perdue never felt Krause was going to agree to a trade.

Annoyed by the column fiasco and Perdue's vocal intentions to be traded, Krause let it be known that if it didn't benefit the Bulls, he sure wasn't going to do Perdue any favors.

Publicly, however, Krause claimed he was rooting for him. "It wasn't a slap at Will when we got Luc," Krause said. "Stacey just couldn't flourish here. Fans were so down on him that he was down on the whole thing. And you can never have enough big people.

"We'd have hoped Will's career had gone better. But I call Bill Cartwright Pee Wee Reese because when he was playing shortstop for the Dodgers, a lot of kids died on the vine or eventually got traded. I figured we'd get three years max out of Bill Cartwright and in the fourth, Will would take over. We ended up getting five."

The day he learned he had not been named to the 12-man playoff roster, Perdue had gone golfing with a friend. It was Monday, the day after the regular season had ended, and the Bulls had the afternoon off. "When I got home," said Perdue, "there were 14 messages on my machine." Most came from Krause, who was desperately trying to locate Perdue before he learned the news elsewhere and before he made an appearance for the Bulls that evening, a prospect Krause thought would be embarrassing for all concerned.

Krause asked him to come to his office at the Berto Center so they could discuss the decision in person. In their meeting, Krause told him they weren't sure what John Paxson could do, given the condition of his knee, and that while they had enough big men, they needed the extra guard on the roster [English].

"At that point," said Perdue, "what was the use of arguing? I just said that I felt it would hurt the team, that if we were going to make it anywhere we would most likely have to go through New York and that for one reason or another, I had had considerable success against the Knicks. But I saw no reason to get ugly about it."

He could, however, get depressed about it. And that he certainly did, moping around his house, staying up at night and trying to figure out if he wanted the team to lose so the season could just be over, or whether he should follow his heart and hope his teammates were successful.

"The decision was made to take Corie [Blount] off," Krause said of the rookie who signed a six-year, $7.2 million rookie contract. "Then it became JoJo or Will and at that time, because we were concerned about Pax, we thought the best thing to do would be to put JoJo on. I told Phil, 'There's only one thing to think about. What gives you the best chance to win?' And he said, 'I think we have a better chance to win with JoJo.' If a coach wants something that strongly, I'm going to give it to him."

For the Cleveland series, Perdue practiced with the team, watched films and attended meetings. "But I still didn't feel part of the team," he said. "They were focused on their goal and I was sitting there [at games] with my suit on."

After the Bulls swept the injury-depleted Cavs, Perdue, who had been given the option to practice, decided to stop. "We went in opposite directions," he said.

His voice trailed off. "It's one of the first things you learn when you come into the NBA," he said. "A, they're paying you a lot of money. B, you have to take responsibility for your career yourself. And C, if you don't do the job, they'll find someone else.

"They really know how to take the fun out of the game."

For B.J. Armstrong, the fun didn't stop as much as the education began. But it sure looked at times over the last two seasons like he wasn't enjoying himself much.

It was always hard to detect with B.J. There would be cryptic comments to reporters like, "You can see what's going on. I don't have to tell you." But to his credit, there were no public displays of dissatisfaction or complaints. Until, that is, midway through the '93-'94 season, when the facade finally started to break away a bit.

The first outright sign that Armstrong was getting restless with the Bulls' system came during a one-point loss at Phoenix in early February. John Paxson played a season-high 35 minutes while Armstrong played just 17, well below his season average of 34. He sat out the entire fourth quarter and was clearly sulking at the end of the bench, failing to join the team huddle. Jackson looked down the bench a few times with the idea of putting him in, but analyzing the body language, decided to keep him there.

A week before, Armstrong had not merely made his first NBA All-Star team, but made it as a starter, having been the leading vote-getter among Eastern Conference guards. Though Armstrong's game had clearly matured, it was also just as obvious that being named a starter was in large part due to his

Around the NBA, Chicago Stadium is known as one of the noisiest arenas in the league. The Bulls are hoping to continue that tradition in the new United Center.

After defeating the Phoenix Suns to complete the Bulls' third-straight NBA championship, Michael Jordan reflected on the team's historic accomplishment: "One or two plays make the difference between being a part of history and not being a part of history. And when you're a part of it, you cherish it. This means so much to all of us. More than I can say."

One of the highlights of a Bulls game is the excitement surrounding the player introductions and the spotlighting of the Championship banners.

The Bulls' coaching braintrust (from left to right): Jim Cleamons (kneeling), John Bach (now with the Charlotte Hornets), Phil Jackson, Tex Winter, and trainer Chip Schaefer. The Bulls have added Jimmy Rodgers for the 1994-95 season.

Phil Jackson (with Pete Myers and Scottie Pippen) is not only one of the NBA's winningest coaches, he is also considered one of the league's more intelligent and off-beat coaches. Under Jackson's guidance, the Bulls have meditated, burned incense, watched obscure movies, and taken a team ferry ride to the Statue of Liberty — all as part of Jackson's pre-game preparations.

No Bulls rookie has ever had as severe an indoctrination to the NBA as Toni Kukoc. But after playing just one season in the NBA, Kukoc became the highest-paid Bull with a new six-year, $24.45 million contract.

While the 1993-94 NBA season saw Scottie Pippen emerge from Jordan's lengthy shadow, Pippen's season will most often be remembered for the off-court controversies: his arrest on gun possession charges (later dropped), his 1.8 second mutiny on the bench, and the swirling trade rumors during the ensuing off-season.

Horace Grant earned a spot on the NBA All-Star team with his tireless efforts under the boards. Grant eventually grew tired of his "blue collar" role with the Bulls, and the bizarre series of negotiations that led to Grant's departure from the Bulls will go down as one of the strangest chapters in Chicago sports history.

Photo by Brian J. Moore

Though B.J. Armstrong is a huge hit with NBA fans — receiving the most All-Star votes among Eastern Conference guards — he is still not comfortable with his celebrity. About autographs, Armstrong says: "Why should someone want mine? Who am I? It makes me very uncomfortable and I think I need to keep that attitude to keep my sanity."

Will Perdue entered the 1993-94 NBA season with a new five-year, $8.5 million contract and with renewed hopes of increased playing time. However, as the season progressed, Perdue spent most of his time on the bench behind new starter Luc Longley and new backup Bill Wennington. Perdue's playing time dwindled to the point where he was eventually left off of the Bulls' 1994 playoff roster.

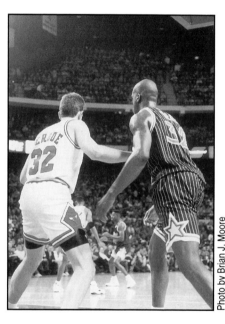

Photo by Brian J. Moore

Photo by Brian J. Moore

Throughout his career with the Bulls, Scott Williams felt that he never received the respect from Bulls coaches and management that his game deserved. Like Grant, Williams left the Bulls via free agency during the summer of 1994, signing a seven-year, $20 million deal with the Philadelphia 76ers.

Pete Myers (shown battling under the boards along with Scottie Pippen) has a pro basketball resume that resembles a travel guide. Shortly after being drafted by the Bulls in 1986, Myers began a basketball odyssey that took him to Rockford, San Antonio, Philadelphia, Spain, New York, New Jersey, back to San Antonio, Italy, and finally to the Bulls as Michael Jordan's replacement for the 1993-94 season.

After a disappointing 1992-93 season with the Orlando Magic, Steve Kerr renewed his career with the Bulls, averaging a career-high 25 minutes per game for the 1993-94 season. Despite his success, Kerr still considered himself a regular working stiff, occasionally taking the commuter train, equipment bag in hand, and then a cab to the Stadium before games.

Bill Wennington thrilled the Stadium crowds with his aggressive, energetic play — especially his patented slam-dunk off the offensive rebound. Growing up in Canada, however, Wennington's sports heroes were Bobby Orr and Ken Dryden. "Kareem and Dr. J were names I heard," Wennington remembered, "but I couldn't tell you if they were centers or guards or who they played for."

Photo by Peter L. Bannon

While injuries during most of his final NBA season frequently left John Paxson in street clothes on the Bulls' bench, his long-range shooting to seal the Bulls' NBA Championships over the Los Angeles Lakers and the Phoenix Suns will forever be etched in the memories of Bulls fans.

Photo by Brian J. Moore

Photo by Brian J. Moore

Bill Cartwright's experience and team leadership have always been his greatest assets. When Pippen's infamous 1.8 second protest was unfolding, Cartwright was the first to approach Pippen on the bench. "It wiped me out totally. I don't think any of us ever saw anything like that before. Ever." Cartwright's planned retirement after the 1994 playoffs was put on hold this summer when Seattle offered him a three-year, $6 million deal.

Since the NBA has become "FANtastic," entertaining the fans during breaks in the action is now an important part of the NBA experience. Entertainment at the Stadium includes something for everyone — from bat-twirling contests, baby races, and a guy juggling his kids, to the Bulls Brothers, free-throw shooting contests, and advertising mascots competing in a basketball game. Two of the regular features at the Bulls' games are the IncrediBulls (right) and the Luvabulls (above). Each year, roughly 1,000 women audition to be one of the 25 Luvabulls who perform at the Stadium.

For fans who can't make it to the Stadium for the Bulls' games, the next best thing is the television broadcast with play-by-play announcer Tom Dore (right) and Bulls legend Johnny "Red" Kerr.

The last NBA game at Chicago Stadium was the Bulls' 93-79 route of the New York Knicks in Game 6 of the 1994 playoffs.

The Bulls' championship banners have been moved across the street, and the new United Center is set to open for the Bulls' 1994-95 NBA season.

popularity with young fans and the fact that the conference's premier guard corps had been practically wiped out with the retirement of Jordan and sudden deaths of Drazen Petrovic and Reggie Lewis.

Jackson, in an apparent attempt to make sure Armstrong would not get too caught up in his sudden fame and always concerned that Armstrong's game demonstrated too many self- ish tendencies, made a pointed crack about Armstrong's popu- larity shortly before the All-Star voting was finalized.

"I noticed in *Seventeen* magazine a couple years ago, he played big," Jackson said. "On the road, there's a section of adoring young fans who are voters in All-Star games, so I know there's that appeal there."

Publicly, Armstrong laughed when someone relayed Jackson's comments. "He's killing me," said Armstrong, who at times was clearly intimidated by Jackson. But tension had been building for some time over the conflict in basketball philoso- phies. Armstrong, a true point guard and team leader at Iowa, had to learn to play without the ball with the Bulls, to become a complementary player to Jordan and a spot-up shooter, but it was an almost constant struggle with his natural instincts. In addition, for a period after the All-Star selection, opposing guards with ruffled egos, such as Mark Price, were applying noticeably more pressure on Armstrong.

The Phoenix incident passed without discussion. But for Armstrong, it was far from resolved and boiled over in Philadel- phia two months later. This time, it started much like the Phoenix game, with Jackson pulling Armstrong earlier than usual in the third quarter after a mistake.

Armstrong kicked a chair over, then wandered from the bench as if contemplating leaving altogether. He eventually deposited himself on the floor, and Jackson never put him back in.

In an interview that was not exactly revealing, but unchar- acteristically emotional, Armstrong slumped against a wall in the lobby of a New Jersey hotel the next morning and told three Bulls beat writers that the night before was "a very low point in my career."

"In no way am I apologetic for my actions or behavior," said Armstrong. "This has been happening a lot during the season, this pattern of substitutions. People make mistakes, and by no means am I excluded from that. But every time I make a mistake, it seems to be magnified .... I have given my life and my dedication to this team, and now I have to do what's best for me."

It sounded, of course, like Armstrong planned to ask to be traded, or at least wanted to be traded. As it turned out, however, he pretty much wanted what every athlete, every employee wants, and that's to be appreciated.

Jackson had gone more and more as the season progressed to a one-guard front with Pippen pushing the ball upcourt. Jackson felt the offense was stagnating at midcourt and had to be opened up, and was often annoyed at Armstrong for bucking the system. Jackson insisted he did not want his players to feel harnessed, but rather to embrace the system, but clearly he did not appreciate Armstrong's methods of disapproval or his timing. "It's certainly not something that should be going on with this team at this point in the season," he said.

Jackson concluded that their relationship had become "a test of wills" and added that he and Armstrong were "alike in so many ways," maybe there wasn't anything to discuss. And indeed, when the two got on the bus later that afternoon, both avoided conflict. "Is there something we need to talk about?" asked Jackson. "Nah," said Armstrong. And that was that.

In truth, Jackson respected Armstrong for his work ethic and felt he had done the most with the abilities he has. But like most coaches and players, Jackson did not think as much of Armstrong's abilities as Armstrong did. And after the season, Armstrong had a more clear-eyed view. "I learned a lot about that, how much I can tolerate, what's really important," he said. "I don't know if it was unavoidable, but I do think you have to fight for what you believe in. If you believe something is unfair, you have to fight for it. Stuff like that happens, and I didn't get to this point by laying down."

Armstrong had begun the season by signing a five-year, estimated $13 million contract extension. This after Krause let it be known earlier in the summer, before Jordan's retirement, that he intended to let Armstrong's contract expire without resigning him, and mold Kukoc into the team's new starting point guard.

But after re-signing, Armstrong grew stronger and more outspoken as the season went along. In late March, when Pippen was ejected for taking a swing at Rick Mahorn in New Jersey, Armstrong was pointed in his postgame comments.

"You would think," Armstrong said in an irritated tone, "that Scottie has been around long enough to know that a guy like Rick is going to come in with some of his tactics and do anything he can to slow him down. I'm sure Rick didn't mean anything by it, but it was just enough to get under Scottie's skin. Whatever was said, it was just unfortunate that Scottie would fall for something like that."

When told initially about Jackson's comments that he felt he and Armstrong were a lot alike, Armstrong was defiant. Later, however, he said he could see where Jackson was coming from. "I thought we were so far apart," Armstrong said, "but now when I look at it I can see that things he believes in, he believes in. And I don't care what I'm doing, if I believe in something, I believe in it. At the heart of it, I wouldn't do anything to hurt the team and I know he wouldn't, either.

"And so maybe that was all good. Maybe that was just the fire he needed to see in me."

While he may not have been ready to call it unavoidable, however, Armstrong did realize that an impasse was bound to occur and that sooner or later, he was going to have to deal with it.

"I have to pick and choose my times," he said. "I don't want to come across as crying, as a baby. And I can sympathize with people who say, 'Why is he complaining? What does he have to complain about?' But at heart, I'm still a kid and I'm going to make mistakes. I have to go through that process. I just happened to make my mistakes in front of 5 million viewers."

There was a resentment about that, about the public image that at once both excited and scared Armstrong.

An only child growing up in Detroit, Armstrong was serious and goal-minded and got used to being by himself. "I stayed home alone a lot because my parents worked," he recalled. "I had to do things myself. There was nobody to fight my fight, so I had to do it myself. I had to believe in myself. And in the long run, I think that helped me."

Armstrong had a list of household chores to complete before he could play and as he saw it, "Most kids can fool around and blame it on so-and-so, say, 'It was his turn to do the dishes.' I couldn't do that, so I got it done."

Though his neighborhood wasn't considered dangerous, Armstrong wasn't allowed to wander outside until his parents returned from work. "The only thing I had to entertain myself was my dog, so I'd make up games in the front yard, dribbling a basketball for hours until they got home," he said.

His goals almost always included basketball and were always incumbent on schoolwork. In the summer, Armstrong had to read a chapter of any book before he could go out and play. "The only thing I had to do was go to school and get good grades," he said. "If I'd get good grades, playing basketball was my reward. If I was on the honor roll, I got closer to my goal. That's what my parents made me believe."

At one time, he was on four different basketball teams. "I always played with older kids," he said. "If I played with kids my age, my dad would say, 'That's no big deal. Go play with the big guys.'"

By 14, he was playing in a semi-pro league with the likes of Isiah Thomas. "And I was getting killed, totally beat up," Armstrong laughed. "But I knew if I could eventually do anything against them, I could dominate my own league. It wasn't enough to just be a good player. You had to have a reputation. That was the key. I always had to be prepared."

One source of his independence has stemmed from watching his mother Barbara cope with multiple sclerosis. "She first had signs of it when I was in ninth grade," he said. "But it was never scary because when you're 13, you just deal with it. More importantly, though, she hasn't let it affect her. I never see her down about it; she never complains. We just look at it like it takes her longer to do certain things. We joke about it, 'Come on, Mom. Hurry up. What's taking you so long?' It's just like, 'That's mom.'"

When it was time to go to high school, Armstrong was torn between wanting to go to the public school in his area and Brother Rice in Birmingham, Michigan, an hour's drive from his house. "I'm not knocking the public school system, but I knew the academy was one of the top schools in the state and so I wanted to go because I knew it would help me get to college," said Armstrong. "At the same time, I wasn't thrilled about leaving my friends."

There were just four other black students in the school. "It really opened my eyes going there," he said. "I met guys with dads who were doctors and lawyers. I saw a different world I hadn't been exposed to before. I never saw guys whose dads had run their own business. These kids had their own cars."

Since his father had to go to work after driving B.J. to school each morning, B.J. would arrive a full hour before school started. To pass the time, he would sit in the hallway and finish up homework or play basketball. And he never let anyone but his parents know of his very serious aspiration to be a professional basketball player. "I didn't want to be stereotyped, especially being a black kid in a predominantly white school," he said.

Prejudice existed, of course, but it often took on subtle appearances that Armstrong said he brushed off easily, aided by his constant distraction with basketball. One summer he took a job on an assembly line loading liquor bottles. "I needed money for school," he said. "I did it for five or six weeks and I hated it. I decided I'd rather practice 20 hours a day."

Going to the University of Iowa, was another shock to his system, but a pleasant one. His senior year, Armstrong struck an agreement with a nearby stable that allowed him to ride a horse ("destined for the glue factory") if he would care for it and groom it regularly. "To me, riding out on an open field, all by myself, is the best," he said. "That's still my favorite thing to do."

On road trips when he had the time, particularly in Florida and California, Armstrong would often spend a day riding and was joined occasionally by Pippen and Grant. "I like golf and tennis, but if I could choose anything to do, it would be riding," said Armstrong, who watched rodeo on television and joked that he would love to take a vacation like the one Billy Crystal's character and friends took in the movie "City Slickers."

"Except that I hear you can't take a shower for like a week," he laughed. "I couldn't stand that."

As an adult, Armstrong is still happiest in his own company on the road, preferring his hotel room or a solo trip to the zoo, rather than dinner, movies or bar-hopping. At home, he will pass up ballgames or concerts because he is sure the experience will be ruined by overzealous fans and, in fact, often lets the slightest disruption in restaurants or elsewhere ruffle him.

As for life in the NBA, he has not so much been disappointed by it, he says, as a bit disillusioned. "At 21, I was really naive as to what the NBA was all about," Armstrong said. "I went through a stage early on where I was like, 'This is it? This is what I've been working my whole life for?' But after that, I realized that you either love to play or you don't and I constantly remind myself what I went through to get to where I'm at.

"When I was a kid, I wanted to be in the NBA because I wanted to be a great player. I didn't want the bubblegum cards or the fancy clothes, but I see how easy it is to lose that innocence, and I try every day not to get caught up in it."

That is why, he says, he eschews personal appearances and dislikes signing autographs. "To this day, that's the hardest thing about doing this job," he says in all sincerity. "I just don't buy into it. I think it's pretty funny. When I was a kid, I didn't really want other people's autographs. So now as an adult, I'm like, 'Why should someone want mine? Who am I?' It makes me very uncomfortable and I think I need to keep that attitude to keep my sanity."

Dear Ms. Isaacson,

I really enjoyed you coming here. I think it
is a good job to work for a newspaper.

It must be fun to go around the United States with the
Bulls. I wish I could do that. Before the game, I wonder i
you play one on one?

I am going to be a U.S. history teacher. If I had a
choice of being a janitor or a newswriter, I would be a
reporter. Do you have lots of stress?

Thank you for coming.

6

DEADLINE HELL

Ah, the glamorous life of a sportswriter. Uh, yeah, right.

This is a concept originated by editors, believed no doubt by many, and a truly ridiculous myth most likely perpetuated by sportswriters themselves. But follow one around someday and it is sure to be squashed just as quickly as our own misconceptions once were.

None of this, of course, has much to do with the Bulls specifically. Consider it a literary intermission. Or perhaps one of those you-learn-something-new-every-day-that-you-never-knew-you-cared-about experiences and try to overlook the fact that you still probably don't.

It is probably safe to say that the first major disappointment once one becomes a sportswriter occurs the first time a former hero treats you like lint when you're merely trying to do your job — like simply asking why he fumbled in the end zone on that crucial play in the fourth quarter, how he felt and what he was thinking while he was doing it.

Or maybe it was that night after covering a prep football game in Okeechobee, Florida, when you were forced to balance a computer on your knee at just such an angle as to catch the reflection of your car headlights since it was easily the best option available to allow you to see what you were writing.

Or then again, maybe it was that night you first found yourself trying to suck Budweiser out of your keyboard. Nothing prepares you for that. But short of carrying a Wet-Vac to each home Bulls game, an industrious reporter can do several things in the event of a beer shower, one of those quirky little things that happened roughly every other night at venerable (*nice word for decrepit*) Chicago Stadium and almost always — as if by intervention of some power much higher, mightier and crueler than ourselves — occurred seconds before deadline.

There's no known proof that the anonymous drunks above the Stadium press box were aware of the inconvenience they were causing when, precisely at 9:45 p.m., they sent their beers cascading into our waiting computers. Perhaps it just seemed that way. Or perhaps Frank Sinatra's voice warbling "My Kind of Town" after each game just got to them, causing their eyes to tear, their hands to tremble and then their beers to pour onto our keyboards.

Either way, these emergencies usually follow this pattern:

1) Beer/Coke (just as lethal, just as sticky) cloudburst occurs, sending a sudden, splattering and seemingly never-ending stream of liquid into your computer and surrounding notes, saturating all.

2) Said victim immediately goes into emergency mode, relying on his or her own personal code of professionalism and experience in these matters to serve as a guide and react something like this:

a) Jump up like pants are on fire, followed by the issuing of a general announcement to all those within yelping distance of impending breakdown — for e.g., "$%#@*, some $#@*& just poured (beer/Coke) into my computer. $#@&*." No one is looking for a thesaurus at a time like this.

b) Scream for napkins, after which Rick, the kindly usher nearby, will set out for the nearest K-mart to procure them. No, seriously, he actually is pretty speedy (elapsed time: 25 minutes) given his experience in such matters and will begin the process of helping dry out the area, which, considering the deep irrigation canals above our heads caused by the roughly thousands of paint chips, should only take another half-hour or so.

3) Everyone in neighboring areas of said flood appears concerned and genuinely troubled by your plight, saying things like, "That really sucks," while hovering over their own bone-dry keyboards and silently thanking God for not afflicting them.

But then, of course, all of this is just a part of the charm and ambience of the grand old — now former — Chicago

Stadium and another in a long list of glamorous aspects of this job we call sportswriting.

Another is dealing with "the desk," or, more specifically, the copy desk, which is in charge of taking a sentence such as: "The Bulls took one look at their destiny Tuesday night and apparently did not like what they saw, opting instead to allow a 30-point lead to crumble in a span of six minutes and the Minnesota Timberwolves to overtake them on this evening of historic embarrassment, 120-105."

And turn it into: "The Bulls did not like what they saw Tuesday night. The Minnesota Timberwolves erased a big lead in the third quarter and won, 120-105."

This is what drives sportswriters to migraine headaches, early ulcers and the habit of filing their stories as late as humanly possible, thereby allowing copy editors as little time as humanly possible to muck things up. Of course, the odds of permitting some teeny-weeny detail like the wrong score to get into the paper rise considerably in such cases. But we can't be expected to worry about such things when we're busy trying to paint a picture. And we have a host of excuses for our various troubles that are completely beyond our control (see above beer storm anecdote), and if any editor-type doubts that, they might consider asking sometime.

In most cases, all of a reporter's most loathsome troubles can be traced to his computer. It would be interesting to ponder what caused the ulcers and annoying nervous conditions in pre-computer reporters. It is, without question, the root of all evil today.

Not to generalize or anything, but one can safely assume several things about the average sportswriter:

1) We consider walking — rather than standing — on the moving sidewalk at the airport to be an adequate exercise regimen.

2) Dressing well is not a prerequisite of the job and considered a sign of weakness by many of our kind.

3) Waking up before 9 a.m. usually means that a fire alarm at the hotel has been triggered.

4) We know nothing about computers.

OK, maybe that's unfair. Maybe not "nothing." Like we know exactly which button to push to send our stories to the newsroom. But do not, repeat, do not ask us anything more.

These questions almost always occur on airplanes when having our computers out as a guise to be left alone is apparently, in reality, a large neon sign inviting the curious microchip salesman sitting next to us to ask the following questions:

Salesman: "Say, is that a floppy disk or a megahurt hard drive?"

Sportswriter: "Unh-huh."

Salesman: "Are you able to transmit via the mouse modem or is this a wireless ram?"

Sportswriter: "I just push this button."

One should not expect a heck of a lot more information should one find oneself seated next to a sportswriter. Of course, there are mutant members of the species who have their own personal computers at home and who will claim to be able to actually define some of the above terms. And then there are those — the honest ones — who have no trouble admitting that having a PC at home simply means asking your computer-literate spouse or loved one to show you which button to push.

There isn't a sportswriter alive in this wonderful techno-logical age who has not been moved to bash in their laptop until the insides smoke. And there are many who have actually done this. In the press room at Wimbledon not long ago, one actually flung his against a wall, doing nothing for his story, but doing wonders for the image of all of us easygoing Americans the Brits already thought were animals.

"What are *you* looking at?" is believed to have been his response when his actions drew some attention.

For the most part, however, we're pretty calm as a people, sportswriters are. We have grown accustomed to deadline situations and laugh condescendingly when our cityside colleagues go out of their minds on election nights. This happens in all newsrooms and never ceases to amaze the sports department. Election nights to your average sports copy desk are no busier than the average Friday night in October, when anywhere from 12 to 13,000 high schools are calling in to either give football scores or get them.

But election night is like Mardi Gras to the rest of the editorial staff, as sports deadlines are moved up to about noon to accommodate all the really important stuff, and the newsroom is put on red alert as everyone is actually required to work. And at night, if you can believe it. Of course, the sports department guys can only be so patronizing. When the food is wheeled in — they always cater dinner on election nights — it would be in bad taste to stuff their faces while laughing at the same time.

People generally do not feel too sorry for sportswriters and they probably shouldn't. It's true. We do get to go to games. Yippee. And there are occasionally a good, solid 10 to 15 minutes when we can actually derive some pure enjoyment from the actual viewing of a sporting event. The rest of the time, we're cursing out the stupid halftime act in Phoenix during Game 6 of the NBA Finals that requires every single light in the building to be turned off to achieve their really neat effects.

Or we're watching a cockroach at venerable Chicago Stadium crawl across our notes. Or, if you're a photographer or cameraman, there's always that exciting moment that seems to happen at least once in every career, when an athlete runs over your face, causing the camera to imbed in your neck.

Then there is the occupational hazard that no one talks about, the one that is probably as responsible for post-traumatic stress syndrome in sportswriters as anything.

Bulls general manager Jerry Krause has often said that if he ever writes his autobiography, he will call it *A Thousand National Anthems*, because that's how many he has heard over the course of his career. But your average sportswriter hears at least that many bad versions.

Most self-respecting singers consider the anthem the most dreaded tune known to man, and if they had any sense, they would never attempt to sing it. Funk, rap, jazz, a cappella and drown-out by every conceivable instrument, a truly horrifying version of our nation's theme song is probably born an average of 20 times per night in sports arenas across the country.

Johnny Bach, an affable man but staunch traditionalist and former naval officer, positively seethes every time he hears one of these goofy renditions. He had to be comforted, however, one night, when a group performing a bee-bop version that sounded a lot more like "Boogie-Woogie Bugle Boy" than "The Star-Spangled Banner" was literally booed off the Stadium court.

Granted, it's not an easy song to sing. If we have learned anything from Roseanne, it is this. But aside from it being sung badly — Carl Lewis holds the all-time record in this category, surpassing Roseanne, for a version they are still talking about in New Jersey, a rendition so thoroughly, utterly awful that he actually stopped, midstream, and apologized — the words are almost impossible.

Some examples? Try "Oh, the ramparts we wash." Try "were so gallantly screaming." Try anything. But please, please, don't try "The Star-Spangled Banner" without extensive experience or a predisposition to public humiliation.

Another little-recognized hazard to sportswriters are courtside hecklers. Now one might think that the media is immune to such things. But in New Jersey, there is no such thing as immunity of any kind.

One particularly loud-mouthed, drunken boob — as opposed to the soft-spoken, drunken boobs normally found at Brendan Byrne Arena — got a big charge out of picking on Luc Longley. The trouble had started years before, Luc explained, when his sister became tired of the guy's antics, walked by his seat and "accidentally" dumped a jumbo Coke in the idiot's lap. The guy apparently took exception to this because he really got on Luc after that.

Where the media came in is a mystery, but it seemed to have been triggered by one reporter, who was caught looking in the direction of the idiot. This, in turn, redirected his focus to the reporter — the game was apparently never his focus — and the taunting began.

"Hey, girl at the press table," he bellowed as the entire Bulls team,] and most of the 18,000 in attendance turned to look, "where did you get your hair done, at the Joliet prison?"

The guy did do his homework.

Press seating is very important to sportswriters. A baseline seat is fine, but midcourt is preferable, especially to those really superficial, insecure types who like to be spotted on television. Some people wonder, especially when sportswriters are seated near the team bench, if we can actually make out what's being said in the huddle and if this aids us in our nightly duties. But bench chatter is not all that technical, despite what you might think and perhaps hope.

For example, when a coach such as Phil Jackson (but not necessarily Phil Jackson) approaches his players during a timeout, he is just as likely to say: "What the fuck are you doing out there?

Are you fucking asleep? You're playing with your heads up your asses. Now go out there and play some fucking basketball, dammit," as he is to say, "Scottie, on the screen roll, watch the back pick, and Horace, you have to help out and double down."

So you see, it's really not all that complicated, as most anyone with a colorful enough vocabulary could coach an NBA team.

Locker room chatter is a whole other matter, for this is where all the really serious pregame preparation occurs. In the Bulls' locker room, where an average of one player — usually someone about to be cut — actually sits around and talks to the media, there's always something valuable to be learned. For instance, whenever a player arrives late for a game, his initials are written on the blackboard, so there is that to record. And assistant coach Jimmy Cleamons is always diagramming the other team's offense, so there is that to stare blankly at.

But the really good stuff comes on the road, especially in dressing rooms where there are no trainer's rooms in which players can hide. It is in those situations where you can really learn what goes through a professional athlete's head as he is preparing for battle. Current events are always a big topic, and the adventures of John and Lorena Bobbitt got plenty of mileage.

It will probably come as no surprise that the majority of Bulls players were not sympathetic to the plight of Lorena. Several were pushing for the death penalty.

In a corner of the locker room, one evening, Bill Cartwright looked as if he was barely listening to the conversation and looked even more serious than usual. As the topic swung around to Mrs. Bobbitt, finally Cartwright spoke. "She must be punished," he mumbled ever so quietly and ever so slowly. "Oh, yes, she must be punished."

Stacey King lauded Bobbitt, in an eloquent soliloquy, for his quick comeback after one story came out about Bobbitt's new sexual conquests. "And that," said one reporter as rumors swirled about King being traded, "is why Stacey King must stay."

Most sportswriters "root for the story," which means that if it's a better story for the home team to win, great. If not, who cares? More accurately, however, most root for their own variant interests.

One writer in New York was absolutely distraught, for example, over the Knicks defeating the Bulls and advancing to the1994 conference finals, where it appeared a good bet they would win and continue playing. Why? Because he coached his kid's Little League team and couldn't imagine missing most of the season.

There are also those who might root like hell—though quietly of course— for a particular athlete to fail if he regularly stiffs everyone for interviews. Rarely, though, does it get that personal.

Once, at the U.S. Olympic skating trials several years ago, the competition, which started much too late to begin with, went past midnight with no clear end in sight. Having taken place in Denver, two hours behind East Coast time, most writers had already seen their deadlines come and go and wanted the damned thing only to end.

To alleviate the boredom, a small pool was set up in the press section. Everyone threw in a buck and picked a skater's name. If your skater fell, you were out. And considering that nearly every skater — except maybe the two or three television actually shows you at the Olympics every four years — falls at least once, it got pretty hot and heavy up in that press section. By the end, sometime after 2 a.m., anyone still in the stands could have looked up to see some highly respected writers from some highly respected papers lunging at each other in disagreement about whether Brian Boitano's finger touch constituted a fall. All in the name of 15 bucks and a little harmless entertainment.

But mostly, sportswriting is a job like anything else. It is one that most take pride in and are responsible about, but one that has plenty of built-in aggravation. And B.J. Armstrong would know all of this if he had just listened, strangely enough, on opening night of the 1993-94 season. Great way to start the year.

It wasn't the computer troubles or the copy editor troubles that Armstrong didn't seem to understand so much as the sportswriter's very existence he was questioning. Why do we do what we do? And why in the world do we do it the way we do it? That was pretty much the gist of this rather futile debate.

The discussion had begun several years before when it first became apparent that this Armstrong fellow was about as open and giving with Bulls beat writers as Nixon was with Woodward and Bernstein. Armstrong's was the only home phone number kept from the regular writers. This was often pointed out to B.J., who when told that even Michael Jordan gave us his number, merely smiled that little smile of his and shrugged that little shrug.

And so it was that the debate began as Armstrong explained that he was warned as a rookie — no doubt by either Jerry Krause or Salman Rushdie — that no good could possibly come from excess publicity, that it would eventually get you into trouble.

And frankly, he had to be admired for maintaining his code during the '92-'93 season when his appearance in the starting lineup was first privately, then publicly scorned by some of the more well-known veterans of the team. No one was looking to hurt Armstrong, but he was a loner, a quiet yet supremely self-confident young player whose on-court style (he liked to shoot) was in sharp initial contrast to that of his predecessor, John Paxson.

So silly did it get that players were even heard to complain about Armstrong's penchant for "woo-wooing" on the court — B.J.'s way of letting his teammates know he was open and wanted the ball — "Woo-Woo."

"What's with that woo-wooing shit?" more than one player was heard to utter. But there was barely a peep from Armstrong, who may have gathered a few grudges but also weathered the temporary storm privately. And afterward, after the sniping stopped and the winning resumed and Armstrong's development as a player continued; after another controversy had arisen, he would occasionally wink and smile and say, "See, that's what I was talking about. It does you no good to open up. No offense, but it just does you no good."

Maybe, but it also catches up to you in other ways. Maybe you don't get quite the same press as some of your NBA contemporaries or quite the same respect. And maybe, just maybe, you start turning bitter and figure that opening night is the perfect time to tell one of the team's beat writers that the profession they have chosen for their life's work is something akin to child molesting.

OK, so maybe that's a bit of an exaggeration, but that was the general tone of the conversation that night as one beat writer suddenly found herself quoting Sally Field's character from the movie "Absence of Malice," a classic newspaper drama in which the Field character plays the part of an investigative reporter assigned to the story of a mob killing in which Paul Newman is a prime suspect.

Of course, the Paul Newman character is completely innocent and ends up sabotaging the efforts of the Sally Field character, who ends up demonstrating all the journalistic instincts and know-how of a flunkie from the *National Enquirer*. But at one point, she sees the error of her ways — after one of her sources kills herself and Paul Newman roughs her up, it should be pointed out — and tells him, "I know you think that what I do is nothing. But it's really something. I just did it badly."

At least this particular writer started to quote the Field character to Armstrong. After getting to the part about doing it badly, she stopped just in time. But the gist of the argument was that, hey, come on, we're not so bad, give us a break. We have all kinds of troubles that you could never imagine, like having Budweiser spilled into our computers on deadline.

His side of the debate boiled down to his notion of what a good game story should say and how a broadcast should be called, and the fact that his version has absolutely nothing in common with our version. Bill Cartwright chimed into this discussion, partly because he agrees with Armstrong but mostly because he just loves to disagree and soon, arguing about the way a basketball game story should be reported started sounding a lot more like pro-choice versus pro-life.

"You guys talk about who scored the most points or who had the most assists," Cartwright said. "You write about the winning play. But you don't talk about the pass before the pass before the winning basket. The one that opened up the defense and made the whole play possible. You don't talk about that play early in the second quarter when the defense broke down and we were able to execute. Or that great screen someone executed."

Explaining the concept of space, and the idea that a decent game story should be somewhat more entertaining than reading the side of a cereal box, did absolutely no good.

"You guys see a game that bears absolutely no resemblance to the one we see. Absolutely none," said Cartwright.

"Oh yeah?" was the clever response.

The debate sort of died after that, mostly because the game was starting and they had to go play, but it picked up again. And again, until someone suggested an experiment of sorts. One game. Our account. Their account. Same approximate length. No real deadline. No beer-spilling handicaps. No benefit of copy editors. Just one honest attempt at being a sportswriter for a day.

"I'll ask my wife," said Cartwright, a closet sexist, but good guy nonetheless.

"And if she says I should do it," he said with a sly grin, "then I'll know I shouldn't."

Needless to say, neither Cartwright nor Armstrong ever quite got around to an experiment that didn't seem all that much fun. There were many other things to occupy their attention, anyway.

After all, strange things happen to professional sports teams, things like previously semi-mature men deciding it would be funny to put Flex-All, a presumably non-toxic, but nonetheless gasolinelike substance in the Ben-Gay family, into the nearest rookie's underwear.

In the case of the Bulls, this would be Corie Blount, who managed to survive that episode in Philadelphia but seemingly found a pair of flaming underwear or an exploding cigarette lighter wherever he went.

The exception to the rookie rule was Horace Grant, always susceptible to the frantically planned, sloppily executed gag. It was easy to get Grant, and Scottie Pippen pretty much relied on the same old standby all season long, beginning with opening night in Charlotte, when he put a lifelike, but 100 percent rubber snake into Grant's dressing stall. Grant fell for it, of course, shrieking loud enough for most of North Carolina to hear. And he fell for a similar stunt in Philadelphia when Pippen deposited another very lifelike, but also very rubber, mouse on a bench behind Grant before the game.

One would think Grant would have known better by then, having been conditioned by a series of similar jokes including one time when Pippen tied a rubber mouse to his boxers. But that was not the case. And the truly funny thing about the gags was not that Grant thought the creatures were real and that's why he was so scared, because even after it sunk in (roughly three seconds after shrieking) that the things were fake, he was still spooked. And if you've never seen a fully muscled, 6-foot-10, 235-pound professional athlete tiptoeing across a room at Mach speed to avoid a two-inch toy mouse, you've truly missed something.

"I'm waiting on someone to invent a remote-control mouse," Pippen whispered conspiratorially. "Then I'm going to put it in his car."

Pippen could get Grant without half trying, like the time he was on the phone with a Bulls public relations assistant after the All-Star voting was finalized and yelped in mock horror and within earshot of Grant, "You're kidding? Horace didn't make it? Who's going to tell him? Jesus, that's terrible."

The weird behavior easily extended beyond the team as the Bulls, even post-Jordan, attracted as much attention as any club around. Hotel lobbies are typically packed with shrewd entrepreneurs cleverly disguised as children and carrying with them everything from trading cards to index cards to various pieces of clothing for players to sign.

But one of the stranger occurrences, speaking of autographs, had to be in a hotel during the exhibition season when the Bulls found themselves at the same hotel as a tattoo convention.

Yeah, a tattoo convention.

Anyway, apparently they're sports fans, too, because Phil Jackson turned around one day and found himself asked if he wanted to tattoo his autograph onto one female fan's, uh, shoulder. At least that's what Jackson said in relating the story. He also said he politely declined the offer.

In general, however, the Bulls traveled in relative isolation. For the last several years, they have had the good fortune to fly to games in a custom-built, private jet, thereby avoiding the agony of having to actually come into contact with real people, a luxury they can't possibly appreciate enough.

For not only do they avoid carrying their own luggage, eating airplane food (the shrimp cocktail they get does not qualify) and squishing into tiny seats, but they also avoid the loud talkers, the non-stop talkers and, of course, the babies.

The Washington Bullets and several other NBA teams without their own planes still must live with this horrible curse. Consider the plight of Bullets center Gheorghe Muresan, who had to figure out a way to fold his 7-foot-7 frame into coach — yes, coach — class, but did entertain his fellow passengers upon arrival one day during the '93-'94 season. No sooner had the stewardess yelled at everyone not to get up until the plane came to a complete stop than Gheorghe reached up, opened the overhead compartment, rooted around for his stuff, found it, removed it and closed the overhead compartment — all from a sitting position.

The move, of course, drew wild applause, not to mention the awe of the stewardesses, who could only stare.

The Bulls, however, were generally spoiled. And so were their coaches, who considered it a major hardship when they had to eat in the media rooms of visiting arenas.

It should first be explained that the Chicago Stadium food is generally considered the best in sports (OK, so maybe not the greatest compliment in the world), and is greatly appreciated. Chef Hans of Bismarck Catering fame is the head chef and maitre d' all rolled into one. He takes great pride in the food, which would fully qualify to garner a positive restaurant review should a reviewer someday pop in.

It might fall flat, however, in the ambience department, prompting a review something like: "Orange roughy is moist and delicate with a sumptuous mushroom glaze. Cockroaches scurrying underfoot, however, detract somewhat from the overall dining experience."

But the road, if possible, was usually worse. Johnny Bach had perhaps the best sense of humor about it. Basically, he had a rating system which began at "inedible" and reached a high mark of "peasant food." That was good. That meant he would grudgingly partake.

The unfortunate part for Johnny was that he had to actually get near the food and maybe even look at it to judge. He couldn't, say, stand at the door and watch to see if his colleagues or the media were eating it. That was a given. Bulls assistant coach Tex Winter actually liked the media room food, which is something akin to liking hospital food, and this was a source of endless ribbing from Bach and Jackson, who would prod him in much the same way Mikey's brothers once did to get him to eat the Life cereal.

"Aren't you going to eat dessert, Tex?" Jackson would say. "That green stuff over there looks good. Go ahead and try it."

Now granted, this is free food we're talking about. And given that, perhaps the diners might consider being kind or, at the very least, diplomatic. But then, that wouldn't be any fun at all.

The worst arena food in the NBA? No contest. It's the beloved Philadelphia Spectrum, and the reason it's no contest is because they don't serve food to the media. Smart folks. How, after all, can we make fun of nothing? Well, very easily, actually.

Legend has it that Harold Katz, the owner of the Sixers, stopped providing food to the media and visiting coaches when one local writer criticized it. So now there are chips and maybe dried pork rinds if Tex is lucky, and that's about it. Oh yeah, and soda, which you're not allowed to bring on the court, of course. They do, however, have scrumptious soybean ice cream cones. We know this because two brave and desperate Chicago sportswriters who went foraging for food one halftime came upon a stand where they advertised ice cream cones.

Being reasonably trusting souls and not quite satiated from the chips, they got into line expecting, well, ice cream. But they noticed something kind of funny, which was that the "ice cream" cones were being displayed behind the counter, kind of like cotton candy. In other words, not refrigerated. At this point, the reporting instinct took over.

Looking around to see the food on either side of the "ice cream" line, one reporter was temporarily blinded by the relatively normal looking french fries nearby. Urged to remain strong and faithful to the task at hand, however, and also considering that the second half was starting and there was no time to re-group for the french fry line, the reporters plunged ahead.

Suffice it to say, neither had ever before tasted warm ice cream that showed absolutely no signs of melting. Suffice it to say also that neither complained much about the chips after that.

Hotels are often a source of terrific, albeit worthless, gossip. Check into any hotel the Bulls stay in on the road, and it will be nearly impossible to avoid having a room-service waiter tell you that Scottie Pippen likes club sandwiches before games or that B.J. Armstrong asked for extra Sweet 'n' Low. If you're really lucky, or really desperate for news, you might even find out that Steve Kerr is the neatest athlete they've ever seen, or Bill Wennington the sloppiest.

"And you should see Will Perdue's shoes," they're sure to tell you, whether you like it or not.

Hotels are a sportswriter's best friend, closest companion and worst enemy. We're not altogether picky, mind you. There are, however, several requirements we demand:

1) More than two cable channels, preferably at least one movie channel, and, of course, ESPN. You know that one cable channel with the stock market information that constantly runs under the screen? The one with the same 12 minutes of news that simply replays over and over throughout the day? Sportswriters watch this. But only when absolutely necessary.

A remote is also mandatory and, surprisingly, not a given. It makes it possible to flip over to Letterman's Top 10 List during the timeout of the UC Santa Barbara-Pepperdine game. The only positive of not having a remote: It fulfills the exercise requirement.

2) Twenty-four-hour room service. Imperative (see above reference to arena food). One sportswriter of local fame actually calls in his room-service orders from the arena. A common scene is one of this writer, sitting amidst others frantically filing stories on deadline, and inquiring on the phone: "How's the prime rib tonight? Can I get an end cut, medium well and a side of onion rings? That's Room 1024. I'll be there in 25 minutes. "

3) Operators not alone on duty and not prone to editorial comment. The first make it nearly impossible to rely on them; the second to retain your dignity. When the same voice answers the phone each time, most heady travelers know to back up the wakeup call with an alarm clock. They also know not to count on anyone actually getting through to the room, which can also be a benefit in disguise when the office is trying to call.

When the same voice answers and comments on your room-service order, such as, "You want the chicken wings and pie a la mode?" it's best just to say, "Never mind," and hang up.

Hotel maids are another subject. One writer tells the story of covering the Super Bowl one year in San Diego, a fine city, a beautiful city, but one of those that falls into the category of small town as well.

San Diego is the kind of city — and there are many, many of these — that tend to try too hard when there's a major sporting event going on. You get the feeling that all the hotel employees have been briefed on a daily basis for months in advance on the importance of efficiency, which is where we get back to the writer, minding his own business and working on a story one day when the maid knocked on his door for roughly the 14th time that hour.

Jumping up quickly to answer it—since screaming "COME IN" didn't work — he tripped over the cord to his computer, sending it careening to the floor. Now one would think that carpeting might cushion the blow, that a three-foot fall might not do too much damage or that the damage would be easily definable, such as it would not turn on after that.

But sportswriters' computers tend to have minds of their own, and one of the funny things they like to do is break in certain ways that hurt said sportswriter the most. Like maybe he can't type John Elway's name anymore without garble eating up the rest of his story. Things like that.

When the reporter tried turning on his computer, he now discovered that it would no longer work on batteries, but only when plugged in. But he figured, OK, I can deal with that for the time being anyway, and so he resumed his work until, of course, the maid came back eight minutes later.

"This time," he explained, "I was careful. I turned off the computer. I unplugged the computer. I carefully stepped around the computer to go get the door. And then I decided to read the paper until she left."

Moments later, he heard a tiny "uh oh."

"She had vacuumed up my plug, completely shredded it," recalled the writer, still with a pained voice years later. "In 11 minutes, she had now rendered my computer completely useless."

Of course, she was very sorry. "You are a sportswriter?" she said in the same tiny voice as she carefully surveyed his room on her next visit.

"Yes, I am," he said, beginning to forgive her already.

"I could tell," she replied. "You people are pigs."

Dear Bulls

I would like to know
If any of you ever were
asked to do drugs an If any
of you ever did drugs and I would
I like to know If any of you
are ~~on~~ or were hooked an achol

Your biggest fan

7

GATE 3 1/2

Bob Rosenberg was thinking maybe the old heap would fight back. That the bulldozers would line up and the wrecking ball would swing into action and she wouldn't budge. "That place is like the Rock of Gibraltar," he said of the building they call Chicago Stadium, the "Old Barn" as it were.

At least that's what Rosenberg, more commonly known as "Rosie," was hoping, because when it finally did go down, he knew a piece of him would go with it.

It was at the Stadium where Rosie met his wife, Linda. "March 18, 1973, Bulls-Pistons," he recalled with absolutely no trouble.

Linda came with her girlfriend, the sole purpose being to meet Bob, so of course it had to be at the Stadium, where he had been keeping score and stats since 1961. He had a streak going, after all. Hadn't missed a Bulls game since the first one in '66.

"It was my birthday and she had made me a cake," Rosie recalled.

Nice gesture for a blind date. The two were married less than six months later. Linda wasn't a sports fan, but that didn't matter. Didn't last long either, for soon she was at Bob's side at the scorer's table, handling the Bulls' stats while he handled the opponents'. She joined him for all the White Sox games as well, where she learned to keep a mean box score.

In 1986, Linda was diagnosed with breast cancer. A partial mastectomy followed, but they figured they had it beat. And when doctors found a malignant tumor on her spine five years later, they were told it was unrelated to the original cancer and figured they had got that, too.

But in February of '93, a bad cough wouldn't go away. The cancer had moved to her lungs. Two weeks were spent on oxygen, and then Bob got a call from his father-in-law at a Blackhawks game at the Stadium. They were rushing Linda to the hospital.

He made it there a half-hour before she passed away. She was 41.

It was the wee hours of Friday morning, and the next day seemed an eternity. Bob's in-laws had planned to go to the Bulls game Friday night. Bob still had his streak.

"If there was one thing Linda wanted me to do," he said, "it was to keep that streak alive."

And so, in a haze, he went back to the Stadium with Linda's parents and accepted the condolences of everyone who knew him. The streak was kept intact at more than 1,200 games. And it didn't stop.

Night after night through a long, lonely winter, when there wasn't a Bulls game, there was a Blackhawks game. "It helped a lot, being around people all day long," Bob said. "And especially being around these people. If I was home, just sitting there alone, that's all I would think about. They made me forget during the time I was there."

"These people," the Stadium people for lack of a better description, form a small community of their own. A subculture of sorts. The scorekeepers, the security people, waitresses, caterers, porters, cheerleaders. They all know each other. Don't like each other in every case. But on any given night from October to June, they are together, many of whom rarely get the chance to poke their heads up to court level, but doing their jobs. Scurrying over, under and around a building they never were quite sure whether to love or to hate.

Charm or squalor? It depends on your perspective of a place where broom handles hung by shoelaces from stray pipes serving as coat racks constructed by desperate hockey officials.

It's a place where one night, Indiana's Reggie Miller was so angry after getting ejected, that he wasn't careful enough navigating the treacherous descent to the visiting dressing room, tripped, missed three stairs and cursed the wretched Stadium all the way down.

It's a place where you never quite knew what was around the next corner and may, on any given night, have found yourself standing in a corridor waiting for Phil Jackson to begin his postgame press conference and instead be treated to the sight of Lance — one half of the Blues Brothers act — abruptly dropping his pants in order to change into street clothes.

Seasoned reporters used to the sight of bloodied and sweaty athletes in various states of undress gasped at the sight while not so silently praying that his partner — the considerably heftier "Jake" — did not follow suit.

But that's the Stadium, where dressing rooms were not a luxury, but a rumor.

Cathy Core, the dedicated manager of the Luvabulls, the Bulls' cheerleaders, had a wealth of stories to relate just a day after raw sewage erupted from the drain in the middle of their "dressing room" late in the '93-'94 season.

This delightful cubicle, somewhat larger than a walk-in closet but not much, had a couple of urinals, which always came in handy for extra storage space, and one toilet, which actually flushed about once every other week when the weather and celestial alignment were just right. There were no lockers, and enough chairs to accommodate about half the squad.

Being the resourceful women they are, the Luvabulls used a large upside-down garbage can over the drain in the middle of the floor to help ward off the strange smells often emanating from it. But on this particular night, odd gurgling noises were heard beneath the garbage can as well, causing the women to back up just a bit and prepare to take cover.

Now these are women who routinely were forced to observe the crazy Stadium house cat meander by with a mouse in its teeth, so they were not easily shocked. They were, however, a bit rattled as the gurgles grew louder. "We thought it was a monster," said Cathy.

Soon their curiosity was satisfied as the drain erupted like a geyser, spewing raw sewage everywhere. Shrieks of "Eeeeeeeew!" could be heard pretty much everywhere as the Luvabulls scrambled to gather their belongings and evacuate.

Down the hall, Benny the Bull, in his nothing-by-nothing-foot room that doubled as the chapel, dressing room for halftime

acts and often resembled the old circus gag with clowns stream-
ing out of a Volkswagen, was getting dressed at the time and
forced to run out in a state of Benny undress that would
definitely have frightened the kids. At the same time, the players
started hearing gurgling beneath the "carpeted" floor of their
dressing room next door and got the hell out as well, as the stink
soon followed.

If you had happened to wander down under the Stadium
at that moment, you would have witnessed the Chicago Bulls,
minutes before tipoff, in a stirring and provocative debate with
their cheerleaders and furry team mascot over who exactly was
responsible for the accident, which now took on nuclear propor-
tions.

Glamorous as it sounds, being a Luvabull isn't always
what it's cracked up to be. For each game during which they
perform (they have to audition for every one), each cheerleader
gets paid $20, which serves as a reimbursement for having their
costumes cleaned, and two Bulls tickets.

Core, also a licensed talent agent, requires each woman to
do six charitable appearances, though she says they put in over
a thousand hours on their own, and books personal appearances
at trade shows, marketing seminars and bar mitzvahs, where
they make their "real" money, anywhere from a couple thousand to $15,000 per year.

Core used to let the women mingle with fans on the
concourse of the Stadium, but stopped that when they started
being asked to autograph bald heads and beer bellies. "I didn't
quite see that as the image we were trying to project," she
explained.

Roughly 1,000 women apply for the Luvabulls audition.
That number gets pared to 225 and then to 50, who must then
attend a three-week mini-camp where the final 25 are selected.
They rehearse twice a week, work up different routines for each
game and are guaranteed only one time on the court each game.

If they're lucky, someone at the scorer's table will give them
a thumbs-up sign during an additional timeout, when they must
then listen to the first few beats of music and look for hand signals
from their captains as to which routine they're performing.

All of this is high entertainment for fans, not to mention
those on press row, most of whom are able to recite the names of
the Luvabulls quicker than the Bulls' starting lineup. In their

defense, good halftime acts are tough to come by. Most, to be more specific, are lame (although this should in no way be considered criticism of one brilliant Bulls marketing concept in which people dressed up as Oreo cookies and Fig Newtons compete in an annual basketball game).

This from the same people who also brought bat-twirling and baby races to Chicago. The baby races are just that, a Neanderthal competition in which infants are forced to crawl the equivalent of about 15 miles across a dusty, sweaty, spit-infested basketball court while 18,000 fans blast their little eardrums and their fathers videotape the whole thing for evidence that could be used against them should there ever be a custody battle with the state.

The bat-twirling thing was apparently also imported/ stolen from another NBA team and entails two, preferably dumb-looking, overweight men in their late 30s, spinning round and round at center court until they are sufficiently dizzy (16 revolutions) but not quite ready to yak. First one to score a basket wins.

The rules — hell yes, there are rules — require that this spinning is done with their helmeted heads resting on a baseball bat. Just standing and spinning apparently wouldn't be nearly as entertaining. The helmet is a safety measure required by law, although in nearly three million bat-twirling episodes and 2.98 million falls, no one has ever actually seen someone fall directly on his head. The far more vulnerable area, one would guess, would be the elbows, which go totally unprotected. And sports-writers covering the Bulls routinely stop what they're doing to watch this fun-filled exercise in the fervent hope that someone will actually crack an elbow and sue the club for millions.

But as far as halftime acts go, one of the most notable ever was, for lack of a better description, Bubble Man. Appropriately enough, Bubble Man appeared at Boston Garden, the place where minimalism was invented. No music during timeouts here. Unh-uh. It might take the fans' minds off basketball and we couldn't have that, although certainly you've got to love any NBA arena that doesn't feature hyperkinetic young men in car wash-style jumpsuits sling-shotting t-shirts into the stands.

Anyway, that's where Bubble Man appeared one halftime during a Bulls- Celtics game, as minimalist an act as it gets as he took the court wearing nothing but a simple body suit and what could only be described as a giant wad of gum on his head.

The routine took all of about a minute-and-a-half and basically consisted of Bubble Man gradually stretching this giant wad over his body until he was engulfed by the entire thing, which by now had taken the shape of a bubble. Eventually, all that was left on the court was a big pink bubble with Bubble Man concealed inside, and the finale had it popping to thunderous applause. Guess you had to be there. But take the word of someone who was, it was both the dumbest and greatest halftime act ever.

Mascots are a whole other story, a genre onto themselves.

Boomer, the Indiana Pacer mascot, is one of the more moronic mascots around. One beat writer's theory about these creatures is that if they were people, most would be sexual deviants. This is what writers do when bored — assess the sexuality of furry, blue, make-believe characters who haven't done anything to us for the most part, except maybe annoy us by their very presence.

But back to Boomer. One of the best moments of the entire season occurred when the furry, blue creature — we're not sure exactly what it is or what it represents (but then it would probably be difficult to reproduce a Pacer) — rigged up an elaborate routine in which a large elastic band was wrapped around the basket support and then around the "waist" of Boomer, who was standing at about midcourt.

The idea, one can only assume, was that he would be launched from there (there was also some extra apparatus involved — a mini-tramp or cannon or something) and end up slamming against the basket support for a really funny finale— which, incidentally, we're still waiting for. Because after the meticulous preparation and setup for this really funny routine, which entailed the small hangup of delaying the actual game, Boomer, instead of being launched, was simply dragged along the court.

If nothing else, it did provide the very important function of cleaning the floor, thereby saving the ballkids wielding the large brooms of doing the job themselves. And, as a very funny mascot timeout routine, it actually ranked among the most entertaining of all time, despite the fact that Boomer stormed off the court and sulked the rest of the evening.

Jordan's retirement was a big theme for team mascots early in the '93-'94 season. Themes are important for these creatures. And wearing a Jordan jersey while swinging everything from a golf club to a baseball bat to a butterfly net proved high entertainment for NBA fans.

Of course, Benny the Bull would never stoop to such depths. Benny, alias Dan Lemonnier, is much more sensitive than the others, which could be one reason why one Bulls beat writer questioned his masculinity on an almost nightly basis — Benny's, not Dan's.

Benny laughs at this tale because Dan is an exceptionally good sport, nice guy and above all, a person with a sense of humor, which comes in very handy in his line of work. Especially the day during the '92-'93 season when Dan, rather Benny, was actually hassled by a fan for the first time in Dan's eight-year career.

"John Paxson's wife was there," recalled Lemonnier, "and I was there, by Gate 7, to meet and greet, take pictures, all that stuff, when this guy who obviously had had a few too many beers starts looking at me funny. Benny has a target on his belly and all of a sudden this guy yells out, 'Yo Benny,' puts his head down and charges me."

The rest of the story is still difficult for Lemonnier to recall, mainly because of where the guy hit him, a place he insists hurt just as much despite all of Benny's red fur serving as padding. Both Benny and Dan were knocked flat, Dan gasping for air but still able to utter Benny's first curse words, to which the idiot attacker responded, "Ooooh, Benny's PO'ed."

You don't really want to know what happened to the guy after that, says Lemonnier, as a pair of handy yellow jackets came onto the scene. "Let's just say the guy needed to sit down for a little while after that," says Dan.

That was the only time Benny and Dan were physically assaulted, unless you count the mauling that occurred in his dressing room one day. This one was of a non-human but infinitely more dangerous variety. To be more specific, it was a dog act that went crazy.

To save the dog embarrassment and Dan possible legal entanglements, the dog's name won't be mentioned. But this was one famous and powerful dog. It's the one who catches Frisbees in his teeth and, according to Dan, an animal that is in a constant state of mange, requiring it to be shaved and leaving it with bare spots all over and, apparently, a nasty disposition on top of it.

Most of the time, however, he's just as friendly as can be. "Until," says Dan, his voice wavering just a bit, "I put on my costume. Then it goes ballistic. One time, it jumped me and got hold of a mouthful of costume. Right on the stomach. On the inside, I'm swearing 'You little SOB,' and on the outside, I'm swinging it around by its teeth."

Thank goodness the dog's trainer was there. He thought the whole thing was so hysterical he could barely speak, especially the part where you could hear Dan's muffled little voice screaming from inside Benny's little smile. And aside from the gaping holes in Benny's stomach that Dan had to have fixed, he actually thought it was fairly humorous. "Mostly because as soon as I got out of the costume, " says Dan, "the dog comes running up to me, all happy and panting like, 'Hey, where have you been? I just chased away that hairy red thing.' "

There is all kinds of interesting history involved when you're talking about NBA mascots. For instance, they used to be able to talk and were even encouraged to do so until the Bango incident. Bango, the deerlike mascot of the Milwaukee Bucks, was reportedly wading through the upper reaches of the Bradley Center one night working the crowd when someone held up a beer and yelled, "Hey, Bango, know what this is? It's venison juice [only he didn't say juice]." So Bango, being the improvisational performer that he is, did the first thing he could think of, pretending to pull down his zipper as if to freshen it for the paying customer.

"Like me," said Dan. "Bango has no pants."

Needless to say, the NBA did not endorse the move. " They told us we couldn't talk to people anymore," Dan said.

They did not, however, mention anything about mime. "That was understood," said Dan.

Lemonnier, who has other endeavors, could make a living off of Benny, which is the property of the Bulls, and does, in fact, devote most of his time to it, making about 300 appearances a year. Once after the Bulls' first championship, Benny accompanied the Luvabulls and several players to the Oprah show. During the show, Jeffrey Jordan, Michael's oldest child, then just a toddler, was caught on camera waving cutely from the audience. Of course, it looked like he was waving to daddy. But as soon as the show was over, he zoomed right past daddy and into the fuzzy embrace of Benny, whom he had been eyeing all along.

Jordan may have a healthy ego but he knew when he couldn't compete, and as they filed out, he peeled Jeffrey off of Benny. "Kiss the bull goodbye," said Jordan, who then asked Dan if he could come to Jeffrey's birthday party.

Only once did Dan really take advantage of his alter ego. He had Benny in the back of his car "airing out" after a daylong summer appearance for a local shoe store chain when he noticed the flashing red light in his rear-view mirror. When the officer walked around to the driver's side, he took a double-take. "Is that the real Benny?" the cop asked.

"Yessir, genuine article," replied Dan.

"Lemme have a picture and autograph for the kid," the cop said.

"Sure thing, Officer," said Dan.

Not counting Benny and the Luvabulls' celebrity status, most of the Stadium subculture consisted of regular people. Two of the original "yellow jackets," the security patrol at the Stadium, are Clarence "C.T." Travis, an investigator for the Cook County narcotics unit, and Augustus "Gus" Lett, a forensic supervisor for the Chicago Police Department. It was the two of them who first began escorting Michael Jordan to his car after games his second year in the league. It was the year Jordan broke his foot and the two would notice him lugging his bag out every night, the last to leave. Jordan mania was about to take off.

"It became obvious he needed us when fans started pulling his clothes off and he had a pair of baby shoes stolen from his rear-view mirror," said Travis, a former bodyguard of Jesse Jackson and once part of the security force for the Jackson Five.

Since then, the two, along with several other off-duty policemen, have provided security and become friends with Jordan, accompanying him almost anywhere they feel he might need protection. They have also become among Jordan's closest friends and fiercest defenders.

After the gambling controversy erupted during the Bulls-Knicks playoff series in '93, Jordan and the team returned home to find a heckler, who brought a pair of dice to the game and was taunting Jordan courtside by throwing them on the floor. Travis quickly grabbed the fan and threw him out of the Stadium.

Another time, after football great Jim Brown raised the subject of whether Jordan was charitable enough to the black community of Chicago, a couple passed out pamphlets at the Stadium urging Jordan to "Give Back To The Community." But they went beyond that, calling his home and asking for money, which they said they would disperse to poor neighborhoods.

Jordan did his own charity work though, most of it quietly, including giving to a local school and, of course, his donations through the Michael Jordan Foundation. He wasn't sure these people were legit and was feeling harassed until Lett and Travis chased them away.

For the most part, it's pretty harmless stuff. That is, until Monday night, January 17, following a Bulls-Sixers game at the Stadium. A bodyguard of the rap star Hammer was shot in the leg outside Gate 3 1/2 by a police officer serving as a member of the Stadium security force after the man had scuffled with a cop and pointed a gun at officers attempting to herd fans out of the building.

Gate 3 1/2 was the port through which everyone without a ticket — Stadium employees, players, media and various big shots — had to enter; a beat-up old door that had become so legendary in status that its picture adorned the cover of the Bulls media guide for the '93-'94 season. It's where the action is, and on this night, it was where this very scary incident occurred.

"There was an end-of-the-game security sweep, as we call it," said Lett. "Ushers and guards start at a certain point and herd everyone out of the building. When it came time for this person to leave, he said, 'You can't tell me what to do, don't put your hands on me,' and pointed a gun at police officers."

It was the first shooting incident at the Stadium and it was a shooting that didn't go by the book, as the officer used his weapon in a crowd and shot to wound.

"He pointed a gun at police officers," said Lett. "He should have been shot between the eyes. That's what I would have done. But there were players and fans out there and he was conscious of that." Nevertheless, the case was reviewed and judged as a justified shooting.

Security obviously tightened for players after that with everyone, whether they asked or not, getting an escort out of the Stadium. For Jordan, however, it had always been that way. "If he wanted us to do something for him or we just thought Michael should have security, we all volunteered," said Travis. "There was never any mention of money."

In return, though they didn't look at it that way, many of the security guys followed Jordan to Sarasota and to Birmingham. They'd show up in various articles and in Jordan's book, *Rare Air*, and even an Oprah Winfrey movie.

But the friendship for many of them went beyond Jordan. And that was true among many members of the Stadium subculture, who did not only get to know each other but the customers as well.

Lett, who stood guard at the northeast corner of the court, exchanges holiday cards with many of the fans in his section. And the waitresses who served courtside season-ticket holders have come to know some of them as old friends over the years, sometimes whether the fans like it or not.

One waitress, for example, became very familiar with her section, so much so that she immediately noticed when one man came to a Bulls game one night with a woman he was obviously chummy with, but who was not his wife. The waitress, who liked the man's wife, whispered loudly, "That's not your wife," and the man promptly slipped her an extra large tip. "And," the waitress said even more proudly, "it was the last time he ever brought anyone other than his wife to a game."

Another waitress pocketed some extra income when a fan offered her $200 for the $35 dollar basketball tie she was wearing. "But you can buy it on the street," she said. "Yeah, but I want the one you're wearing," he told her, and she figures it was, in part, because of the generous, some might say goofy nature of many of these people that she was able to put herself through college.

For Wally Barabasz, who worked the Gate 3 1/2 parking lot for 22 years and has seen it all, including a few things he wishes he hadn't, there were similar fringe benefits, but also some obvious drawbacks.

He too has never seen more than a minute or two of either a Bulls or Blackhawks game. "I was told my first night on the job by my boss at the time, 'Hockey fever is like pony fever. Once you catch it, you'll never let it go.' So I've never watched a game. I never felt my job was inside."

Besides, there's way too much good stuff going on outside.

One young attendant who no longer works at the Stadium (we'll call him Joe) was new on the job several years ago when one of the neighborhood cops nearing retirement needed a car to sneak over to the nearest gin mill for a quick pop.

"I can't get my car out," said the cop, "can you lend me one?"

"Well, uh, I don't know," said Joe.

"Look, it'll be fine," said the cop. "I'll be right back."

The cop settled on the brand-new Cadillac of a friend of Blackhawks owner Bill Wirtz. "I'll be back soon," he said as he sped off. But two hours later, there was no sign of him.

Inside the Stadium, the clock ticked down with just minutes remaining in the game. But still no cop and no Cadillac.

With visions of being retired swirling about him, Joe suddenly turned and saw a tow truck with the Caddy attached, pulling up to the gate. Out jumped the cop.

"What happened?" Joe stammered.

"Oh these damn new locks," said the cop. "I left my keys in the car and couldn't get them out. My cousin drove me over in his tow truck."

Nervously, Joe went over the car. No scratches. No dents. The car was fine. He jimmied the lock and pulled it into its space just as its owner walked out of the Stadium — none the wiser.

Wally had a similar experience with a well-known season-ticket holder (now in jail, incidentally) when the guy left his car in the street outside the parking area, keys in ignition and engine running.

"Park it for me, will you, Wally?" the man said as he ran past him and into the Stadium.

Problem was that Wally barely heard him in the middle of trying to park a half-dozen other cars and didn't remember until the man came out of the game two-and-a-half-hours later.

"Wally, where's my car?" he asked.

"I brought it back out to the street for you," said Wally without batting an eye. "It's all ready."

"Great, thank you," said the man, handing him a $2 tip. "And it's even facing in the right direction."

Of the basketball support staff, Rosenberg has been there the longest, logging more than 4,200 games in various sports. So much a fixture of the scorer's table at the Stadium, Rosenberg is known and trusted by athletes and officials alike. "One time, a ref came by," Rosenberg recalled, "and I asked, 'Who was the foul against?' And the guy said, 'Bob, I really don't know. Pick one out for me.' "

At times, Bulls players have counted on him as well. "I would flash to Michael what he needed on rebounds and assists if he was close to a triple-double," Rosenberg said. "If a player is going for something, there's no reason you can't tell him."

Players often tell Rosenberg they have been gypped a steal or rebound, or flat out have asked for an extra assist. But it isn't as bad as it used to be. Dick Klein, the original owner of the Bulls, once told Rosenberg he wanted to give Tom Boerwinkle and Dave Newmark more rebounds. "I said, 'But the guards are complaining they're not getting enough assists,' " said Rosenberg. "He said, 'Well, we can cut them back so we can pay them less.' In those days, it was pretty routine."

Jackson pays numerous visits to the scorer's table during games. "He'll say, 'Can't you turn that damn music down? We can't hear in the huddle.'" And Rosenberg will shrug, for it is out of his control.

The job does have its dangers. Former Bulls coach Doug Collins once lost his temper and accidentally whacked Rosenberg in the face with a giant cooler of Gatorade. "Oh, God, Rosie, I'm sorry," wailed Collins.

"That's OK, Doug," said Rosenberg, "it's nothing new."

And then there's Walter. And you really need not say anything more to any of the Stadium people, for everyone knows Walter, who has achieved something of a cult status in his role as good-luck charm/pregame mascot.

Walter Owens, a 30-year-old liquor porter for Bismarck Catering, became part of the Bulls' pregame routine in 1989, a year after he began his job and discovered that Jordan was not only approachable down there in the pits of the Stadium before games, but downright chatty. So the two would talk and play-wrestle and before Walter would scoot away to do his real job, he would peek into the Bulls' huddle, which convenes before every game at the bottom of the steps leading up to the court.

There, where cameras have long since caught them, is the place where first Cliff Levingston, then Scott Williams yelled the now-famous "What time is it?" and the rest of the team responded "Game time, (ooouuugghhhgrunt)."

And funny, but the Bulls got on a hot streak after Walter joined that huddle, with Jordan's blessing, perched on the third step, so that at 5 feet 4, he could peer over their shoulders and see what was going on. So obvious were Walter's charms to the superstitious Jordan that when he couldn't get over there in time one game, the Bulls waited until someone tracked him down.

Soon it became tradition. As did the songs Walter occasionally crooned until the players came out of their dressing room and did their stretching and huddled up. "Just gospel stuff or maybe the Coca-Cola song," says Walter, who obviously has a wide repertoire. Sometimes he'll even take requests. Stacey King always asked for the national anthem, though why anyone would want to endure that twice in one night is anyone's guess.

The Stadium patrons would have to go thirsty before Walter would miss this ritual, which didn't always sit well with his superiors, who told him a couple years after he started to cut it out. By then the Bulls were world champions and their intimate little ritual was being replayed for national television audiences, and you didn't have to look too closely to see Walter's mug right there in the middle of it all.

They told him he was on TV too much and that he should stop it. But when he informed them just as coolly as can be that the Bulls' coaches and players wanted him in there, well, then, "We guess it's OK," they said.

So now, Walter huffs proudly, he's a pretty famous guy, ticking off the names of the people Jordan has introduced him to, like Magic Johnson and Ahmad Rashad. And don't laugh, because it's all true. And even if he can't produce the picture, there's one more thing that few people know about.

After the Bulls won their second NBA title and their first at the Stadium, defeating Portland in Game 6, Walter carried the champagne into the room the Bulls used as their dressing area that night. Off that room was a smaller one used for the officials' dressing room, in which just a small group convened after the initial cork-popping had ceased. In that room, Jerry Reinsdorf, Jerry Krause, Phil Jackson, Michael Jordan, Scottie Pippen and Horace Grant gathered briefly to light some cigars and have a private toast to their success. Walter, peeking in at the door, was spied by a security guard and told he would have to leave, but Pippen piped up, "He's family. He doesn't go anywhere."

And so there, beneath the court in which they had triumphed and later danced; behind doors that no one even knew about; in the relative sanctuary of quiet though joyous reflection; the principal parties of the NBA champions gathered for a private photo — Reinsdorf and Krause and Jackson and Jordan and Pippen and Grant . . . . and Walter, of course, kneeling right in the middle and holding the Larry O'Brien Trophy.

Dear Chicago Bulls,
Congratulations on the first two games!
If you could send me a needel
of who you have to play if you beat
Milwakee, I can write and tell you
what it you will probaly have to
do! I should know, I've watch every
team in the A.B.A. and I know what
to do against each team. So If
you decide to take my word ar to
cock Jackson's just let me know

8

BILL PERDUE AND PETE WHO?

Tough as it may be to believe, there was no one defining moment when Pete Myers made like the Wesley Snipes character in the movie "Major Leagues," walked outside the locker room door and performed a quick moon walk in silent celebration of not just earning a spot on the Chicago Bulls, but of finding out he would be starting at Michael Jordan's recently vacated position.

"I was too scared," Myers said, and he wasn't talking about the notion of taking on such an imposing new job. He was talking of being cut, a very real possibility that haunted "the new guys" of the '93-'94 Bulls, even after January 10, the deadline when all players are guaranteed their salaries for the rest of the season.

"They can still waive you," Myers reminded anyone who dared ask. And at $150,000 per, which is what Myers, Bill Wennington and Steve Kerr earned that season, it certainly was an affordable option for the Bulls.

Thing was, they happened to be holding the team together early on, particularly Kerr and Wennington, whose roles on the second unit became every bit as important as Scottie Pippen's and Horace Grant's were on the starting five. After early December, when the bench began outscoring the opposition with regularity, it became apparent that the legends of former Bulls reserves Cliff Levingston and Craig Hodges — not to mention Bobby Hansen, Trent Tucker and Darrell Walker — had nothing on the newest Bulls. People stopped wondering who these guys were and simply wondered how the Bulls found them.

Of course, it wasn't as if they were discovered on some playground in North Dakota. All three were NBA veterans, and Wennington and Kerr came from bona fide college programs. But the reality was that having played in Europe the year before joining the Bulls, Myers, who turned 30 in September of '93, and Wennington, who was 31 in April of '94, were looking hard at the prospect of life after basketball. And Kerr, who had a disappointing '92-'93 season in Orlando the year before and turned 28 in September of '93, was thinking about his European options.

Myers knew all about the organization, having been drafted by the Bulls in June of 1986 behind Brad Sellers of Ohio State, Larry Krystkowiak of Montana, Ricky Wilson of George Mason, Scott Meents of Illinois and Jimmie Gilbert of Texas A&M and ahead of Robert Henderson of Michigan, whom the Bulls selected with their seventh-round and final pick.

If Myers stuck with the Bulls, it would have been a miracle, as far as he was concerned. But back home in Mobile, Alabama, his buddies were telling him, "Man, that's where Michael Jordan plays. You're going to play with Michael Jordan. It's going to be great." And knowing what he did about his own history of beating odds, he probably should have been a little more confident.

Growing up, Myers was a football and baseball fan. Football, because that's what you did if you grew up in Alabama. Baseball, because that's what his father played as a young man, and Pete idolized his dad.

"My man," he says now of Eugene Myers, a longshoreman and hard-working man who wanted only for his children to get a proper education. The elder Myers had a good relationship with all three of his children — his oldest child, Walter, who also played basketball, and only daughter, Helen, who played basketball and volleyball in junior college. But it was Pete whom everyone said was most like him.

"My pop was very laid-back, easygoing, didn't say too much," said Pete. "Whatever my mom said, he would never argue. He was a person who got along with everybody."

Together, father and son would often watch basketball games on television.

"I can remember watching if the Celtics were on," Pete recalled, "and I can remember my pop being crazy about Jo Jo

White, Charlie Scott, that crew. He would tell me I should try to pattern my game after Charlie Scott."

Pete's dad and his mom, Helen, owned a lounge called the Brown Dot Social Club. "A small community club" is how Pete described it, and it was there where his view of life and his lingering childhood were irreversibly altered. For it was there, in the early-morning hours of Sunday, May 21, 1978, that 45-year-old Charles Wilkes aimed a gun at a man he had been arguing with, but killed Eugene Meyers, standing behind the bar, instead.

Myers was 46. Pete was 14.

"He was a neighborhood guy who only lived four or five blocks from us," Myers said of the man who killed his father. "He turned himself in. It was accidental. My brother took it real strong, but it was real tough on me and my sister. And it was really tough on my mom. She had to go to court over and over. It was like you knew pretty soon, me and my brother would have to pretty much start taking care of my mother."

By then, Pete had picked up basketball. "Only because my brother played," Pete said. "They called me 'Little Walt.' "

And indeed, he was little for a basketball player. At 5 foot 8 his freshman year, Pete was the smallest boy on the freshman basketball team at Lillie Williamson High School. "I had some talent in football but it just wasn't in me, and my mother didn't like football so she didn't encourage me too much," he recalled.

"She really encouraged me to play baseball, but once I got to high school, I just dropped it. Basketball was it. It was exciting watching my brother play. It was so different. I barely made the team. I was probably the 12th guy to make it, and I think I only made it because my brother played."

But he worked at it and had fun at it, and when the pain started in both knees, he tried his best to ignore it. Trouble was, he couldn't. "If you just grazed me," he said, "I had pain." The doctor's recommendation? Stop playing basketball. One year at least, probably two. "He told me I was growing too rapidly [he would end up sprouting nine inches over the next two years] and that's why I had so much pain," he said. "But I didn't want to hear it."

Pleading with his mother to allow him to return to the court, but to no avail, Pete suddenly found himself without the man he loved and the game he loved. At times it was too much to bear.

"It was tough," he said. "I couldn't concentrate academically. I wasn't focused, because I really couldn't enjoy life as a youngster. That doctor took the best thing I had going for me away, so I couldn't really deal with it. And my mother was like, well, until you get your grades up, you're not going to play anyway. It was hard for her because she knew how much I loved the game."

For two years, Myers had to be content with playing pickup games at the park whenever he wasn't in too much pain, and he played a little AAU ball. "But that didn't mean anything," he said with all the emotion of a frustrated 15-year-old. "Guys are walking around with their letter jackets and I knew I should be a part of that, but I couldn't. And those guys were improving, while the guys in the pickup games, the guys I played with, couldn't really play."

In his spare time, Myers worked at a flower shop. "Anything to just take up time and take my mind off it," he said. He managed to stay out of serious trouble. "But thinking back, it could have happened easily," he said. "Every day, I'd go home, do my homework, go to the park and play, so these guys became my friends. Now I'm back at school and these are the same guys who want to skip school. You find yourself getting caught up. My mother and my brother talking to me daily kept me out of trouble.

"My brother became my father figure and I resented it. He was always on me and I'm thinking, 'You're only five years older than me. I'm a young man, just growing up, you should understand.' But really he was trying to tell me something, that for later on in life, now is the key. You have to get control of your life now. And I knew I wanted something better out of life than just shooting hooky from school and not graduating. I come from a good family that really pushes you toward education, and I think that was a big plus."

A big plus, too, was coming back his senior year measuring 6 feet 5. "Now I come back and I'm one of the tallest guys on the team with skills a lot of big guys didn't have, because coming in as a young guy at 5-8, I had lot of ballhandling skills. So I wasn't behind at all."

Myers' high school team ended up going to the state tournament that year, but lost to Huntsville Butler, whose star, Bobby Lee Hurt, went on to play at the University of Alabama and later in the NBA. Myers' team was one of balanced scoring, and at 8.8 points per game, with no basketball camp experience and practically no basketball history beyond one season, Myers didn't draw much attention from college recruiters.

Once again though, his big brother came in handy as the coach from Faulkner State, Walter's junior college team, came calling. "My brother had fun, so I figured I'd go," Pete recalled. "I figured if I got the chance to go to college, it would be a plus just to go to college for free."

He was accompanied to Faulkner State, just a 30-minute drive from home, by his best friend, Michael Clark, and Myers' cousin, Kenneth Worthy. "I've played in the shadow of many guys," Myers said, and this situation was no different as Clark and Worthy were the ones to draw attention from the "big colleges."

After two years at Faulkner State, Myers was recruited by an assistant coach at Arkansas-Little Rock who came to call at the supermarket where Myers was working. Myers told him he couldn't talk because he wasn't on break yet. The coach waited.

Myers would again go with his buddies. The star of the Little Rock team was a kid named Myron Jackson, who roomed with Myers. And often, Jackson's cousin, a quiet, skinny kid named Scottie Pippen who played down the road at Central Arkansas, would come visit Myron during the summer and sleep on the floor of their apartment.

In Myers' last year at Little Rock, the Trojans were the talk of the NCAA tournament early on, defeating Notre Dame in the first round before losing in double overtime to an N.C. State team that had Chris Washburn, Nate McMillan, Charles Shackleford and Vinny Del Negro.

"My cousin and I had a good tournament," Myers remembers, "but Myron was getting all the publicity even though I led the team in scoring during the tournament. Everybody was excited about him because he was a good shooter. I was a jack of all trades, considered an athlete maybe more than a basketball player.

"He'd tell me all the scouts he had talked to, and I was trying to be happy for him, but I was like, 'Oh, man, no scouts are calling me.' My coach was telling me to finish my education and come back as an assistant and I was thankful for that."

Myers remembers the day he was drafted as starting in truly lousy fashion. Jackson was drafted in the third round and local television reporters came to their apartment to record his reaction. When the knock on the door came, it awoke Myers from a nap he dearly needed after a tough day with rowdy kids at the basketball camp where he was a counselor.

"I'm thinking, 'I'm not going to get drafted.' I was depressed and just trying to get some sleep," Myers recalls. "When the TV guys woke me up, they told me I had been drafted in the sixth round by the Chicago Bulls. Then I talked to Jerry [Krause] and he told me to come in shape and be ready to play. They didn't have a good team, but they had Michael. I knew I was a long shot."

Myers didn't have an agent and didn't figure he needed one. The NBA minimum then was $75,000, which sounded pretty good to him when he signed a standard one-year, non-guaranteed contract. Only six Bulls in camp that year had guaranteed contracts.

Myers knew of Jordan, of course, but had not seen him play much. He knew Jordan was coming off a 63-point performance against Boston in the playoffs. And he knew his buddies were making him crazy telling him he was going to play alongside the great Jordan. "And I'm just thinking, 'OK, Michael Jordan,' " recalled Myers.

It was Doug Collins' first year as coach of the Bulls and Myers rightly figured that this would work to his advantage as Collins wanted to bring in new faces. Pretty quickly, Myers became a human teething ring for Jordan. Years later, in fact, Jerry Krause would avoid bringing in young two-guards with Myers in mind. "Michael would just tear him up every day," Krause said. "I didn't want another young kid to go through that. It can't be too good for your confidence."

Myers ended up handling it pretty well, but the memory of practicing against Jordan all season is indelibly etched in his brain. The first night of two-a-day sessions in training camp, Myers was assigned to guard Jordan, who, halfheartedly and in typical first-day shape, scored a rather mortal 18 points on the rookie in a scrimmage. Bulls coaches praised Myers while veterans like Charles Oakley gave Jordan endless grief. "I'm thinking, OK, he's good but he's not *that* tough," laughed Myers of his first youthful impressions.

The next day, Jordan strolled up to Myers, looked him in the eye and announced, "I want Pete Myers to guard me. I want Pete Myers."

Recalls Myers: "He had about 55 that day." He laughs about it but still marvels at the thought. "How can you play on that same level — game, practice, game, practice— all season? But Michael did. I go to practice, playing only 23 minutes a game, and I'm thinking today I have to ease off a little bit. But Michael came in every day the same. One night that season, he scored 61 against Detroit and the next day in practice he kicked my butt like he didn't do anything the night before."

"You're destroying this kid," Bulls assistant coach Johnny Bach told Jordan after this routine repeated itself daily. "I have to get myself ready, Johnny," Jordan would shrug.

When the Bulls opened the '86 season with Myers on the roster, he was the second-lowest drafted player in the league. But his professional career after that was something of a blur. After being waived by the Bulls before the next season began, Myers would make stops in Rockford, San Antonio, Philadelphia, Spain, New York, New Jersey, San Antonio again, and Italy, where he would meet and become friendly with Bill Wennington.

Wennington can relate to Myers with a pro resume that also resembles a travel guide. But like Myers, Wennington is also thankful for every minute after a childhood that hardly resembled that of a future professional basketball player.

Born in Montreal, the oldest of three children adopted by William and Elswyth Wennington, Bill and his wife, Anne, have already planned their first vacation after he retires from basketball. It will be somewhere cold and preferably snowy, and include as many winter sports as they can cram in. Growing up, Wennington never heard of kick the can. And he certainly didn't know anything about basketball. "Every community had their own outdoor rinks and that was our entertainment," he recalled. "We'd play hockey and ice skate. And there'd be a little chalet where they sold hot chocolate. That's what you did."

Wennington tried to play hockey because that's also what you did, but at 6 feet 2 by age 11, agility was not one of his strong points, particularly on ice skates.

"Guys would check me and they were so much smaller than me, I couldn't do anything," he said. "I checked someone once and hit them pretty hard and knocked him down, and for the whole rest of the game, their whole team was after me. One guy, I remember, came after me in the corner. I tried to brace myself against the boards and he just bounced off of me. I just started laughing."

By his own admission, Wennington was "so bad" that he started. He had to. "They could only put me on with all the starters so it wouldn't matter."

Being tall was not any sort of badge of honor back then. When you're the tallest person in the school in the sixth grade—teachers included—you're strange not special, and Wennington struggled with it. Not that he wasn't used to it by then. "When I was younger, my mom said people would look at me and say, 'Why is he acting like a seven-year-old?' And she'd say, 'Because he's six.' And they'd say, 'Oh, I thought he was 13.' "

As he approached adolescence, it only became tougher. His parents were in the midst of a divorce and only the help of a kind seventh grade teacher made life bearable.

"Thank God for Mr. Patrick," he said, recalling his teacher's name with ease. "I was starting puberty, my sweat glands opened up and my classmates complained about me. I was mortified. I had no idea what they were talking about. One day, Mr. Patrick called me aside and said, 'Bill, did you shower this morning?' And I was like, 'Yeah.' And he said, 'Maybe you should start using deodorant.' "

Soon after, Wennington developed what he called a "fuck-you attitude," as a sort of defense mechanism. "I didn't give a damn," he recalled. "I wanted people to like me and I'd try, but they still wouldn't like me because I was too different. I decided

I didn't care. People were either going to like me or not. I wasn't nasty. I just stopped caring."

Basketball would be his savior.

Looking up to hockey legends Bobby Orr and Ken Dryden, Wennington barely knew the game of basketball existed until he was 12. "Kareem and Dr. J were names I heard," he said, "but I couldn't tell you if they were centers or guards or who they played for."

One Sunday afternoon, while swimming at the local YMCA, a man named Doug Alexander, a reporter for a nearby suburban paper and a friend to all the neighborhood kids, asked Wennington, "How old are you, 16?" Wennington was 11.

"He said, 'Do you play basketball?' " Wennington recalled. "And I was like, 'What's basketball?' I mean, I knew what it was, sort of. But not really."

Wennington went home, asked his mother for permission and signed up. He topped 6-2 by then and by his own account was "horrible. We played on eight-foot baskets and that first year, if I scored eight points in one game, it would be a lot. I was the biggest, but I was also uncoordinated and I didn't understand the concept. But the next year, I started to enjoy it."

One really good reason was that for perhaps the first time in his life, he gained acceptance. Simply put, "Basketball started getting me more friends," he said. Wennington played soccer, hockey and volleyball, and was on the swim team. But he had found his sport.

"In basketball, I wasn't so much better, but I was so much bigger that in this sport, everyone started respecting me."

They began calling him Bill *Winnington* because every team he played on for the next several years seemed to win whatever title it played for.

At home, however, life was no fun at all. His parents had divorced, his mother had moved out when Bill was 11, and his father remarried when Bill was 16. He had "conflicts" with his stepmother from the start, refusing to accept her as any sort of authority figure, and resenting her three children, who joined a family that already had three and only seemed to make matters worse.

"She was very intimidated by me, and I would speak my mind," Wennington said. "I still do. My dad was a very good man, but he was trying to make everything work out and we'd get taken advantage of. Or at least I thought so."

Wennington's stepmother would accuse her husband's children of being spoiled, and Bill would hear none of it, insisting that her kids were the ones causing the problems. At the time, Bill's younger sister was 15, and the restlessness of adolescence gave way to monstrous fights that more often than not left the younger and considerably smaller sibling in tears.

That summer, Bill visited his mother and her new husband in New York. While he was gone, his stepmother's message to his father was simple: "If he comes back, I'm leaving."

"My mom and stepfather took me to a bar and they told me," Wennington recalls. "And my first instinct was, 'I want to go home.' Then they said, 'Well, they don't want you back.' And I insisted, 'I want to go home.' All my friends were there. Then I thought about it all of 10 seconds and thought, why do I want to go home? We didn't get along. She made my life miserable. So I said, 'OK, I'll stay.' "

If there is now a disarming sense of humor in the adult Bill Wennington replacing the anger of a 16-year-old boy, it is clear there is still pain as well. But there is also time and distance on his side, and maturity as he looks back to days that eventually turned out to be a blessing to his basketball career.

"My dad let me go," he says. "I still can't understand it, but I can accept it. I see why. He didn't want to grow old by himself. He had three kids and he had to meet someone who wanted to be with him. He found someone he loved and he didn't want to lose her."

Life in New York was a shock. A friend of the family had recommended a private school, a Lutheran high school on Long Island, and it wasn't long before Wennington discovered that the game he had been fooling around with in Canada was a serious sport in the states, and a sport he was hardly well-trained to play. "I often joked that I played basketball, but until I came to the States, I wasn't an athlete," he said.

It was that sort of innate modesty that allowed Wennington to blossom into a national college prospect, though it sure didn't come easily. At 16 years old, he had now grown to 6 feet 10, but was a portly 240 pounds and hardly disciplined.

"I grew up drinking beer," he recalls. "Being so tall, I could walk into a liquor store and not get carded when I was 13 (the legal age was 18). I was popular for that, but who was I popular with? Not the people who are going to be good role models and be successful in life. I was hanging out all the time. I didn't care about school. I didn't care about anything. I wasn't a bad kid. I never got arrested. I never got involved with drugs. I was just kind of a wise guy and I wasn't disciplined."

His foundation in basketball was shaky at best. Hardly a major program at his high school in Canada, practice often consisted of an hour of nothing more than fooling around. "Basically, me and this other kid would run practice," Wennington recalled. "If we didn't feel like doing anything one day, we'd just say, 'We're not doing that' and do layups and scrimmage and that was it. And that's what we did."

Wennington's first clue that life in New York would be different was his first summer camp experience shortly before he moved. "I thought I was in shape, but I couldn't run up and down the court four times without stopping to catch my wind," he said. "I had a beer belly, I was 6 feet 10 and these guys who were 6-6 were just killing me."

It was then that his new high school coach, Bob McKillop, decided a little discussion was in order, a talk that went something like this:

Coach: So, what do you know about basketball, Bill?

Bill: It's fun.

Coach: Uh-huh. And what do you want to do with your life?

Bill: I haven't really thought about it.

"At this point," says Wennington, remembering the talk, "I'm not even sure I knew you could get a scholarship to college by playing basketball."

Coach: Well, do you want to be a good basketball player?

Bill: Yeah, sure, I want to be good.

Coach: Because you have to really want it.

Bill: Yeah, sure, I want it.

Coach: I can help you make it if you really want to be the best basketball player you can be. But do you really want it?

Bill: Yeah, sure.

Coach: OK, then from now on, you do as I say and how I say

it and ask no questions, and I'll make you a good basketball player.

Bill: What do you mean?

Coach: You can't ask, "What do you mean?" You have to do what I say.

Bill: But . . .

Coach: You can't say "But. . ." Now, will you do what I say?

Bill: OK, I guess that sounds cool.

Says Wennington now: "I'm walking out thinking, 'OK, how bad can it be?' "

He found out quickly. After the first two weeks, throwing up in trash barrels was pretty much a routine part of Wennington's daily practice regimen as he quickly shrunk to 215 pounds. Thoughts of quitting also occurred daily as coach and student clashed.

One day, running that delightful drill all basketball players recognize and many refer to as suicides—sprinting from baseline to free throw line and back, then to mid-court and back, to the next free throw line and back, and to the far baseline and back, touching each line as you go, and normally running it several times in a row—student crumpled to the court in a cramping, moaning heap.

Coach (standing over student): Get your lazy ass up, Wennington, you stiff.

Bill: Auuuuuuggghhhh.

"Now we've already run 10 suicides after a three-hour practice," recalled Wennington, "and he's yelling at me, 'Every second you stay on the floor, the whole team is going to have to run three more with you.' And I can't move. My legs are shaking, I had cramps in my stomach, my hamstrings were knotted. I'm almost crying on the floor. And I'm thinking it's not worth it. And the whole team is standing over me saying, 'Come on Billy, don't do this. Come on, get up.'

"So I get up and we run two more. And I'm throwing up and we go in the locker room and I'm thinking, I'm going to quit. I don't need this bullshit.

"Then I thought, no, I'm not going to quit. You can't break me. I actually got sick from it. I ended up missing two days from school. But I decided I liked this game and I wanted to be good at it. For me, it showed I was a good kid in the wrong lane. I would have eventually become a bad kid. But this was a big turning point for me."

Wennington stayed close to his new home when he opted for St. John's and Louie Carnesecca over every major program in the nation, including the five others to which he had narrowed his choices: Duke, Virginia, Providence, Davidson and South Carolina.

He did not crack the starting lineup until late in his sophomore year, played for the Canadian Olympic team during the summers, and did not consider the NBA a realistic goal until his senior year.

The third offensive option on a team that featured Chris Mullin and Walter Berry, Wennington averaged 12 points and seven rebounds per game his senior year. But by then, he had grown to his present height of seven feet and had developed a work ethic and toughness that had scouts talking.

"I had agents calling me, but I still wasn't sure where I stood," he remembers. "And even though I played college basketball, I wasn't a big sports fan, so I wouldn't run home and watch all the games on TV to find out what was going on."

When draft day rolled around, Wennington's agent told him that Denver would pick him at No. 15, though there was a slight chance Utah might take him at No. 13. The 13th pick came and went with the Jazz snatching Karl Malone. At 15, the Nuggets picked Blair Rasmussen.

"So I'm thinking, 'Now what? Who did I talk to?' " said Wennington. "I remember I talked to Jerry Krause and my agent said, 'It'll be 18, Chicago. So I'm thinking, OK, Chicago. Then I start watching and I hear, 'With the No. 16 pick, the Dallas Mavericks pick Bill Wennington,' and all I can think of is, I'm going to get interviewed and they're going to ask me questions and I don't know one player on Dallas. All I knew was that Detlef Schrempf was drafted eighth and Uwe Blab 17th. I had no clue. I didn't even know who the coach was."

And things sure enough got off on a bad foot when Wennington elected to stay in New York and finish one remaining class toward his degree in communications rather than attend a press conference in Dallas. It got worse soon after he arrived, and a local columnist ripped him.

"I was a bad guy already for not coming to media day," said Wennington. "Then this columnist called at 10 one night. It was the first time a reporter ever called me at home and he asked me a couple questions I didn't know the answer to. He called me an arrogant pig. That was a real eye-opener."

Another was playing 125 minutes over the entire season his third year there, John MacLeod's first as head coach. "I went in," said Wennington, "and said, 'I'm obviously not in your plans. You've got to get me out of here. I want to play somewhere.' And they said, hey, no, you're definitely in our plans. And I'm like, 'You've got to be kidding me, 125 minutes and I'm in your plans?' "

Wennington could have kept complaining, but this was a talented Mavs team, with Sam Perkins and Roy Tarpley playing ahead of him at center, and things did get better the next year. But it was a tough learning experience.

"Everything goes through your mind," Wennington said. "First you start to doubt yourself, then everyone around you. You think, God, I can't be that bad. I can't go from being a great player to being nothing. But I tried to put everything into perspective. As bad as anything got, I knew my life was probably still better than the rest of the country. It's all how you look at it. But everything really changes when you have a child [Wennington and his wife have one son, Robbie]. You feel like you want to be remembered, like you want to make a little mark."

Wennington's last year in Dallas, the '88-'89 season, MacLeod was fired, Richie Adubato took over and the Mavs set their sights on obtaining Rodney McCray from Sacramento, where Wennington's first NBA coach, Dick Motta had relocated. "We got along well in Dallas," Wennington said of Motta. "And he was trying to sell his system in Sacramento."

Wennington and some draft choices were swapped for McCray and some more draft choices, and Wennington learned what serious losing was all about as the Kings proceeded to win just one road game all season and set an NBA record with 35 consecutive road losses. "Losing sucks, no matter how you put it," Wennington said. "I'm a competitor and I don't like to lose.

It was fun to play more and I loved Sacramento, but losing all the time isn't fun."

That was the last year of Wennington's contract and by then, after six years in the league, he had readjusted his goals. The day Wennington went to Italy, he could have signed a four-year guaranteed deal with the Knicks starting at $300,000 a year, which would have had him backing up Patrick Ewing the rest of his career. He chose Italy, partly because he ended up making more than $800,000, though he missed out on an earlier $1.2 million offer because he delayed his decision. But money was just part of it.

"I had been in the NBA for six years and the most I ever played was in Sacramento [19 minutes per game]," Wennington said. "I wasn't ready to say that it wouldn't get any better than backing up Ewing. I didn't mind being a journeyman-type player. But one of the reasons I went to Italy [the next season] was to see what I actually still had in me since I hadn't played much."

Wennington made his final decision and was in Italy within four days of getting their second offer. He left his wife, Anne, expecting Robbie, in Sacramento. "It was heart-wrenching," said Anne. "I don't even know how to describe it. We didn't want to let go of each other. Bill was worse than I was. At least I had a support system at home. He was going somewhere where he knew no one, he didn't know the language and didn't know what he was getting into, leaving me crying and pregnant with our son."

Two weeks later, his mother-in-law called to tell him that Anne was going in for an emergency C-section. The team [Knorr Bologna] had originally told them he could return for the birth, but now was saying they had a game and he couldn't. A week later, he was able to come home for three days.

Ultimately, however, Bill and Anne agreed it was a good decision to go overseas. "It was the most difficult decision I ever had to make in my life," said Bill. "It was sad, but it was one of the best decisions I ever made. Basketball-wise, everything was saying, go over. It was a team that didn't want me to score 30 points a game, but just rebound and play good defense. I knew I'd fit in well."

The second year in Italy was considerably better than the first. Anne and Robbie were with him full-time. He played well, averaging 12 points and seven rebounds. And his team won the Italian championships.

Bologna was perhaps the only town in Italy in which basketball was bigger than soccer and the fans were rabid. "They thought nothing of calling Bill at home before and after games to give him their opinion, good or bad, and tell him what they thought he should do," Anne said. The Wenningtons asked to get a non-published number but were told by the team that it had always been that way.

The Italians enjoyed Wennington's outgoing personality and charm. He would try to speak the language, which they appreciated. "But usually what would happen," he said, "is that I'd start out my answer in Italian, then halfway through I'd throw in a few French words, then I'd finish off in English."

The Wenningtons became close friends with Myers and his wife, Donna, who lived just a few blocks away in Bologna. "We spent New Year's Eve together one year," remembered Bill, "and all of a sudden, we hear pop, pop, pop. We look out the window and they weren't shooting off fireworks, they were shooting off guns in the streets."

Italy took some getting used to, to be sure. When Wennington's team won the Italian championships, many of the 7,500 fans stormed the court.

Suddenly, Wennington was surrounded as fans tried to pull off his jersey. "I really wanted to keep my jersey; it was important to me," he said. "So I was arguing with them and they got it over my head, and now I'm hitting and pushing. Next thing I know, my shorts are down to my ankles and now I'm really pissed. Now I'm punching fans.

"Finally, I work my way off the court and I'm pretty upset because it lost a little bit of the fun for me, and I look over at my teammates and three of them are totally naked. A couple even lost their jocks. It was pretty wild.

"A long way from the NBA."

All you have to do is look at Steve Kerr to know he has bucked the odds. At 6-3, 180 pounds, he still looks like a college freshman who hasn't quite bulked up yet. He was six when he decided he wanted to be a professional athlete. "But as soon as I got old enough to realize how difficult it was," he said, "it never entered my mind."

Nonetheless, whatever sport was in season, Kerr took it up and excelled in most — even football, which he played in junior high in Pacific Palisades, California. "Then I broke my hand and separated my shoulder and called it quits," he recalled.

Kerr was born in Beirut, where his father had been born and raised and where he then worked as president of the American University of Beirut. The family moved back to Los Angeles less than a year after Steve was born, with Malcolm Kerr accepting a position as a professor of political science at UCLA.

Every few years, however, he would take a sabbatical and the family would live overseas — in France and Tunisia when Steve was four and five; in Cairo when he was 11 and 12 and again when he was 14 and 15. More than any of the other three Kerr kids, Steve didn't care for being uprooted.

"They all actually really enjoyed it," he said. "And I did, too. But in sixth grade, it was a tough age to do that and I thought I was being taken away from playing basketball. That was tough, because I thought I was falling behind."

It turned out to be better than he thought. He attended an American school, played on the basketball team and ended up touring Europe competing against other American schools. "The level of competition wasn't nearly as good as it was at home," he recalled, "but it was a lot more fun flying to Greece to play a game, than it was taking a bus in Los Angeles."

His freshman year of high school was spent in Cairo. But the first semester of his sophomore year, Kerr lived with friends in Pacific Palisades in order to play the basketball season, then returned to Cairo for the second semester. "I had friends from all over the world," he said. "It was really neat and something I especially appreciate now.

"While I was there, my [American] friends would always complain, 'There's no McDonald's, no movie theaters.' But meanwhile, while we were complaining, we were being creative and finding things to do to have fun."

While the kids back home were scarfing Big Macs and going to the movies, Steve was riding horses in the desert and climbing the Pyramids. "It was incredible," he said. "One of the Pyramids, the bigger one, originally had steps, but there was a covering on the outside so you couldn't walk on it. But another was completely stepped and you could climb up all the way."

Except for one problem. "It was forbidden by law," said Kerr. "There was always this old guy with a rifle sitting at the base of this pyramid. So what you'd do was get there very early, at dawn, and you'd bribe him. He'd be waving his rifle, screaming, 'Go away, go away,' in Arabic and we'd take out 10 bucks and he'd say, 'OK.' We did that a few times. It was pretty neat. I mean, you'd climb to the top and you could see the whole city.

"For experiences like that . . . " his voice trails off. "And the kids at home were playing Nintendo."

Kerr and his friends would also rent sailboats, called *philugas*. "You'd sail up and down the Nile for a few hours and you'd get drunk and get crude and have a little party," he said, as if discussing cruising some main drag in Pacific Palisades.

Going back to California was tough after that. "That's when I saw the so-called ugly American side to people," he said. "It was emphasized even more when you came back to it. Over there, we were doing all these things and having all these friends from different backgrounds, and then I got back to Los Angeles and all of a sudden it was a big competition over who could outdress each other and who had the cooler car, and I had a hard time. I was not at all cool in high school. The only thing I had going for me was sports."

Basketball and baseball were Kerr's favorites and, like most kids, he wore out the driveway shooting hoops with his father and older brother. But in high school, it was clear he was among some pretty serious competition. "I always thought I was too slow for college ball," he said.

His family had moved back to California for Steve's junior and senior years of high school. With the situation tense in Lebanon, his father spent a year in New York during that period as acting president for AUB.

"My mom [an author and teacher] made a big sacrifice," said Kerr. "The reason we stayed in L.A. was so I could finish high school there. My mom likes to say she stayed back to help with the recruiting process and then nobody recruited me. But she was ready anyway."

By his senior year, Kerr had received letters of interest from several schools and was originally recruited by seven or eight, including Gonzaga, where he took a visit and considered attending. "But they pulled their scholarship back," he said. "They all backed off."

Kerr had played basketball and was a baseball pitcher and third baseman, and considers the highlight of his high school athletic career playing in the city finals at Dodger Stadium, even though his team ended up losing 13-0 and getting no-hit by a kid named Bret Saberhagen.

In basketball, his team was decent and Kerr made the starting five as a junior, but he had no illusions of becoming a star. "I was humbled at an earlier age than most athletes," he said. "A lot of future NBA players are pampered in high school, go to all-star games all over the country and are named in all these magazines. I didn't have any of that, but that helped me in college because I realized I had a lot of work to do."

That summer of '83, Lute Olson left the University of Iowa to take the head coaching job at Arizona, inheriting a program that was 4-24 the season before. Six scholarships opened up through graduation, transfers and academic ineligibility, so Olson recruited several solid prospects and saved one opening for a wild card of sorts.

He first saw Kerr in a summer-league game. "I could really shoot the ball at the time," Kerr said, "but I sure didn't have a feel for the game like I do now. I didn't have some of the skills that have made me a pretty good player. I didn't have the passing skills, the ball handling, and my feet were really slow. Really, really slow. So he kind of took a chance on me. Also, I think he was really trying to get a kid he knew would go to class and be a pretty good scout team player or whatever.

"I didn't even let myself dream about the pros then. I knew I loved sports and wanted to stay in sports. So I figured I'd get my degree and maybe go into coaching. But I knew I loved it too much to just walk away and get a real job somewhere."

The Wildcats continued to struggle Kerr's freshman year, and as the third guard, he played about 20 minutes a game. "Practicing every day helped me get quicker, stronger, everything," he said. "Everything just improved. And the following year, the program really took off."

By then, Kerr had advanced enough to make the starting lineup and that's where he would stay for the next three years, eventually leading Arizona to the Final Four, setting a Pac-Ten record in three-point shooting and being named a second-team All-American. "There was a lot of great timing there for me," he said with typical modesty. "If we had a great team right away, I wouldn't have played as much. I think about fate all the time. It's amazing how fate shapes all of our lives. That's why it's tough to plan your life."

If he had, of course, he would have planned it differently.

By 1984, his father was well-established as the foremost authority on the Middle East. A civil war was ravaging Beirut and Malcolm Kerr entered his second year of presidency at AUB. He had told his family of his fears of returning to Lebanon, but was committed to the job and decided he could not turn it down.

Steve was 18 and midway through his freshman year at Arizona when his father was assassinated by Arab extremists on the AUB campus the morning of January 18, 1984. Malcolm Kerr was 52.

"It made me angry, but how it changed my life, I don't know," Kerr said. "The way you cope with something like that is just to continue to live your life. That's not just for me but anybody who has dealt with a death in the family. You have to just go on with your life. It was somewhat easier that I had basketball, because it gave me something that I really enjoyed and it took my mind off it for a while. It was very therapeutic.

"But it was strange. My family had always seen each other in the summer. And we're all letter writers, so we'd always kept in touch. But after it happened, we'd go on road trips and it always seemed everybody had their families at games. That was one thing I really missed, not having my mom there and especially my dad. He was the one who was a real basketball fan. He never saw me play in college because it happened my freshman year. He saw me play in high school and I sent him a videotape of a couple games at the beginning of [college]."

Easygoing in nature, Kerr would be tested in the years after his father's death with repeated inquiries and, unthinkably, even cruel taunts from opposing fans while he was still in college. "It wasn't so much painful as tiresome," he said. "Every single story about me was about the same thing, over and over and over again. Then I hurt my knee and people started drawing comparisons and that kind of made me angry. How can you compare that to a knee injury?"

Kerr is from a family of scholars. In addition to his parents, there are his sister, Susie, who holds a doctorate in education from Harvard; an older brother, John, with a Ph.D. in economics from Stanford, now working in India; and a younger brother, Andrew, a political science major at Arizona, now on the staff of the National Security Council at the tender age of 26. Steve, working on his master's in sports administration, is fortunate, he said, that his parents never discouraged him from a career in athletics.

"I'm lucky my parents recognized that basketball wasn't a good-for-nothing pursuit, but that it was what I really loved to do," he said. "They helped me realize my studying was very important and they always emphasized that, but they also allowed me to play sports and pursue them with a passion."

That passion, he said, comes from his father. And it would no doubt serve him well in the years to come. "Coming out of college," he said, "the scouts were saying 'He's too slow. He can't create his own shot,' the same things they always said about me, the same things they're still saying about me, really. And it's true. Aside from All-Stars, most NBA players do have weaknesses. The key is to try to cover them up the best you can, then develop your skills the best you can, then be in the right situation."

He caught a break, he said, in being selected by Phoenix in the second round of the '88 draft. The Suns were looking to clean up their image after a drug scandal and so they looked no further than the local kid. "I think they made a commitment to keep me not so much as a favor to the school but just to give me a chance," he said. "It was public relations, almost. But just to stick around for a year and get to practice with Kevin Johnson and Jeff Hornacek every day was great."

The next year, Kerr was traded to Cleveland, and with a little confidence and improving three-point range and ballhandling skills, he found himself backing up Mark Price and playing 20 minutes per game. Kerr fit in well with the system and with the personalities of a largely friendly, easygoing group of guys.

That first year in Cleveland, he led the NBA in three-point shooting percentage, but saw his numbers gradually decline as the Cavs signed John Battle to a five-year deal and then brought in Gerald Wilkins. Nevertheless, Kerr was content. "I was on the verge of signing a new contract [before being traded to Orlando]," he said. "I was going to sign it because of the financial security, even though I knew I wasn't going to play a lot. This was a place where I was happy and I wasn't going to take any chances."

"[Coach] Lenny [Wilkens] didn't want to trade me, but [general manager] Wayne Embry said I wasn't going to play a lot and that Orlando was a good situation for me. I let myself be talked into it and on paper, it looked good. I figured Shaq, double teams, jump shots, sunshine. I probably should have given it a little more thought."

They say you can't survive professional athletics without at least one brush with the reality of big business. Kerr's trade to Orlando was his. "I knew from other players that you can get caught up in numbers and business moves, but that was my first experience with it," he said. "I wanted to be traded by Phoenix because I knew there was no future there for me. But when I went to Orlando, I ended up taking a pay cut and adjusted my salary structure to fit in because they told me I was going to play. The general manager [Pat Williams] told me that, but the coach had other ideas and I got caught up in that business grind, and that was the first time it really hit me hard.

"Initially, I kept looking back and asking myself why I ever left Cleveland. And I spent a lot of time regretting that decision."

Going to the Bulls meant starting over. With his contract expired in Orlando, Kerr knew he would probably have to accept a major pay cut and have to earn a spot all over again. "All of a sudden I was back to square one, but that was also a break because I got to get rid of the money focus," he said. "The whole focus over the summer [of '93] became: Where can I play? Where can I fit in? Where can I enjoy myself?

"If I had had a decent year in Orlando [he averaged three points in 9.4 minutes per game in half a season there] and a few teams offered me good money, my focus wouldn't have been which team is best for me, but where can I get the most money. So now I was looking at the whole league without looking at money, and I knew Chicago was a great spot for me."

In addition to the fact that the Bulls were three-time defending world champions and had Michael Jordan, Kerr had long admired John Paxson and fashioned himself somewhat after Paxson as a player, envisioning himself as heir apparent when Paxson retired.

Initially, Kerr didn't know if the Bulls were interested. "Right after the ['93] Finals ended, we called Jerry Krause, but we didn't get any response the first two months of the summer," Kerr recalled. "I was disappointed because Chicago is where I wanted to go."

Eventually, Kerr was promised only that there would be at least one spot open on the roster if he came to Bulls camp [Trent Tucker was not offered a guaranteed contract and thus opted not to come].

"I talked to Phil [Jackson] before I even considered coming and he assured me I had a great chance of making the team," Kerr said. "I could tell right away he was being straight with me and that was important to me because in Orlando, I felt I got caught up in a situation where there were different opinions and different agendas, and I needed someone to tell me outright what the situation was."

When he heard that Jordan had retired, Kerr, who had been in Chicago only a week, was as upset as any Bulls player. The first thing Kerr did was call Wennington, with whom he had already struck up a friendship and was staying at the same hotel, and the two went out and shot pool for a long time.

"Everybody for years had said that the Bulls without Jordan were a bad team," said Kerr. "So we wondered, 'Are we on a bad team now?'

"Not only did I think the team was going to suffer, but I really thought my role would suffer. I thought playing with Michael would have been good for me because I had watched Pax and B.J. and I saw their success playing alongside of him, so I was pretty discouraged at first. But then after I got a chance to think about it, I realized another guard spot had opened up and as it turned out for me, it has probably been good for my career."

If it was good for Kerr's career, it was vital for Myers.

Krause had remembered Myers from his first stop in Chicago and was impressed when Myers had refused to back down against Jordan in an exhibition game later in his career.

The night Jordan retired, Krause contacted Myers' agent, Steve Kauffman. Myers, who still lived in the Chicago area, had a plane ticket for Sacramento, where he was to go the next morning to attend the Kings' preseason camp. "I can't tell you why," Krause told Kauffman, "but Pete is going to be here. Don't let him get on that plane."

Myers' expectations of signing with any NBA team were low. In July, just three months earlier, he had undergone a hernia operation and wanted only to use NBA camps to get back in shape so he could finish his career overseas.

"It was pretty much like every other summer," recalls Myers. "I was looking to pack to go to Europe. I thought maybe if I was lucky, I'd only have to go for five months instead of eight months."

Every year, the big question for Myers and his wife is whether to keep Pete's son, Eugene, with them [he was eight the summer of '94] or send him to stay with his natural mother in Alabama, where he can attend the same school all year.

In his six years in the NBA, Myers never had a guaranteed contract. "I didn't go to a big, glamorous school," said Myers. "I was fortunate to be drafted in the sixth round and was blessed to be able to stick with Chicago [his rookie year]. But I felt I never got an opportunity to prove myself anywhere because I didn't come in as a project. Each year, coaches always had to make a decision on me.

"It makes it so difficult because everyone thinks you're just playing that particular game, but basically you're playing to survive. That 15-16-foot jump shot becomes difficult because you think it's going to make the difference. I never felt I had it made with the Bulls or with anyone until after the trading deadline."

What made it harder on Myers with the Bulls was the fact that he occupied their most vulnerable position. "Every day you read in the papers all these names of guards the Bulls want or are considering," he said. "I'm realistic, believe me, but I also think I did a good job, especially in the playoffs."

Before the season started, Jordan talked to former Bull Trent Tucker and predicted that Myers would start in his place.

When he worked out with the team one day early on, Jordan pulled Myers aside and gave him advice. "Don't worry about anything," he told him. "You're doing great. Just learn the offense, understand it, find your shots. And above all, play hard."

Myers may very well have shone above all the first-year Bulls in the playoffs, particularly against the Knicks, when he thoroughly frustrated John Starks, still recuperating from knee surgery. But Starks was certainly not the only player all year that Myers frustrated.

By the second game of the season, he was already getting harassed by the Miami Heat and retaliated for a Steve Smith elbow with one of his own, drawing a $5,000 fine. For the most part, however, opponents just resented Myers for even being on the court.

"It was a situation where I wasn't an established player in the league, so a lot of guys felt they should be able to do whatever they wanted to me and I shouldn't be able to do anything back," said Myers, who once very nearly ran onto the Stadium court with his name misspelled on his jersey. "It was definitely a lack of respect. They looked at me as a rookie."

Smith was particularly incensed, and remembered their faceoff at the Stadium when the Bulls traveled to Miami on April 13. Smith, apparently frustrated by a first half in which he picked up three fouls— including two offensive as Myers took the charge—started cursing Myers as the two made their way from the locker room to the court at the end of halftime.

"If you have a problem, then let's take care of business," Myers told him.

Myers was the only Bull in the vicinity while Smith was with his team, who had to restrain him after he lunged at Myers and took a swing.

On another occasion guarding Stacey Augmon in Atlanta, Myers found himself on the deck each time he fought his way around Kevin Willis' screens, only to catch an elbow. About the fifth time this happened, Myers retaliated with an elbow back.

Willis flung him to the floor. "Fuck you," he yelled at Myers. "You'll be back in the CBA before the trade deadline."

"It was funny," said Myers, "but everybody made these CBA references to me and there's nothing wrong with the CBA, but I was only there for two months, back in '88. But it really didn't bother me. It actually motivated me."

He certainly was never ashamed of his two stints in Italy, either. "It's tough going through your career without ever getting a chance to prove yourself," he said, "and that's one reason why I chose to go to Europe [after spending his first five years in the NBA with five different teams]. They only have two foreigners on every team and we'd have the responsibility of carrying the team. Every player wants that kind of responsibility.

"I spent a whole career as just another man on the team. Every year you worry about the trading deadline. You're in this city, out of that city. Europe gave me satisfaction."

For Wennington, like the others, this go-around with the Bulls constituted a new life in the NBA. Years before, while he was sitting on the bench in Dallas, fellow '85 draftee Uwe Blab once posed a question: Would he rather make more money and not play, or make less money and play? For Wennington, it was no contest: he'd rather play. And that mentality was certainly put to the test with the Bulls.

From the beginning, Wennington was the longest of long shots, expected to make the team as the fifth center and perhaps stick for a month or two to allow Bill Cartwright to ease into the season.

"I was thinking I was going to go out there and try to improve my situation, my market value," he said, "so if they cut me, another team would pick me up. "

He was also thinking retirement. "We thought about wrapping it up," Wennington admitted. "It was getting harder every summer to wait and wait. It was so frustrating not knowing where you're going and leaving your family. It makes your whole life miserable and it was playing on me a lot."

But Wennington's high school coach, Bob McKillop, to whom he remained close, talked him into perservering. "He told me, 'That's ridiculous. You have to play until they throw you out.' "

When Jordan retired, Scott Williams went down in the preseason with a freak injury and Cartwright was forced into action, Wennington was thinking maybe he would last until the new year. He was still being mistaken for Will Perdue and called "Bill Perdue" more often than not, but he had to know where he stood.

On November 30, however, after spending two months in a hotel room and, more importantly, two months away from Anne and Robbie, he asked management where he stood.

"I went in to Phil and Jerry and said, 'Look, normally you'd never see me, but I'd like to see my wife and son in December and I'd like to know where I stand.' "

He was told he would definitely make it until January 1, and so his family joined him and they rented an apartment. And waited. Hours after Wennington had his meeting, Pippen played his first game for the Bulls in three weeks, and they would proceed to win 30 of 36 games going into the All-Star break.

Suddenly, they were the hottest team in the league again, and Wennington, Kerr and Myers were as much a part of it as anyone.

Wennington brought to the Bulls a whole new dimension at center, an aggressive, energetic presence in the mold of the still-injured Williams, but also someone who was a very effective shooter within 15 feet.

"[Jackson] opened up the offense for me because normally, the post person stays in the post, passing," Wennington said. "He allowed me to step out and hit the outside jumper, but I knew my boundaries. I had to rebound. I couldn't go out and shoot three-pointers."

During that period, Wennington also developed into something of a crowd pleaser, with a patented jam off the offensive rebound, a move he had worked on in Europe.

The one thing that Wennington, Kerr and Myers seemed to share was the willingness and common-sense approach to filling their roles. "Everyone in the NBA can play relatively well. It's just getting on the right team and in the right spot," said Wennington, and the rest agreed. "I think some guys never realize that. Some guys can't accept a role."

But there was always that gnawing sense of insecurity that didn't truly leave him until the guarantee deadline, January 10.

"I was talking about it once [the possibility of being cut]," Wennington recalled, "and Pax looked at me and laughed, 'Are you kidding? Phil doesn't just like you, he's counting on you.' I felt better after that."

Kerr never had to worry about being cut by the Bulls, though he didn't have a guaranteed contract either. But with Paxson not up to his usual form and the Bulls desperately looking for solid jump shooting, Kerr fit the role well.

For much of the season, he even led the NBA in three-point shooting, though he would jokingly beg reporters not to tell him what he was shooting or where he stood for fear of putting dangerous feelings of superiority in his head.

Kerr was much more comfortable laughing with Paxson after a rare driving layup. "I've got the whole package," Kerr would joke. And his self-deprecating ways would extend to evaluating all facets of his game. But not his shooting. "Some guys were born to run, some guys were born to jump," he said once, "but I was born to shoot. That's why I've lasted this long. That's what I do."

Kerr could be called a nine-to-fiver, that is, he came to work, did his job and then went home to wife Margot and son Nicholas. And he often resembled just any other working stiff, occasionally commuting by train into downtown Chicago, equipment bag in hand, and then transferring to a cab for the short ride to the Stadium.

"If the weather was bad or my wife needed the car, I'd take the train," said Kerr matter-of-factly, as if every professional athlete does it. "I kind of liked it. I could take a book along and not have to worry about rush-hour traffic."

Before coming to the Bulls, Kerr talked to Atlanta, Indiana, Dallas and the L.A. Clippers, and said he had Europe to fall back on. But in the end, most of the options eliminated themselves, and Europe wasn't much of a choice.

For one thing, big men are most coveted and most highly paid in Europe. For another, Kerr did not want to do that unless it was his only option. "Before my rookie year, I thought of going to Germany," he said. "And before going to the Bulls, I looked into Europe. But I never wanted to give up any chance of playing in the NBA. It's such a great league. And I know [Cleveland teammate] Danny Ferry felt his game deteriorated over there. I was always concerned about that."

For Kerr, the Bulls did not merely represent by far the most playing time of his career at 25 minutes per game [he averaged 21 minutes in Cleveland his second year in the league], but also restored his faith in his ability and career. "I always knew if I could get some playing time, my shooting would reflect that," he said. "That's the way it has always been for me."

He ended up shooting 50 percent during the regular season, third on the team behind two big men, Grant and Cartwright. The only tangible disappointment was the New York playoff series, when the Knicks' physical play left Kerr often picking himself off the floor and severely limiting his effectiveness.

There was never any pretense about Kerr. "I never had any illusions about being a star in the league," he said. "I just wanted to be in the league."

And it was that desire that he shared with Wennington and Myers.

The '93-'94 season was a pleasant surprise to all of them, a much-needed breath of life into careers that only needed a little reviving.

"Bill would come home during the preseason," recalled Anne Wennington, "and say, 'They don't need me. They already have four centers. Just one more year and then I'll retire.' And as a wife, I wondered what to tell him. Do I say, 'You have the ability, you have to keep going.' I always thought, no one knows what Bill can do. Or did I want him to stop suffering from the constant uncertainty?

"The whole scenario with the Bulls was nothing we ever imagined, and that was what was so sweet."

"It was a blessing," said Myers. "Just to be able to finally have the chance to prove your worth, to earn your money, is great. My whole career has been a blessing, but this was special."

Dear Tony,

     My name is Tim. You are my favorite basketball
player. I was mad that you didn't play in the Allstar
Game. I have the same haircut as you. I am 10 years ol
I am tall for my age. I hope that when I grow up, I'll
be just like you. Please send an autographed picture of
you. I think you should give Scottie Pippen a big
nuggy.

                    Your fan,

9

A NEW WORLD

Perhaps no Bulls rookie has ever had as severe an indoctrination to the NBA as Toni Kukoc.

This is not said lightly, nor is it to imply some secret, fraternity-like hazing was perpetrated on Kukoc. To the contrary, nearly everything Kukoc had to go through — from his recruiting, to his signing, to his performance during his first year in the league — was done under a very public glare and the harshest scrutiny.

He was, as Michael Jordan said, done no favors by Jerry Krause, who trumpeted his second-round draft choice to unreceptive ears. And Kukoc had the added burden of a cultural barrier that hindered his transition.

Krause, genuinely enthusiastic about his find, had told everyone from players to coaches to media in advance of Kukoc's arrival in the summer of 1993, that not only was this one nice, personable kid, but that his English was flawless and basically, any writer who suggested differently was just another lying, stinking so-and-so.

But the truth was, Kukoc was not fluent, and his wife, Renata, could barely speak the language at all. Oh, Toni could speak quite well enough to communicate, surely much better than most Americans would do in a foreign country. But understanding was a different matter. And that contributed, as much as anything, to his slow adjustment to the Bulls' system and specifically, to Phil Jackson's instructions.

"I understand what he says to me 99 percent of the time," Kukoc said at one point, about two-thirds of the way through the season. "But the thing is, he's speaking English and I understand in English, but I have to translate into Croatian to be sure what we're talking about. So sometimes he's talking to me when there are a lot of things he's saying, and I have to think about all those things he said to me. And then he's saying, 'Do you understand?' so I say 'Yes,' even though I have to keep thinking.

"What I want to say is, 'I know what you're talking about, just give me time.' Usually I really understand only about two, three words he's saying. But it's easier to say, 'I understand, I understand.' "

This would generally frustrate Jackson, who couldn't figure out early on why, if Kukoc said he understood, he was still screwing up.

Many times when Jackson would be screaming, Kukoc would have a completely puzzled expression on his face or give Jackson his patented Toni shrug. "Sometimes I think I'm doing on the court the things he wants me to do when he's yelling at me," Kukoc said. "And I want to say, 'I don't know why you're yelling. I'm doing what you tell me to do.' But most times he's trying to help me and make me a better player."

And aside from whining to officials, a habit that may have been justified but was increasingly bothersome to the coaching staff, Kukoc never really fought back. "There are different kinds of persons," he tried to explain. "I never was a person who was aggressive or something like that. I am in control of myself as a person. But I am the youngest, a rookie, and I know I could be like, pissed or something, but I know I must learn."

Krause denied it for reasons no one ever quite figured out, but he made sure to hire someone in scout Ivica Dukan, a Croatian who could not only communicate with Toni but befriend him as well.

Jackson was not always so sure that was a help to Kukoc. "A lot of support factors probably retarded his assimilation into our society," he observed. "His parents were here for over a month. The guy on staff [Dukan] was his idol as a kid and played on the same club he played on at Split. We hired him for his basketball abilities but make no doubt about it, the reason he's here is because of Toni Kukoc. "

Jackson was admittedly rough on Kukoc all season. He did, however, often inject humor into his tirades, such as the time the Bulls were playing Washington in late February and Kukoc took an ill-advised three-pointer with plenty of time left on the shot clock. As Jackson met Kukoc at mid-court, his favorite place to berate him, Kukoc tried to explain.

"But I haven't taken a three-point shot all night," he pleaded.

"Toni," Jackson intoned, "they don't have to be an addiction."

More often than not, however, he yelled. And mostly stuff like, "Toni, get the fuck downcourt." It wasn't like Jackson was always picking on him. In fact, most of the time Toni was in something of a dream world on the court. Or at least he appeared that way.

"He has a tendency to be irresponsible defensively and play the ball more than his man because he's used to zone defenses, so it causes some irritation to his teammates," said Jackson. "I think they realize this kid is going to do some wonderful things for the team so they're willing to put up with it, but they want to see growth in certain areas. And they want to make sure if they get chastised for their mistakes, he does for his."

An obviously gifted player in many ways, Kukoc found it difficult to pick up the jargon of NBA basketball. And who, after all, could blame him, with such terminology as "blind pig" and "pinch post," two common terms in the Bulls' lexicon?

Fortunately for Jackson, screaming was a common denominator in all languages and one particular word was a universal expression.

Early in the season, Jackson was clearly the bad guy, seemingly caught on camera every time he ever uttered a harsh word to Kukoc, who always responded with a sad-looking, hang-dog expression. Letters came in to Kukoc and to the Bulls' offices sympathizing with the rookie and critical of the mean old coach who figured by about the new year that Toni was no longer taking him so seriously.

"He knows now that I do a lot of kidding and I say a lot of things just to kind of shock him a little bit and that I'm not really serious about it, that I'm having fun," Jackson said in late December. "He's childlike, naive in many ways, and that's a really winning thing for him because he looks vulnerable.

"But he can take it. I watched how coaches handled him in [Croatia] and Italy. They were all over him. Everyone was all over one another all the time. Italians and Yugoslavians are very similar. It's 'I fucked up, you fucked up,' the coach saying 'We all fucked up.' But they work hard and have a sense of fun, a real penchant for the game of basketball."

Kukoc grew up the youngest of two children in a modest home in Split, a beautiful seaport resort on the Adriatic. He described his family as middle class. "I had nothing if you compare me to guys with big dads or moms who got a car when they were 15 years old," he said. "For us, never. What I got was love, big love from my dad and my mom, and that was the most important thing. And they gave me everything I needed at the time."

As a child, his ideal days were spent deep-sea fishing with his father. "I was always a happy child," said Kukoc, who has a sister, Sandra, four years older, who was a talented swimmer at a young age. "Me and my dad always went against each other in soccer and tennis [ping-pong] in the basement."

His true love, however, was and is the sea. "Every summer, that's all we would do," he recalled fondly. "We never had our own boat but early in the morning, I would go out with dad fishing. Even now, a lot of times, that's what I want to do. I'd like to be a deep-sea fisherman one day. That's my idea. It's nothing for me to spend four or five hours and just fish."

It wasn't until the age of 15 that he took up basketball — "my No. 3 favorite sport" — and he took to it immediately, a bona fide star by 16 on the junior national team and one of the better players on the national team by 18. In 1988, at 19, he led Yugoslavia to a silver medal in the Seoul Olympics and he was no longer a secret.

The Bulls, in Krause's mind, had messed up by passing on a chance to scout Vlade Divac years before, and when Krause was told in the spring of '89 about this 6-10 white kid who could handle the ball like Magic Johnson, he was not about to make the same mistake again.

Less than a year later, Krause was in a Barcelona hotel room with George Karl, then coaching in Spain, watching the "Toni tapes," a marathon session of eight games that had Krause convinced he wanted to see more.

"The first time I saw him," said Krause of the European championships soon after, "I thought he was going to be an outstanding player, but he was so skinny I thought he was liable to break in two."

When the next NBA draft rolled around, in the summer of '90, Krause used the pick they had traded for Dennis Hopson and held his breath. "Nobody picked him the first round," he said of Kukoc, "because no one expected him to come over. But I felt with Chicago having the largest [Croatian] population outside the country, that we had a good chance to sign him."

Krause's infatuation with his new draftee would only grow when he and Jackson went to watch him play in the Goodwill Games in Seattle two months later. "I was pretty high on him already," raved Krause, "but we go to Seattle and he's dunking over Alonzo Mourning and going past Kenny Anderson and I'm going, 'Holy shit, look what we did.' And Phil's looking at me like, 'We ain't this smart,' and I'm like, 'I know we aren't.' We got lucky. This kid was better than we thought.

"I remember sitting there, and the whole NBA was there, and there was a look of envy in all of their faces like, 'You lucky SOB, you stole him.' And then everyone's thinking, 'That SOB can't sign him.' "

Krause and Jackson spent several hours over dinner with Kukoc, whom they had to literally sneak out of camp, and his two agents, Europe-based Luciano "Lucky" Capicchioni and Chicago-based Herb Rudoy.

But Jackson particularly charmed and impressed Kukoc, and all walked away thinking he would soon be coming to the NBA. Said Krause: "The courtship began."

"His English got good enough to where we could talk on the phone," said Krause. "And a relationship formed between he and I."

In December of '90, the Krauses made their first trip to Split. "Renata [then Toni's fiancee] didn't even want to talk to me," Krause said. "She was very, very much against Toni leaving and one night she didn't even come to dinner with us. She wasn't happy and we knew that was going to be a problem."

In the spring of '91, Krause went back to Split, this time with Jerry Reinsdorf, and they made a serious pitch to their young draftee, then playing for the Split team Pop 84. According to Krause, the Bulls had found a loophole in the salary cap that allowed an exception for foreign players the year after they're drafted. It would have allowed the Bulls to essentially use the same cap money twice and thereby free up money for Scottie Pippen, who was demanding a new contract.

Kukoc drew an annoying amount of attention as the Bulls made a bid for their first NBA championship, but Krause persevered. "We were going to try to take advantage of the loophole by mid-March," said Krause.

About the same time, however, civil war would begin tearing Yugoslavia apart, and basketball was not exactly foremost on people's minds. Once, when Dukan was talking to Krause by phone, he suddenly shouted, "I've got to go, I've got to go. They're bombing." For five days, no one could get through.

"Toni got scared and Renata got scared and at the last minute, they decided to sign with Bennetton [Treviso in Italy]," Krause said. "Toni's mother was very influential in the decision. She didn't want him to go far, and Toni's very loyal to his parents."

It's an hour plane flight from Split to Italy, or an overnight boat ride across the Adriatic, which was necessary during the war. "It was a tough decision," said Krause, "and I think Toni deeply regrets it."

Kukoc, indeed close to his parents and Renata to hers, would never go that far publicly. After all, he wasn't exactly in purgatory with an annual salary of more than $4 million as well as a 10-room villa and BMW given to him by the team.

"I don't know exactly why I didn't sign with the Bulls earlier," Kukoc said. "I was 21, 22 years old. I didn't want to sit on the bench. There weren't so many European players at that time [in the NBA] and they were sitting on the bench. So I said maybe it is better for me to play in Europe than to sit on the bench in the NBA."

Krause let him know what he thought in an urgent sales pitch two years later. Ten games into his first season in Italy, Kukoc had broken his ankle. But after surgery and what Krause considered inadequate rehabilitation, Krause thought Kukoc had become less of a player. "He wasn't nearly as explosive," said Krause, who maintains "the old Toni Kukoc" still hasn't emerged but will eventually return.

When Krause met with him again at the European Final Four in Athens in the spring of '93, he claims he told Kukoc that this would be the Bulls final offer. "I told him, 'If you don't come now, we're not interested,' " Krause said. "In another year you'll be 27, you're not weight training and you've gone backward, not forward."

For Kukoc, the decision came down to one thing and sounded not unlike Jordan's decision to leave the NBA. "When I won all the things in Europe [three-time European Player of the Year, a member of three European championship teams and two-time Olympic silver medalist], I had nothing to prove anymore and then I decided," he said.

"When I started basketball in Europe, I would see videos of players like Magic, Bird, Michael and we would try to make the perfect assist like Magic, shoot the ball like Larry, jump like Michael ... After the ['92] Olympics, after that first game [against the U.S.], there was no more doubt I wanted to try the NBA. I saw that I must come here and if I can't do it here, I will return to Europe and at the end of my career, I will say to myself 'No problem. You were only a good European player.' But now I'll try to be more."

After Kukoc signed—for $17.6 million over eight years with a one-year escape clause, which he exercised in the summer of '94, re-signing for $26 million over six years— the Bulls went over him like a prized racehorse. Among the first things they did that summer of '93, was decide he needed his tonsils out because he was getting sick too often.

Jackson was against it. "I'm not the type of person who thinks anything should be taken out of the body. I think everything is there for a reason," he said. "So I was a naysayer on the tonsils issue, but I was assured by people who know more about medicine that it would take away the sickly nature he had the last few years in Europe."

Jackson would soon have other worries as well. Krause had decided Kukoc needed to gain weight and strength and put him in the capable hands of strength coach Al Vermeil with those orders. Jackson, never a proponent of weight work despite the proven results Vermeil had had with players such as Horace Grant and B.J. Armstrong, saw only a kid who, in his mind, was out of shape.

When his conditioning didn't seem to improve, coaches and teammates grew impatient. All rookies hit the proverbial wall, usually midway through the season, about the time when their college seasons would have ended. And granted, Kukoc's season in Europe, though longer than college, would not normally have more than two games in a row and never back-to-back. But Kukoc was seemingly always tired, and theories were floating around.

"I had to ask," recalled Jackson, "because I know a lot of European kids smoke, 'Are you a smoker?' [Dino] Radja [a fellow Croatian, friend and rookie with the Celtics] had a two-pack-a-day habit he had to break. But he assured me no, he wasn't a smoker. So I asked him if he was sleeping well, if he was adjusting to the food. It's the little things, like Europeans drink in the middle of the day and expect to go out and play that night."

The players weren't sure about the smoking. A few claimed to have heard that he indeed was a smoker, but Kukoc steadfastly denied it. The one thing they did know was that his diet was horrible. Jackson insisted on hiring a nutritionist for him when he caught on that vegetables and Toni were strangers.

And his teammates were stunned whenever they saw him eat. Four hours before a game, he would be eating multi-course Italian meals complete with antipasto, pizza, pasta, bread, cheese, watered-down wine and often beer as well, and topped off by a rich dessert. More and more, modern-day athletes were adhering to strict no-fat, low-sugar diets. B.J. Armstrong was a health freak who never ate meat. Michael Jordan gave up Big Macs midway through his career, hired a nutritionist and raved about the results. And for even the biggest, bulkiest Bulls, loading up was uncommon.

As far as Toni's sleeping habits, Jackson was worried as well. The couple's toddler son, Marin, often slept in the same bed with Toni and his wife, waking them up as early as 5 in the morning after a game the night before or, worse, after a road game in which he would not get home until 3 a.m. and had to be at practice by 9:30.

Kukoc said he had two problems with conditioning. One was that the Bulls were stressing his weight too much. He put on about 10 pounds over the first few months of training and said he ended up feeling lethargic. His other problem was that while the Bulls had a far superior weight and conditioning program to the one he was used to in Europe, he missed doing the one thing that really helped him there and that was running outdoors.

"I need that," he said midway through the season, when he started to run outside again. "That was the usual way we practiced in Europe before and after the season. When you're doing something the same way for nine years and you feel good, why not keep doing it?"

The Chicago winter was clearly a shock to his system. "In Italy, maybe one or two months are cold, but I don't think it's below 30," he said. "To me, it's terrible [in Chicago]. I hate it. I can't stand being inside all the time because during winter in my hometown, you walk almost every day outside with a jacket or sweater and it's enough."

Not helping matters in Kukoc's adjustment to the NBA was the fact that the Bulls had to rely on him immediately after Jordan's retirement and Pippen's early-season stint on the injured list. He was devastated by Jordan's retirement. "He was dying to play with Michael," said Rudoy. "The idea of playing with him was a big selling point."

As much as Krause crowed about Toni's early success — he would score 10 points and grab five rebounds in his debut in Charlotte and hit a game-winner at the buzzer in Milwaukee in his fourth — Jackson was not altogether happy. Kukoc was no more ready to be an NBA starter than most rookies, and Jackson worried if he was being set up for a big fall.

"I had a mind-set going in," Jackson said. "I had wanted him to come off the bench and learn how to play basketball. I wanted to be able to milk-feed him to the NBA. If he had to start, I felt he might get chewed up by the incredible duress that goes into that high, intense energy at the beginning of each half, that he would find himself in foul trouble and that guys would exploit his defense and lapses."

Jackson saw the bright side. "It was fortunate in some ways that he had to start games eight through 12 because all of a sudden he was faced with that responsibility and he had some real positive moments as well as some really down games. But I think he got a real feel for it. Also, it helped the organization understand what to expect from this guy and where can we go.

"Then when Scottie came back [from a sore ankle after missing 10 of the first 12 games] and Toni went back to the bench, it was easier to pick spots to slide him into and he could be really effective and an end-game player. "

There were certainly times when he struggled during his first NBA season. A player bound by no rules in his basketball infancy and moved by creativity in the tradition of Jordan and Pippen, Kukoc nonetheless found himself often tight, constrained and unusually uncomfortable on the court. "We don't always understand each other," he said once early in the season when his dramatic passes were flying out of bounds with some regularity, "and then the ball, it just bounces."

He would internalize his frustration, walking around for days on end, it seemed, with a sour expression. "Especially when we were not playing well some games and you're trying to do something and you think it's good but everything is wrong and nobody understands," he said. "I don't even like to talk about that."

By the time the Bulls' first extended road trip in mid-November was over, something else was developing as well. As Kukoc began to struggle with inconsistency, with learning the NBA game and getting to know his teammates, Krause was unwittingly getting in the way.

Players would sneer in their direction as Krause came into the dressing room after games — particularly on the road early in the season — drape one arm over Toni's shoulder and whisper apparent words of consolation in his ear. The resentment had begun years before, when the Bulls were courting Kukoc while players like Pippen, Cartwright and Paxson were not getting their way in contract negotiations. And Jordan was open in his feelings that the Bulls and specifically Krause, should be worrying more about his own players under contract, than some skinny kid who never played a day in the NBA.

Krause and Kukoc are fond of one another, no secret to the other Bulls, and that too made things tough, though Krause insisted he did not contribute.

"I've been tougher on Toni than any other rookie in this franchise," he snapped. "This stuff about him being my boy is bullshit. What I couldn't do was have the 11 other guys say,

'You're Jerry's boy.' We didn't go out publicly after the first summer. But Toni's a good person and I like him."

Jackson tried to serve as watchdog. "They both knew inherently that their relationship was going to have to end when the season started," he said. "Jerry was very aware of it and he knew it was going to be very hard on him because it was a relationship he liked and nurtured over a two-year period of time to the point where he felt fatherly in a lot of ways.

"But he understood the impossibility of Toni being on equal footing with the other players if they saw him giving too much support to him. That's also one of the reasons why I've been very hard on him is because if I'm not, I think the other players are going to get on him."

And they most certainly did when they heard that Kukoc's new home was being built in the same subdivision where Krause was building. Krause said that was merely coincidence. He said he and his wife bought the last lot in the place. And indeed, Toni and Renata had seemingly settled on a home in another area of town. But later in the summer, the couple bought a model home a half-mile from the Krauses.

"Did I know Toni was going to move there?" said Krause. "No. Did I care [what people thought]? No."

Kukoc said he didn't, either. "Jerry was always good to me, so I didn't know what kind of relationship he had with the rest of the guys," he said. "He was OK with me. He said, 'You might have some problems with that early in the season because guys don't know you that well,' but it was just joking and it was fine.

"Scottie and Horace were once considered Jerry's kids and now they put me in that position. After I knew it was a joke, I was fine. Jerry to me was a normal person. So why should I change our relationship? I didn't."

As far as Pippen and Kukoc's relationship was concerned, the best anyone could realistically hope for was that Pippen would give him a chance. "He really wants to be Pippen's friend," said Rudoy. "Toni's like a big puppy."

In practice, Pippen was relentless, covering Kukoc all the way upcourt during scrimmages and generally harassing him in a way Pippen compared to Jordan's treatment of rookies. "I think he helped me, though," Kukoc said. "If somebody doesn't care about the way you play, he doesn't do that. But every day I came to practice knowing he's going to try to stop me from scoring, and I was trying to stop him."

Pippen never really tried to get to know Kukoc, but expecting them to be fast friends would have been truly ridiculous. They came from two different worlds and the Bulls, like a lot of NBA teams, were not a chummy bunch off the court anyway. More often than not, players went their separate ways, either staying in their hotel rooms or going out with friends or relatives.

Kukoc was not at all used to this after the clublike atmosphere in Europe. He said it did not bother him, but there were times when he would literally beg teammates to go out to a restaurant with him on the road, and he could not help but notice a certain coldness emanating from Pippen's direction midway through the season.

Pippen, frustrated by the lack of action by Krause before the Jan. 10 trading deadline and further annoyed by the Bulls' slide after the All-Star game, had lashed out on the last day in February. Criticizing the crowd for booing, he suddenly brought Kukoc's name into it, saying he had never heard them "boo a white guy," then singling out Kukoc's bad game that night as an example.

"I never thought it was something real personal with Scottie," Kukoc said after the season. "If I thought it was, I would find a way to clear it up so we'd know between us. Maybe we're not going to go out to dinner, we're not going to be friends and we're not going to speak. But on the court, we have to be together and good together."

Kukoc, by that time, had grown almost deathly silent around the media, and was clearly distressed by his performance and his health after missing games with a strained back and the flu. Teammates started speculating that he would exercise the escape clause in his contract and go back to Europe after one year in the NBA. "If that happens," cracked Horace Grant, "they're going to have to send Jerry to [the mental hospital in] Elgin."

Kukoc said he was staying, though never very emphatically, and made it clear in his understated way that this was not his idea of team unity. "This is sport," he said a few weeks after the Pippen episode. "And as long as you have a good group of people, they're going to understand each other and they're going to play together. That's the most important part of team sport.

"I always try to have people around me who are positive. We don't have to go out and drink beers or go looking for girls together, but in practice and on the court, you have to think and play like brothers. I can't tell because it's my first year here, but I'm sure they had that the last couple years because without it, it would be almost impossible to do the things they did."

That had to be among the toughest adjustments Kukoc had in his first season. "Maybe it's because there's too many games and traveling," he theorized. "When you see someone every morning and every game, you kind of get tired looking at the same faces and you might want to have a change a little bit and escape basketball. But it's a lot different in Europe.

"In Italy, the first couple of days [of each season], guys invite you to go out to dinner and the beach with them. When I first came here, everybody was OK and it was good. Then you'd leave here at 12 or 1 p.m. and it was bye-bye. So OK, I went home to my wife and kid."

As for adjusting to American life, everything was different — the food, shopping, television, all of which, incidentally, Kukoc ended up loving. At first, he said, his wife became something of a McDonald's junkie and he had to stay away from it. But Renata Kukoc is also a fabulous cook, and the two mostly stayed home to eat. As for shopping, the two could often be seen at Northbrook Court, a mall near the Bulls' training facility, and especially at a big-name toy store chain that delighted Kukoc, who bought goodies for his son and sent gifts overseas to family back home.

Television was a new adventure and for Kukoc, American movies ("The Deer Hunter" was a favorite) were a preference, along with sports.

As for the new culture: "Sometimes, I did feel out of place," he admitted. "And other times, I felt really out of place."

In general, however, he got a kick out of America and Americans. "I like it here, but it's a lot different than Europe," he said. "When someone here is speaking about past history, it's the American Indians and World War I and II and those kinds of things 100 years ago. What we learned in school about history was the Roman Empire. My hometown of Split was from that time; that's when they started to build the town. That was history."

But Kukoc was intrigued by American history and was especially excited by one excursion he made while in Washington with Steve Kerr, Bulls equipment manager John Ligmanowski and broadcaster Tom Dore.

Kerr's brother, Andrew, is on the staff of the National Security Council, so the group was treated to a private tour of the White House that included the Oval Office, the Cabinet meeting room and the Situation Room, where George Bush spent much time during the Gulf War.

"Toni loved it," said Kerr. "I mean, we stood inside the Oval Office for probably 10 minutes."

"I couldn't imagine a foreigner being able to do that in any other country in the world," marveled Kukoc. "There were a lot of things to see and learn about American history. It was really special. I would never have had an occasion to see this place."

His favorite stop was the Cabinet meeting room, where he tried out the president's chair. "Knowing the situation in Croatia, I was joking that I should have left a note on the president's chair," he said. "But I'm a sportsman and not a statesman."

And what would he have written in the note, he was asked? "I'd ask him to save all the kids who aren't guilty for this war."

After Jackson regaled him with the history of Thanksgiving as the team dined in Dallas, Kukoc nodded. "Maybe after the war," he said, "Croatia will have a Thanksgiving."

No matter where he was, the war was never far away. "It was hard just to go to Italy," he said. "The first year, I didn't care too much about basketball at all. That was the first year of the war, and basketball was the last thing I thought about.

"Talking over the phone with my family makes you know they're fine. But after that, you see the TV and bombs are all around and all the other bad things, and you know that any minute, any second, something bad can happen to them. I was calling morning, afternoon and night just to check on the firefights and see if they were OK. Then you come into practice or play a game and you're still thinking about your family."

His first year in the U.S., Kukoc said, was a little less worrisome. "Split was maybe the only one the enemy didn't touch," he said. "Only a few days of light bombing, so I think they'll be fine. [The family] doesn't want to leave. That's not the solution."

Kukoc had an awkward relationship with Serbs in the U.S., even fellow NBA players like Divac, who said he wanted to be friendly with Kukoc. And Kukoc tried to explain to people who couldn't possibly relate. "It's very difficult to explain because against each other, there's not hate but still it's difficult to explain to people in your hometown that you're supposed to be friends," he said. "They say, 'They're Serbs and Serbs are killing us. They're destroying our cause and you're still friends? You're like a Serb. I don't want to see you anymore. Stay with them.' It's why I don't have a good relationship with them."

The politics that are an intrinsic part of his life may have also made Kukoc feel somewhat alienated from teammates, who worried about money or playing time or even girlfriends while he was checking on firefights. But he often used humor as a disarming tool; his subtle wit, razor-sharp.

Once, for example, shortly after Pippen's arrest on gun possession charges, many Bulls were asked for their reaction and opinion, with most staying away from the media entirely. Kukoc, who would submit, though somewhat uneasily, to most interview requests, zipped through the area in the Berto Center where reporters were gathered that day, with a twinkle in his eye but nothing to say. But those who listened very closely to the song he was whistling got a chuckle, for it was the theme from "Bonanza."

Before the season started, Kukoc joined Jerry Reinsdorf in the owner's box at Comiskey Park for a White Sox game. Days later, Kukoc was still shaking his head. "Maybe it's a famous game in America, but I don't know," he said. "Everyone said, 'Wait until you see the fireworks.' So I said OK. And after seven innings, it's 0-0, no home runs, no fireworks, no nothing. I don't know."

Another time, he was asked if he was prepared to play in some "hostile" NBA arenas where fans did not worship the Bulls. Sacramento, an unusually loud place, was given as an example. Kukoc shrugged. "Yeah," he replied, "but in Sacramento, they don't throw coins."

Rudoy saw many examples of Kukoc's sense of humor but most clearly recalled one occasion in October, when he talked to

Kukoc from Israel. Rudoy, who had traveled there on business, had asked Kukoc previously to name his least favorite place to play. "Albania," Kukoc replied. And the best? Israel, especially Jerusalem, his favorite city. And when he found out Rudoy was going, he attempted to explain to him about this "crying wall" he had visited.

"If you go and pray and leave a wish, it comes true," he told Rudoy of the Wailing Wall. Twice Kukoc had left notes in the past and both times his teams had won European championships, he explained. And so he wanted Rudoy to leave another note, this one for the Bulls. "God," it read, "please let me have a great season and the Bulls win another championship."

The night he spoke to Rudoy from Israel, however, was October 5, and he had just heard the news about Jordan retiring. "Herb, forget the note," Kukoc said. "Leave a book. We're in big trouble."

When Kukoc would talk about his new home or his new life, he would make it clear that everything else was secondary. He was in Chicago for one reason only and that was to play basketball. But if he had a passion, one greater than any other, it was being a father.

"The kid," as Kukoc frequently referred to him, could do no wrong. A playmate and continual source of wonder, it was only when talking about Marin, who would be two at the start of the '94 season, that Toni truly opened up.

"We play soccer and play with our dog [Asta, a German shepherd], all kinds of games and go out everywhere," he said. "My dad never could take me to Orlando to see Disney World, but I know with my kid, we will take him [during the off-season] and seven days after that, he's going to dream about it. He talks about Mickey Mouse all the time.

"We're going to go there and we're also going to see all the animals in the zoo. Those are the kinds of things that, if you're a kid, make you happy. We went to the zoo one time and during the night, he started talking about the big elephants and monkeys."

Jackson was right when he talked about Marin getting in bed with Toni and Renata. That was regular practice in the early morning and Toni was not about to change his favorite time of the day. "First thing in the morning he comes in the bed and we watch cartoons and Barney and Big Bird," said Toni. "Then we go to gymboree and play 'Itsy-Bitsy Spider.'"

Still learning to speak, Marin often confused English and Croatian. And sometimes, like any toddler, he would merely confuse the concepts. He would, for example, watch Bulls games on television and shout "*Tya* (the Croatian word for daddy) and "*Tya Daddy.*"

But if father and son were watching a tape or highlights together and Toni pointed himself out to Marin and asked who it was, he would shout, "Toni Kukoc."

"I would tell him, 'Say Pippen, say Cartwright,'" Toni laughed, "and he would say, 'Toni Kukoc.' Tya and Toni Kukoc are not the same person to him. He's starting to understand, though."

It did not matter, of course. "If I'm depressed about my game or practice, I come home and Marin makes me feel better," Kukoc said. "He's always ready to smile and play and he never asks me about basketball."

If he had, Kukoc would tell him he had mixed feelings about his first year in the NBA. A chronic perfectionist, he would finish with respectable numbers — 11 points, 3.4 assists and 2.8 steals in 24 minutes per game. And though he would struggle with his shot for the first time in his career at just 43 percent, he also showed a fire and unmistakable "big-time" abilities with game-winning shots in three regular-season games and, of course, Game 3 of the Eastern Conference semifinals.

"It was the way I expected, maybe a little bit tougher," he said. "The language, coming from Europe, learning the NBA, all these things made it difficult. But the end of the season made it good.

"I really enjoyed the playoffs. I really thought we were a better team than New York. And when it was all over, I really wanted to play more games."

Dear John

    I want to thank you for the years of basketball. you effort And sportmanship was Always a pleasure to watch. And I wish you The best in The future. I am also writing to see if you can send Me An Autograph picture

Thank you
Tony

10

THE BEAUTY PART

"I should write down how I'm feeling right now and then read it a year from now when I'm thinking about playing again."
—John Paxson, October 21, 1993

"My body's talking to me again."
—Paxson, January 24, 1994

Fact 1: Professional athletes do not particularly enjoy talking about retirement.

Fact 2: They enjoy actual retirement even less.

This is not to say that John Paxson and Bill Cartwright did not take time to savor the positive aspects of the 1993-94 season. Nor is it to say that they dreaded the last game, which they believed in all likelihood would mean the end of their careers.

And it is not to say that once that last game is behind them, that athletes do not find adventure and fulfillment in the next stage of their lives (see Chapter 1 for the adventure part).

But is anyone ever 100 percent, unequivocally at peace with the decision of giving up something they have been doing for most of their lives? Even with the pain that dogged the final years of Paxson and Cartwright's careers, both thought of basketball as more a way of life than a career, still a game when it came right down to it.

Paxson never lost sight of that. One day, not long after he came off the injured list after missing the first 31 games of the season with persistent knee pain, and not long before he went back on for another 15-game stint, Paxson left a courtside chat to jog onto the court for pregame shooting practice.

"Excuse me, but I have to go to work now," he said, then looked back at the reporters he was talking to with a twinkle in his eye. "Heh, heh, did you hear that? Work. What a life."

He never did forget that and neither did Cartwright, who had to be talked into going on the injured list virtually every time, and who looked back fondly on what many would consider a low point in his career.

At the time, Cartwright, an NBA All-Star as a rookie, already had put in nine years in the league and was playing behind Patrick Ewing in New York in what he figured would be his last season. "But I was having fun that last year in New York," he recalled. "I was playing 10 to 15 minutes a game. I didn't have any bruises. I'd say to [wife] Sheri, 'Guys complain about this? You gotta be kidding.' "

This does not mean, however, that there weren't some regrets and second thoughts at times. For Paxson, the perfect ending could well have been his famous three-pointer with 3.9 seconds left in Game 6 of the 1993 NBA Finals against Phoenix to put the Bulls up by one and give them their third consecutive championship.

But while everyone was talking about Michael Jordan leaving on his own terms when he announced his retirement and walked out on the three years left on his contract, Paxson could not see turning his back on the $800,000 he was to earn for the 1993-94 season. Especially when he was feeling pretty good.

After taking a rare summer off, he said he "never felt better" early in the '93 training camp, so much so that he removed the wrap on his left knee so as not to remind himself of the two surgeries he had had within eight months before and during the '92-'93 season.

Paxson remembered the ordeal of his last contract. The Bulls had not planned on asking him back after the '90-'91 season, the year he ended up rallying the team to its first NBA title with 20 points in the deciding game against the Lakers. The Bulls had wanted to move B.J. Armstrong into the starting point guard position, which eventually happened anyway, and they still needed money to pay Toni Kukoc.

Paxson's base salary the year before was a paltry $320,000, supplemented by a $200,000 bonus, and he was looking forward to being a free agent. After surviving a small army of job competition during his tenure with the Bulls, Paxson had found his role as Jordan's backcourt mate, an unselfish complement to Jordan's extraordinary talents with the smarts and ability to be a valuable spot-up shooter.

Three years before, when rumors surfaced of the Bulls looking to trade Paxson to the L.A. Clippers, Jordan shocked some by saying, "If you trade John Paxson, you might as well trade me."

Jordan had a soft spot for Paxson, respecting his unselfish nature, and asked his agent, David Falk, to handle the negotiations.

Paxson had an interesting history with agents. Actually, the better way to put it was that he had no history with agents before Falk. Choosing an agent after being drafted out of Notre Dame by San Antonio, Paxson decided to follow his brother Jim's example and use Larry Fleischer, then head of the NBA Players Association. What he didn't realize was that the Spurs owner at the time, Angelo Drossos, had a running feud with Fleischer.

"It was always a contest of who could come out better," Paxson recalled, "and I got caught in the middle."

He ended up signing a deal that paid him $85,000 the first year and $95,000 the second year, but he ended up reporting to camp two weeks late. "I was treated like a criminal," said Paxson, who received an instant education on the business of basketball. "I was totally naive. I didn't know if I'd ever play again after that. That experience really soured me on the league. I realized a lot of things are out of your control."

In addition to souring him, it gave him a phobia about contract negotiations. "It got to where I dreaded it so much that after my first three years with the Bulls, I just decided to negotiate my contract on my own because I didn't like the thought of confrontation." he said "I didn't want to do anything that would rock the boat."

But he always wondered if couldn't have done better than $1 million over three years leading up to his last contract, and thought perhaps it was time to get someone to represent him. "I asked Michael real innocently if David Falk would represent me," Paxson said. "I knew he had a lot of well-known clients and I didn't know if he would accept me or have time to handle my deal.

"I sure wasn't thinking blockbuster contract. But I knew I would start [in '90-'91]. I had the year before and averaged 10 points per game, and we were one game from the Finals. I just knew if I had a solid year, I would get another contract. That was all I was thinking."

But as the '90-'91 season progressed, Paxson, then 30, grew more and more sure he wasn't going to be re-signed. He definitely knew he wasn't hearing from the Bulls. And as it turned out, it wasn't until his former team, the Spurs, offered him a three-year, $4.4 million deal that the Bulls came back with an offer of three years at $1.25 million per year and Paxson accepted the offer because he and his wife, Caroline, wanted to stay in Chicago. "No one will ever know how close I was to leaving," Paxson said then.

Of course, his playoff performance provided the perfect bargaining chip. "They could have gotten me for a lot less if they would have signed me earlier," he said.

Before the Spurs' offer, the best the Bulls said they could do for Paxson was $867,000 per year. And remembering all that, Paxson was not about to retire without everything that was coming to him.

Cartwright's circumstances were seemingly even more precarious, with the Bulls holding the option for the '93-'94 season, which would pay him $2.4 million. When most of the summer went by and he still didn't know if he would be asked back, the assumption was that he would be fairly annoyed at being left dangling. But Cartwright is one of the few Bulls with a close relationship with Jerry Krause, and he said he understood.

"Jerry was waiting to see who else he could get," said Cartwright, matter-of-factly, "but I wasn't insulted by that at all. I had been a part of three world championships. If I wasn't going back, I certainly had a great time. And I knew it was nothing personal."

He once tried to explain that concept to his son, Justin, when he coached the 13-year-old's basketball team. "I'd yell at the kids, giving them direction," Bill said. "And finally Justin comes up to me and says, 'Dad, the kids don't like you yelling at them.' So I got them together and told them, 'Look, I'm doing it for you, for the team. It's nothing personal.' I don't think they understood."

But Cartwright did, and he had other, more obvious reasons for not holding a grudge against the Bulls. He was forever grateful to Krause for getting him out of New York and into a situation where he would contribute to three NBA championships. Largely because of that, he was even able to overlook some rather intense contract negotiations in the summer of '91.

At the time, Cartwright and his agent, the late Bob Woolf, accused Krause and the Bulls of reneging on a three-year contract offer. Originally, the deal was three years, two guaranteed, for an average of about $2.2 million per season. But a day after that deal was unofficially struck, Cartwright said the Bulls had decided to limit their offer to two years at about $2 million per season. Cartwright was thoroughly dismayed at being treated in a manner he thought disrespectful and unfair, and uncharacteristically lashed out publicly at Krause, saying he felt he was being handled "like dirt" and that his relationship with Krause was "over."

Days later, Cartwright ended up signing for the original deal and wrote off his earlier comments to emotions running high at the moment. "That happens and no one wants it to happen," he said, "but once you get to know Jerry and see why he does what he does, it's very interesting. I'm always asking questions of him. Why did you do that? What are you looking for? And he always has a reason for everything. Things don't just happen with him."

It was hard for Cartwright to ever stay angry at Krause for long. "Jerry gave me a second life," he said. "Guys would tease me and say, 'Jerry's your boy,' and I would say, 'He sure is. He got me out of New York. Whatever he wants, he gets.' If Jerry doesn't make that deal for me [trading Charles Oakley to the Knicks in return], I would have quit for sure. My contract was up the next year."

With a new life, however, came some serious new adjustments that, frankly, frightened Cartwright. "Once I was traded to the Bulls, it was a huge challenge," he said. "Now all of a sudden, I have to come in and play again. Now I have to be geared up. It was such a different mind-set. And it wasn't like I was really welcomed to the team, either."

The first player Cartwright felt he had to win over was Dave Corzine, starting center at the time. "He's a great guy and I had no problems with him," Cartwright said. "But I said 'Dave look, I remember coming into the league when Marvin Webster was with the Knicks and we were trying to kill each other in training camp. It was crazy.' I told Dave the same thing I told Patrick [Ewing]. 'We're not going to kill each other, we're going to try to help each other.' "

The other players weren't nearly so easy to win over, beginning with Jordan, who was a close friend of Oakley's and openly against the trade. "Michael gave me as much support as putting a training bra on Dolly Parton," Cartwright laughed. "Michael ruled the team. Then on top of it, when I came in I had always been my own person. I didn't care what anyone thought of me and Michael didn't know how to take me. But he knew he couldn't mess with me.

"I had a lot of appreciation for him as a player and competitor, but I was not going to go up and try to be buddy-buddy with him and I think that kind of helped me and hurt me."

Cartwright said his biggest influence, unwittingly, may have been on Pippen and Grant. "I came in at a time when Scottie and Horace were still trying to find themselves [in the second year in the league for both]. They saw that Oakley was buddies with Michael, and now they saw someone who didn't have to be. They saw someone who came in and didn't bow down. I could say, 'Fuck Michael,' and no one would care. So they saw Michael couldn't control them."

And while Cartwright and Jordan never developed what anyone would call a friendship, they did develop a healthy respect for each other. "As you play together, give up your body to one another and get to know one another, a certain respect develops," said Cartwright. "But we have different personalities. Some things he does work for him that wouldn't work for me. But there's no right or wrong."

Paxson, who spent nine seasons in Chicago, had an even rougher entry with the Bulls, though it never had to do with winning people over off the court. "Every year," he said, "I felt I had to fight for my position. I always felt a little anxiety around the trade deadline."

Paxson had signed an offer sheet with the Bulls on October 29, 1985, the same day Jordan broke his foot in a game at Golden State, an injury that would keep him out of the lineup the next four-and-a-half months. And so began a Bulls career in which Paxson would outlast Kyle Macy, Steve Colter, Sedale Threatt, Rory Sparrow, Sam Vincent and Craig Hodges before becoming the regular starter at the beginning of the '89-'90 season.

For years, Paxson read and heard that all the Bulls needed to win a championship was to get the right pieces around Jordan. "One of those pieces was point guard," he said, "so it was like I had this thing attached to me. When we weren't real good, they were always searching for names to play with Michael. At the time I had to bite my lip. After all, who was I to complain? It wasn't until we became solid as a team that what I did became a little more noticeable."

One thing he figured he had going for him was that Jordan genuinely liked him. But he also knew his personality would only carry him so far. "I contend and I always did that all you had to do on our team was gain Michael's confidence," Paxson said.

Paxson had a reputation for making clutch shots, which he thought probably stuck in Jordan's mind. But one shot in particular, his first as a teammate of Jordan's, gave him a good start.

In the summer of '82, the two were together on a U.S. national team selected to play in the FIBA Games in Europe. Their first two games were against the 10 best players in Europe. "And they just drilled us," Paxson recalled.

Their next game came against Yugoslavia in a tiny, decrepit gym with windows smashed by rocks. Before a hostile crowd, Paxson hit the game-winning shot at the buzzer. "The big thing was just gaining his confidence," Paxson reiterated of Jordan, "and a lot of guys who came through [the Bulls] couldn't do it."

Colter was one. "He had some problems making outside shots," Paxson remembered, "and you saw it right away. Michael would challenge him in practice and you could see right away it wouldn't work. You saw it with Brad Sellers and Rodney McCray. He wanted guys to play well and want to win as much as he did."

Paxson's 20 points in Game 5 of the '91 NBA Finals against the Lakers spurred the Bulls to their first world championship, and almost forgotten was an 8-for-8 performance in Game 2. "For me, it was almost vindication," he said. "Not only to win it, but to be a big part of it. It had been rough for me. You had all these experts around the league saying the Bulls needed a point guard to win the championship. No one likes to be hammered down like that."

When it became obvious that a changing of the guard was inevitable, with Armstrong taking Paxson's spot in the starting lineup, Paxson would not allow it to become a rivalry. Both publicly and privately, Paxson pledged his support for Armstrong and the team, and that is but one reason he will be remembered fondly by Bulls fans. "I learned as much from John Paxson about what it means to be a professional as I did from anyone," said Armstrong.

Perhaps no other Bulls experienced as much daily physical discomfort as Cartwright and Paxson. Cartwright remembers how it used to be.

"When I first got in the league," said Cartwright, "God, I remember playing and it didn't matter what you had, banged up or beat up, knee twists, ankle sprains, bruises, you could run through a wall without anything really bothering you, because that's what you're supposed to do. You just wanted to play, to prove yourself. And back then, you'd heal pretty quickly. You'd twist or sprain something and two days later, it's gone. But before long, you don't recover like that anymore."

There were times during his last season, Cartwright said, when suddenly and inexplicably after feeling good all day, a knifing pain would engulf his knees and he found it difficult to even walk, much less run. But he said he never became fearful. "You try to be aware of what's happening," he said. "I mean, I knew my knee wasn't going to explode or fall apart."

No, more than the pain and the fear was simply the frustration involved. "John and I were always saying, you don't want to go out there and embarrass yourself," Cartwright said. "You knew certain things you could do five years ago, you couldn't do anymore. John would say, 'I used to run right by that guy,' and that, more than anything, is what bothers you. You're out there talking to yourself: 'Dammit, get there, get there.' "

Financially, of course, it's pretty tough to retire. "Guys now are making so much money, they want to play as long as they can," said Cartwright, who eventually decided to delay retirement after being offered approximately $6 million guaranteed over three years by Seattle. "Charles Barkley may talk about quitting, but he doesn't want to quit when there's money to be made. You can never have enough money."

Paxson and Cartwright, however, were caught off guard by Jordan's retirement. "John and I came back with the understanding that Michael was coming back," Cartwright said, "with the idea that we would get ready for the end of the year to win another championship. What a great thing that was. I was looking forward to that all summer.

"Jerry [Krause] and I talked about how great a season it was going to be, and he said at a certain point, 'We'll start gearing you toward the season.' "

"If Michael had come back," echoed Krause, "Bill wasn't going to play until December, and Pax, maybe longer than that."

Needless to say, Jordan's announcement was a bit of a shock to everyone's system. "Scott Williams goes down," said Cartwright, "and it was like, Holy Jesus, I'm playing 30 minutes a game."

"When I found out about Michael," said Paxson, "I can't say I was the most motivated guy in the world."

To their advantage, Cartwright and Paxson were aided by a coach and general manager who understood an aging player's needs.

"For my standpoint," said Paxson, "Phil was great for me. All year long, he knew I wasn't going to play much or contribute much, though I think I surprised him sometimes. But he just let me go with it and I think he felt having me around was a good thing."

In Cartwright's case, his playing and practice status was almost always up to him. "Phil and Jerry were definitely great for me," he said, "because they really allowed me the freedom to do what I thought best. It's a Catch-22 a lot of times, because they allowed me to be responsible but I was so eager to play, I'd rush it sometimes. And the bad thing about my situation was that you don't know how far you can go until you push too hard."

One of the strangest but most frustrating injuries with which Cartwright walked away from the game was a damaged larynx. A larynx is supposed to be V-shaped. But Cartwright's, because of the number of whacks he has taken to the throat area, is U-shaped. The subject of good-natured jokes and Stacey King's imitations, Cartwright's voice was as much a part of his lasting image with basketball fans as his pointy elbows.

But it wasn't always that way, and it wasn't a joke to either Cartwright or his wife. "I know this is unbelievable, but my voice used to be beautiful," Cartwright said.

Shortly after he retired, Bill and Sheri ran across a tape from about 1988 of the two singing in a karaoke bar. "Bill," Sheri cried in amazement, "I can't believe you could sing like that."

Said Cartwright: "I remember being hit in the throat at least once every year. In December [of '93], we were playing Indiana and I was hit especially hard. Chip [Schaefer, the Bulls trainer] called the doctor in and he asked, 'Does he always talk in that voice?' Everyone laughed. But what I didn't realize then was that blow fractured it and put it over the edge."

In order to repair the larynx, he would have to undergo an extensive operation his doctor does not recommend, which would require re-breaking it. It's a tough decision but Cartwright said if he is considering a career in which speaking is required, it may be necessary.

"If I don't do it," he said, "it will always alter the things I want to do."

Krause, who said he has discussed a possible future career in coaching with Cartwright, said he is hoping he has the surgery. "It's one of the things we talked about and I told him, 'First, you've got to have the voice fixed,' " Krause said.

"To be a coach, unfortunately, you have to make yourself heard, and Bill can't make himself heard. The reward from surgery may be greater than the risk."

In general, however, neither Cartwright nor Paxson expressed any serious fears about debilitating after effects of the game. Referring to the conditions of Jackson, who has had back fusion surgery, and Bulls play-by-play announcer Johnny "Red" Kerr, who required a hip replacement, Cartwright shrugged.

"That was a different era when Red played, and they don't have the technology that we have now," he said. "Their training camps were like boot camps. You got into shape during training camp. Today's athletes are different, because we stay in shape year-round.

"There are a lot of things that are different. Guys are better athletes now. They're better prepared. And obviously, they're compensated more. Then, guys had summer jobs. Now when you come into this league, this could quite possibly be the only thing you have to worry about."

Paxson had the same reasoning. "Toward the end of the season, more people were saying stuff to me about my health down the road," he said. "But that's the tradeoff. That's what we do."

For Paxson, the last season especially was a frustrating tug-of-war between his pride and high level of competitiveness as a player, and the reality of his body's increasing limitations. "I told myself when I came back after the first 31 games that my only goal was to have fun," he said. "But it's not that easy. You still want to play and contribute, and when you don't feel good, you feel you're a liability on the floor. The hardest part is not being able to do what you did just a couple years before."

Athletes' bodies are generally the first to betray them, but there are other, subtler signs of age that surround them as well. Cartwright was constantly amazed at the changing behavior of coaches and players as his career went on.

One day as he looked across the locker room at Corie Blount, he could no longer contain himself. Now Blount had already established himself as the symbol of today's youth and, perhaps, today's NBA rookie in his fashion choices. Namely his choice of jean jackets. Paxson could hardly keep a straight face one day early in the season as he examined Blount's latest purchase, an elaborately designed, fluorescent painting of the rookie in a Bulls uniform, his name taking up much of the portrait. Blount seemed enormously proud of the "artwork," which looked as if it belonged on velvet rather than on denim, and on sale at a corner gas station rather than on display in the locker room.

Nevertheless, he loved it. And wore it. And later, he turned up in another denim jacket, this time with the words "Three-time NBA Champion Chicago Bulls" adorning the back. No problem that Blount had not been a member of any of the world championship teams. He was a member of the defending three-time champs and proud of it.

Still, Cartwright was puzzled one day as he observed what Blount was wearing — baggy jeans worn low down on his hips and an oversized shirt. "I was asking Corie about that, " recalled Cartwright. "I said, 'Is that comfortable to wear your pants down like that?' And he's like, 'This is just how it is. This is the way you wear them.' I'm always trying to get my kids to be neat and tuck in their shirt, so I was asking Scott Williams, 'Scott, why don't you tuck your shirt in?' And he just said, 'Because it's just not comfortable.' And that's fine, I guess."

Cartwright laughed because the very least of the changes in player attitudes were of a fashion variety. He recalled the story of former Sixer Maurice Cheeks, who one day had a cold and was not playing very well, and being told at halftime by coach Billy Cunningham, "If you're sick, get dressed and get your ass out of here."

Another time, the president of Madison Square Garden, Sonny Werblin, came into the Knicks' dressing room when Cartwright played in New York and cussed out the team at halftime of a particularly brutal game. "After the game, which we ended up winning," recalls Cartwright, "the guy comes back in laughing. 'See, I told you, you could do it.' Picture that kind of thing happening today."

Cartwright often saw signs of selfishness in younger players but never was there a more glaring and, to him, galling example than Game 3 of the '94 Eastern Conference semifinals.

Months later, Cartwright was still emotional about Pippen's conduct, saying, "It wiped me out, totally. I don't think any of us ever saw anything like that before. Ever."

The shock, he said, was palpable. "It's like when you play with somebody a number of years," he said, "and come to know somebody and grow to depend on them and trust them, and then they do something you would bet your life would never happen, even more than your wife cheating on you. I would have imagined more of a chance of my wife having an affair than Scottie Pippen not playing a basketball game with 1.8 seconds on the clock.

"If he had a broken back, you would bet the ranch that he plays in that situation."

Cartwright was the first Bull to approach Pippen on the bench that night, and his first reaction was impatience. "I was obviously yelling at him," said Cartwright, "trying to convince him to go back in the best way that I could. At one time, I'm telling him, 'Scottie, this is not the time for this. We can't win this basketball game if you're not on the court.' "

The time, of course, was fleeting as Jackson called a second timeout. But Cartwright felt hopeful that he was getting to Pippen. "He was ready to go back, he really was," said Cartwright. "He didn't say it, but I felt he was ready to go back. But then Phil broke the huddle and just said, 'Fuck it, we'll do it without you.'

"The whole thing is like being in Vegas and winning 20 grand and deciding to put it all on the line. Now if you're dealt a bad hand, you can't say, 'Dealer, I want new cards.' Phil dealt that hand and now, in front of 18,676, Scottie wanted to give them back. He wanted to throw in the pot. But in the end, everyone else's money is on the table, too."

When Kukoc made the shot, Cartwright's anger toward Pippen deepened. "Even though he made it," said Cartwright, "it was still like, how could you do that? What's more important? That we won the game or that you won the game?"

Cartwright could never understand why some of the veterans, like Pippen, weren't more understanding of the new players. "Toni didn't have an easy time fitting in," he said. "Steve Kerr, Bill Wennington, Jo Jo English, none of them had an easy time. But those guys killed themselves, and we should do everything we can to help them.

"When a new guy comes in, go over and introduce yourself. Help him out. That's what Scottie should have done with Toni. The better Toni is, the better the team is. That's what he didn't understand. Those guys would try to kill Toni, try to embarrass him. They saw him as a threat. But I think they'll grow out of it."

In a way, Cartwright understood that this was inevitable. "A lot of things have changed from when I came into the league," he said. "It used to be when you were a rookie coming into the league, you were taken in by the older guys and shown around. Rookies come in now and they're your highest-paid players. You don't show them around. They're making the money, they're going to get all the minutes and they have everything. In that way, basketball has changed. It's giving guys coming into the league a huge opportunity to prove themselves right away. If you're going to pay Shawn Bradley all this money, he damn well better be great on the court. But all it does is put more pressure on them to play right away."

When Cartwright considers the changes that have taken place since he entered the league, he's actually more amazed at attitudes toward opponents.

"It's kind of weird," he said. "Like I never remember when I was a rookie, people sitting around and talking about other players like our team does. I mean, with respect to other players. Like, 'Man, did you see what he did there? Wow, did you see that move?' "

Cartwright was talking about one game he remembered in particular, when the Bulls were playing the Nuggets in Denver and he found himself on the bench at the end of the game seated next to B.J. Armstrong.

"This kid [Kevin] Brooks came in," said Cartwright, "and B.J. was going, 'Hey, watch this guy. This guy can score, I'm telling you.' It was so weird. We never did that. We were like, 'Hey, let's shut his ass down. He isn't that great.' "

Yet Cartwright appreciated the fact that Armstrong was a student of the game and said that's what he liked about Krause. "It's so nice talking about basketball to someone who's so excited about it. That's a real basketball person, who can watch just for the pleasure of it. That's Jerry. B.J. has that, too. He enjoys when someone does something on the court. John and Steve Kerr are like that as well. I like that."

Paxson will no doubt ease into retirement with his fame level and tolerance much the same as it was pre-retirement. He's not likely to ever walk down a Chicago street without someone thanking him for his heroics in the NBA Finals.

After the '93 Finals in particular, Paxson spent much of the summer pressing palms and listening patiently as fan after fan recounted how they either predicted he would hit the last shot or dreamed about it the night before. "No kidding," Paxson would say pleasantly. "You're the first person who has told me that."

A word here on fans. Some can be very persistent, others incredibly rude. And still others are just flat strange.

They will, for instance, walk past a Bill Cartwright in a shopping mall and find that merely staring and whispering is not sufficient. Instead, they will yell out to no one in particular, "THAT'S BILL CARTWRIGHT," and then, so as to make sure Bill Cartwright knows who he is, walk up, point and shout "YOU'RE BILL CARTWRIGHT."

Eyewitnesses can vouch that Cartwright, like Paxson, is quite polite and will generally smile and nod and maybe even respond, "Yes, I am." But often, this is not enough, and the fan will then speak to Bill as if he is, say, a carnival ride. "BILL CARTWRIGHT," the person will shout again, perhaps expecting Bill to be devoid of any three-dimensional characteristics. And Bill, still polite though suffering some moderate hearing loss by now, will respond again. "Yes, I am. How are you?"

This throws the fan, who is not expecting to make any real conversation, though if you were to ask this person if he might like to someday meet and talk with Bill Cartwright, he would, in all likelihood, say that he'd love to. And Bill would probably just as soon have a nice, albeit brief, conversation in return as opposed to simply having his name shouted at his belly button.

But give said fan the chance in a nearly empty shopping mall to maybe say something, anything, and nine times out of 10, Cartwright will have to withstand "BILL CARTWRIGHT" instead.

Very strange.

Of course, there are fringe benefits galore to all of this. For every 10 fans who scream your name at you, there will be at least five who will buy you a drink, pick up your dinner check or invite you to take advantage of free dry cleaning at their local establishments.

Dining at a suburban deli one afternoon, one Bull barely blinked when the manager handed him a shopping bag full of "goodies" as he was ready to leave. Common practice. "And that's fine," said the player, "but then you better expect the guy to ask you for a picture or an autograph. Some guys have no problem taking stuff, but do have a problem when that person wants something in return. There's always a price."

Another time, a Bulls player found himself at a downtown cafe that served muffins. The player wanted corn muffins, which the restaurant did not have. So the manager scurried out of the restaurant and to a store down the street for muffins. When the player was ready to leave, he was given a bag of corn muffins to take with him. "And I didn't even like them," he said.

One local place of business gave Bulls players free car phones. When word got out, nearly the whole team made its way over. "When you'd ask the guy how much you owed him," said one player, "he just gave you his business card and said, 'If you ever have any extra tickets, call me. I won't bother you.' You love that kind of arrangement."

And some of the players actually remembered the guy. Sometimes, however, the price was too steep. Many Bulls have car deals for the season or half the season, where they will give two season tickets (each player gets four for the year) in return for use of a Mercedes, BMW, Jeep, etc. Some players, however, say they feel the price is too high.

"I'm not a wheeler-dealer," claims Scottie Pippen, who bought a car dealership during the '93-'94 season. "I feel like I'm selling myself if I do that. Friends give me cars, and maybe once in a while call and want tickets, but it wouldn't be a consistent thing. The value of my ticket is worth much more than its face value. In the end, they're walking away with their cars, but I'm not walking away with anything for my ticket. If you want tickets for a year, give me a car from your dealership."

In general, the price of fame is more than fair. An autograph or signed picture to put on the wall is hardly a lot to ask for free meals, preferred seating and reservations, and assorted goody bags. And don't for a second think athletes balk at the favoritism, subtle or otherwise. Paxson grew to appreciate it.

"The neat thing about that summer [after his game-winning shot in Phoenix] was how many people said, 'I was with my family or a group of friends when you hit that shot and it's one of those things where I'll never forget where I was.' I liked hearing that. And I don't think I'll ever tire of it.

"When people approach me for an autograph or picture, they always say, 'You probably hate doing this,' or 'Sorry to bother you but . . .' But I always say, 'In five years, you may not know who I am.' I'm going to enjoy it while I can. Plus, my kids get a kick out of it."

Of course, the flip side is the knowledge that virtually every public encounter is being examined and analyzed.

Once while he was playing in San Antonio, Paxson remembers leaving a restaurant after dining, paying and tipping, only to return later because he wasn't sure if he had tipped enough.

"You feel like you're being scrutinized all the time," said Paxson. "One thing I rationalized as an athlete is that you make a great sum of money. But at the same time, there aren't too many jobs where your performance is out there for the public to see and scrutinize daily. People say, 'Yeah, well I'd do it for that money, too.' But there's a tremendous amount of stress involved.

"I don't know if I'd say it took years off my life or anything, but it's just the constant desire to succeed. In my case, it was coming in each year and trying to earn a spot on the team."

One often stark reality of retirement, especially involving athletes from successful teams in large markets like Chicago, is that giving up basketball does not just mean saying goodbye to a substantial regular salary and maybe free muffins, but to many other perks as well.

Endorsements, appearance money for card shows and autograph signings, car deals, and other arrangements, usually end with an athlete's retirement.

"I've taken advantage of a lot of opportunities and the fact that we won three NBA titles," Paxson said. "When I first came to Chicago, I was lucky to get $500 to $1,000 for an appearance, but it has changed so much in the last few years."

Paxson is one of the rare exceptions among athletes who will still be in some demand after retirement, particularly in the Chicago area, and, in fact, has a deal with Coca-Cola that is to continue after his retirement. He also plans to continue working for the Bulls for the '94-'95 season, doing color commentary on their flagship radio station.

In comparison to the rest of the NBA, Bulls players have been extremely marketable over the last few years, obviously due to their three championships.

Will Perdue, for example, who did not have a highly visible role in the playoffs over the years, still earned nearly $100,000 in additional revenue in 1993, including his $67,000 playoff share.

Every NBA player, per his contract, is required to do six personal appearances and six team appearances during the season. But that does not always happen, especially among the bigger-name Bulls like Pippen, who asked for at least $20,000 for an appearance. Grant asked anywhere from $12,000 to $15,000 and Armstrong, who asked and normally received $7,500 in 1992, raised his asking price to $12,500 after Jordan retired.

Pippen said before the Bulls' first championship, he was paid anywhere from $5,000 to $7,000 for an appearance. After the first title, he raised his price to $10,000. After the third, he was up to $20,000. "I figure if they really want me, they'll pay me," he said. "Guys get mad when other guys go cheap because it drives everyone's market value down."

Perdue, one of the more personable Bulls and one willing to do charitable appearances as well, earned $7,500 for one appearance during the '94 Super Bowl, spending an hour and a half at a party goods store in the Chicago area, then spending another hour and a half during the game at the house of the winner of a drawing.

Williams asked and received $6,000 for all appearances within the city limits of Chicago and $7,000 outside. Kukoc, a first-year Bull but a high-profile player, received up to $7,500 for appearances early in the season. Compared to big-name players around the NBA, and even to other Chicago athletes, the comparisons are staggering.

Former Bears quarterback Jim Harbaugh, for example, would accept appearance fees as low as $500. When perennial All-Star Dominique Wilkins was in Atlanta, he could command $7,500, but that would be for a half-day appearance. Teammate Mookie Blaylock, also an All-Star, could get only $2,000 to $3,000, and Kevin Willis, another All-Star, only $1,500.

Blount was like the proverbial kid in the candy store when he joined the Bulls as a rookie in the '93-'94 season and turned down almost nothing, going to bar mitzvahs for $1,000 and other appearances for $1,500.

"When I first got here, I was doing two appearances a week, whatever I could get," admitted Blount. "The guys would mess with me — 'Are you doing *another* appearance?' But I'd just say, 'Hey, if you won't do them, I get your leftovers.' "

Most of the veterans quickly tired of appearances. "You burn yourself out real fast and you get tired of it, the fans hounding you," said Pippen.

Pippen stopped doing official autograph signings years ago "once I found out the backgrounds of what the guys do with the cards and autographs," he said. "They'll pay you for two hours at $10,000 and they'll make $60,000."

Paxson could command up to $10,000 for an appearance, but agreed with Pippen that it did not hold the same allure to him as time went on.

"It gets old and time becomes more important to you," said Paxson, who has a wife and two young sons. And the way Paxson looked at it was that any income from outside appearances was a bonus. "I just feel very lucky to be in a position where I was able to make the money I was," he said. "Business people work 30 years to get to the position I'm in."

Paxson said his perspective was obviously shaped by a salary history in which he was perennially underpaid. And he didn't figure on any huge lifestyle adjustments upon retirement. "The only thing I've tried to do for my family is buy a nice house and hopefully send the kids to good schools," he said. "That's the only extravagant thing and I don't plan on being crazy in retirement."

Cartwright was open to a range of possibilities after leaving the Bulls, including coming back to Chicago part-time to help coach the Bulls' centers. He was also planning on continuing his correspondence studies toward a Master's in sociology, his major at the University of San Francisco.

Cartwright said he started worrying about a life after basketball fairly early in his NBA career. "My first three years in the league, I wasn't worried about it," he said. "But I played with Paul Westphal in New York and Paul was nearing the end of his career, and it really used to bother me thinking, 'What in the world am I going to do?' So one day I asked Paul, 'What are you going to do when you get done playing?' And his reply was 'I don't know.'

"And I think that's pretty normal, that you really don't know for sure. You might have a pretty good idea that you can do a lot of different things, but you really don't know. So from that point on, I decided I wasn't going to worry about it as much. I was going to leave myself open and obviously consider a lot of different things to do."

When he looks back on his last year in the league, Paxson fondly recalls returning to Phoenix the season after the Bulls' third title and walking to the spot where he launched one of the biggest shots in team history. Teammates playfully teased him about it, encouraging him to shoot from there, but he never did among his three three-point attempts that night, not even in warmups, though Phil Jackson did consider him for a last-second shot that could have won the game.

"It wasn't my sense of the dramatic," Jackson said at the time. "It was my sense of being ironic."

"My feeling," said Paxson, "is that was something that could not be duplicated. So I wasn't sitting out there hoping it would happen again. I stayed away from the spot before the game. I figured lightning wouldn't strike twice. And I didn't want people to think I was out there trying to duplicate it."

He also remembers his first game back from the injured list, when he scored six points on 3-of-6 shooting and the crowd showered him with cheers of affection and appreciation.

"I'll miss being in the Stadium," said Paxson. "That was special every time, and I really tried to look around and savor the moments there."

And despite the pain that still lingers in his knees and the days when he wished he could will himself onto the court, he does not for a moment, he says, regret any of it. "I'm definitely glad I went through it," he said. "And mostly not for basketball reasons. I'm not so sure I was glad when Michael retired, and the pain was tough at times. But one of the great things about this profession is the new guys I met; guys like Steve Kerr, Luc Longley, Bill Wennington. If I wasn't around, I wouldn't have had a chance to socialize with those guys and I enjoyed that immensely."

But what he'll miss most will be the little things. "One thing I've enjoyed is just getting on the plane and the whole routine with your teammates," he said. "Whoever I sat next to on a particular flight, just talking things over with Steve Kerr or walking over and sitting next to Horace and Scottie and joking around. I know I'll miss that. And the next game . . . .

"I had a bunch of people tell me to retire on that last shot in Phoenix. But the more people said that to me, the more I knew that would have been wrong. It would've been too easy. It would've said, this is a perfect world and life is great.

"I needed a year to test my will and my heart and my desire. I learned a lot staying around this business. And I know absolutely for sure that I did the right thing. If I had only been in one game all year, I still would've been happy just to be around."

Cartwright had the same sense of sentimentality when talking about retirement. "I won't miss the hanging out so much as the feeling you had," he said, struggling for the words to explain. "Coming into practice has a certain feel, a certain smell. Getting ready for games had a certain feel."

His voice trails off . . .

"But the reality of it is that the greater part of our lives is ahead of us and a great challenge is ahead of us. And that's the beauty part. That's what I'm ready for."

EPILOGUE

Scottie Pippen laughed at the question. Was he surprised to still be a Chicago Bull? Surprised that here it was, October 6, 1994, one year to the day after Michael Jordan's retirement, and here he was, once again surrounded by microphones and being asked if he was equipped to be the leader of this team?

In the span of one year, everything had changed. His buddy for so many years, Horace Grant, was gone, as were championship team members John Paxson, Bill Cartwright and Scott Williams. As Pippen looked to either side of him, he saw NBA veterans and Bulls newcomers Ron Harper and Larry Krystkowiak. Hovering just inside the gym was rookie Dickey Simpkins and nearby, refusing to answer questions about his apparent continuing role as sixth man, was Toni Kukoc.

Everything had changed.

In the span of a year, Pippen had been thrust into a leadership role he alternately embraced and resented. He had watched as Jordan left the game for baseball and left the responsibility of on-court leadership to him.

He saw himself succeed in bringing the Bulls to the All-Star break as the surprise team of the NBA, a team that suddenly was being talked of again as a championship contender. And he saw firsthand how very fragile celebrity can be with misdeeds that cost him MVP consideration and cast doubts on his character.

Everything had changed.

This was not as much fun as he thought it would be, Pippen said more than once. And he wondered as he looked around the locker room, how long even this seemingly charmed Bulls team would last in its current form.

The playoffs were its own nightmare, one that he would never quite fully comprehend in a summer filled with hurt and anger. Trade rumors swirled about and then one night, he found himself in a surrealistic scene, watching TV and listening as they talked about a move that was imminent—one that would send him to Seattle and away from the city in which he had recently built a house, the city that he had finally begun to call home.

Everything had changed. Grant was on his way to Orlando. Assistant coach Johnny Bach was unceremoniously let go and was now working in Charlotte and recovering from a heart attack. And if that was the way they wanted it, Pippen would be gone too. And he would leave in the best shape possible, for this was a rare lengthy summer break in which he had set his sights on becoming stronger, improving his three-point shooting and making a run at league MVP that this time, no one could deny.

He would watch as the Bulls finally conceded Paxson's retirement; as Cartwright entered a ninth life with the SuperSonics as a sage reserve center; and as Williams signed with Philadelphia for $20 million.

Pippen would see the Bulls fail in their continued attempts to trade him and instead, focus on re-tooling a team they claimed could still contend. Harper, a good friend, would be signed, thereby hastening the departure of Pete Myers, a warrior and Jordan's 82-game replacement at off-guard who deserved better.

Back would be Steve Kerr and Bill Wennington, Luc Longley and Will Perdue, B.J. Armstrong and Corie Blount and Kukoc, re-signed to a $26 million deal that put Pippen third in line on the team's payroll.

And now here he was again. Facing the microphones. Another October in Deerfield. Being asked if he was capable of leading this team, being asked how far he could take them and if he could survive the transition period.

Pippen laughed. Nothing had changed.